ALSO BY ROBERT M. GATES

Duty: Memoirs of a Secretary at War

From the Shadows:
The Ultimate Insider's Story of Five Presidents
and How They Won the Cold War

A PASSION FOR
LEADERSHIP

A PASSION FOR LEADERSHIP

Lessons on Change and
Reform from Fifty Years
of Public Service

Robert M. Gates

ALFRED A. KNOPF   NEW YORK   2016

THIS IS A BORZOI BOOK
PUBLISHED BY ALFRED A. KNOPF

Copyright © 2016 by Robert M. Gates

All rights reserved. Published in the United States by Alfred A. Knopf,
a division of Penguin Random House LLC, New York, and distributed
in Canada by Random House of Canada, a division of
Penguin Random House Canada Ltd., Toronto.

www.aaknopf.com

Knopf, Borzoi Books, and the colophon are registered trademarks
of Penguin Random House LLC.

Library of Congress Cataloging-in-Publication Data
Gates, Robert Michael, [date]
A passion for leadership : lessons on change and reform from fifty
years of public service / by Robert M. Gates.
pages cm   Includes index.
ISBN 978-0-307-95949-2 (hardcover)
ISBN 978-0-307-95950-8 (eBook)
1. Gates, Robert Michael, 1943–   2. Cabinet officers—United
States—Biography.   3. Organizational change—United States.
4. Leadership—United States.   5. Public administration—United
States—Anecdotes.   6. Administrative agencies—United States—
Reorganization.   7. United States. Department of Defense—Officials
and employees—Biography.   8. United States. Central Intelligence
Agency—Officials and employees—Biography.   9. Texas A & M
University System—Biography.   10. United States—Politics
and government.   I. Title.   II. Title: Lessons on change and
reform from fifty years of public service.
E897.4.G37A3   2016   352.2'93092—dc23
[B]   2015010209

Jacket photograph by Charles Ommanney/Getty Images
Jacket design by Chip Kidd

Manufactured in the United States of America
First Edition

This book is dedicated to all who serve the Public Good

Contents

1. Why Bureaucracies So Often Fail Us   3
2. Where You Want to Go: "The Vision Thing"   23
3. Formulating a Strategy   39
4. Techniques for Implementing Change   63
5. It's Always About People   98
6. Stakeholders: Friends and Foes   131
7. The Agent of Change: "Mirror, Mirror on the Wall"   157
8. Money, Money, Money: Reforming in Scarce Times   186
9. Reform: The Never-Ending Story   203
10. A Flaming Heart   219

Acknowledgments   231
Index   233

A PASSION FOR
LEADERSHIP

1

Why Bureaucracies So Often Fail Us

Everybody hates bureaucracies, even those who work in them. Yet in twenty-first-century America, apart from a handful of hermits and survivalists living off the grid, dealing with impenetrable, impersonal, infinitely complex, obdurate, arrogant, and often stupefyingly incompetent bureaucracies is an everyday travail for everyone. Think about it: Social Security. Medicare. Local, state, and federal taxing agencies. Getting a driver's license. Obtaining documents for business, remodeling your house, or getting a building permit. Any federal department or agency. Dealing with the phone company, your credit card issuer, a credit bureau, a billing error by a big chain store. Navigating airport security, health-care insurance, university and public school administrations.

Hardly a day passes in the life of any American without his or her having to confront one or another bureaucracy, standing in line, dialing a telephone number, only to enter an automated labyrinth seemingly devoid of humans and humanity, being placed on indefinite hold, trying to access a bad government or business Web site, or being shuffled from one office to the next to find that one person, the anomaly, who can fix a problem. Encounters with a bureaucracy almost always have stress and frustration as by-products. And finding someone in a bureaucracy who is pleasant *and* can solve one's problem quickly is so unusual as to be very nearly a life-altering experience. President Lyndon Johnson once said, "If the first person who answers the phone cannot answer your question, it is a bureaucracy." Don't we all know it.

Despite political paralysis in Washington and elsewhere, bureaucracies inexorably—day by day, year by year—intrude ever more pervasively into our daily lives. They influence our health, our safety, our economic well-being, our children, what we eat, what we drive, and every business, farm, and educational institution in the land.

Yet even as bureaucratic tentacles extend their reach into every nook and cranny of America, the litany of their incompetence and arrogance grows exponentially. Many of these institutions are now indispensable, but their repeated and highly publicized sins of omission and commission have shaken the public's confidence that they—that government in particular—can do *anything* right. Just a sampling of lapses and failures in recent years regardless of who was minding the store in Congress or the White House is profoundly disturbing: 9/11 itself, a failure of intelligence and law enforcement of monumental consequence; the failure of virtually all our financial regulatory and administrative bodies to anticipate and prevent the abuses that led to the financial meltdown in 2008–9; the Federal Emergency Management Agency's handling of the aftermath of Hurricane Katrina and other disasters; the lack of planning for post-invasion Iraq in 2003; the scandalous treatment of outpatient wounded warriors at Walter Reed Army Medical Center; the multiple failures of the Veterans Affairs Department; challenges to the integrity of the Internal Revenue Service; lapses and scandals of the Secret Service; the initial handling of the Ebola crisis by the Centers for Disease Control; the botched rollout of the Affordable Care Act (ObamaCare); the ever-changing and inconsistent rules relating to airport security; the extraordinary waste of development dollars in Iraq and Afghanistan; underperforming public schools; the inability to control our southern border; and so much more. The institutions—the bureaucracies—responsible for these disasters and embarrassments are crucial to us. Some of them have previously been among our most respected organizations. Now they are failing us.

One of my favorite sayings about government—attributed to Napoleon Bonaparte, of all people—is "Never mistake for malice that which is easily explained by stupidity or incompetence." No one set out to make bureaucracies the enemy of ordinary people, resistant to change, impervious to new realities, and incompetent. Few if any individuals choose public service as a career because they want to make life miserable for people or to work for some hapless bureaucracy. Indeed, I can attest from decades of working with talented and dedicated public servants, the opposite is often true. And yet the humorist Will Rogers could say decades ago, "I don't make jokes. I just watch the government and report the facts."

The world of business—the private sector—as I have observed it both as a customer and from the corporate boardroom has its own issues with bureaucracy. While the obstacles to cutting costs and becoming more efficient are more onerous for the public sector—local, state, and federal—leaders in both the public and the private sectors face multiple barriers to innovation and reform to cope with new and changing circumstances. For example, leaders in both sectors often encounter entrenched cultures that make real change difficult, as well as lower-level organizations resistant to guidance from the top, determined to preserve their piece of the cake and their status. Trimming organizational deadwood can be as challenging in the business world as in public institutions. It is a rare soul who has not been frustrated and maddened by multiple business bureaucracies—not to mention disastrous business decisions that cost jobs and create economic turmoil and heartache.

But for most businesses, success and self-preservation require that leaders and employees work hard every day to innovate and change with (or before) the times, to overcome sluggishness, poor customer service, and the stifling effect of layer upon layer of management that inevitably delays and complicates decision making. As a rule, companies that do not promote innovation, strive to reduce overhead costs and managerial layering, and become more customer-friendly don't do well in the long term.

The public sector, however, faces multiple unique obstacles to reform, whether it's cutting costs, becoming more efficient, encouraging innovation, or changing to cope with new challenges or changed circumstances. And no matter how different in purpose or size, for nearly all public bureaucracies those obstacles are the same.

The everyday experiences of Americans make a compelling case that bureaucracies do not work and cannot be reformed, that we are stuck. After so many highly visible failures, public opinion polls show that, as I've said, a majority of our citizens have lost confidence in our institutions and in government itself. The political Left is too often indifferent to obvious bureaucratic incompetence and failure because it believes that whatever the problem, government is the solution. It's tough making the case for more government when what we have works so poorly. The political Right welcomes bureaucratic incompetence as proof that government rarely does anything well, and thus it reinforces its belief that whatever the problem, government involvement will probably only make things worse.

We can—and will—continue to argue endlessly about the proper role of government in the United States, but the fact is we have a bunch of it and most of it doesn't work very well. Because we actually do need government, failure to fix it imposes huge financial costs in terms of incompetence, time wasted, and inefficiency, not to mention the cost in public cynicism and the loss of credibility of both government and those who lead it.

In truth, virtually every bureaucracy needs to reform: to modernize, get rid of paralyzing procedural and operational barnacles that have accumulated over decades, reduce waste, and become more efficient and effective. When in 2010 we could find $180 billion to cut (over a several-year period) in bureaucratic overhead in the Pentagon in just a few months, you have some idea of the "opportunity" offered by far-reaching reform. Defense is far from alone in this regard.

I believe bureaucracies can be fixed: changed, made more cost-effective, user-friendly, efficient and responsive, and shaped to meet new problems and challenges even in an age of austerity. I know because, with the help of some great colleagues, I did it at three very different institutions I led—the Central Intelligence Agency and the other dozen or so U.S. intelligence agencies; Texas A&M University, now the nation's fifth biggest; and the Department of Defense, the largest and most complex organization on the planet. All three, and virtually all other public institutions, have similar challenges to change and reform. And my colleagues and I at all three places showed that a dysfunctional political environment is not, in itself, an overriding impediment to bureaucratic reform.

You may fairly ask what three apparently unique organizations—the CIA, A&M, and Defense—have in common and what lessons they offer for leaders at all levels of government and in business as well. Let me suggest just a few examples. While everything I did at the CIA was supposedly secret, everything at the university was public, and Defense was a mix, in reality I had no secrets from any of my overseers—the White House, the governor's mansion, Congress, the state capitol. And between aggressive media and leaks, I had few secrets from the public either. I had to do much of my business at all three in the public eye. This feature is common to virtually all public-sector bureaucracies. The influence of elected officials on Pentagon programs and funding was far more prevalent and political than at either the CIA or A&M, but even at the latter two every dollar the institution spent had to be approved by elected officials, who were not shy about making clear their priorities and preferences. The role of politicians in the everyday life of any public organization is significant; it's just that their influence is applied differently depending upon the agency or department.

Also, at the CIA and Defense I supposedly could tell people what to do, whereas persuasion was my only recourse at A&M. However, while I could give orders at the CIA and the Pentagon, no successful leader of either ever did so; on the big issues, like the budget, the list is long of directors and secretaries whose ambitious plans crashed and burned because they failed to consult and persuade the intelligence professionals and the uniformed military to go along with their plans. In sum, when it comes to the fundamentals, these three organizations have much in common.

Similar traits can be found in most other institutions. I entered government nearly fifty years ago and, working for eight presidents, had the opportunity to observe the federal government at close hand—including many departments and agencies not associated with national security. As president of Texas A&M, I had a ringside seat to watch how state government and bureaucracies operate. And over the last twenty years, I have served on the board of directors of ten companies, where I had ample opportunity to observe the challenges of bureaucratic bloat, turf protection, empire building, and resistance to change facing their CEOs. And now I am national president of the Boy Scouts of America, which, like any big, century-old organization, has its own bureaucratic problems. Despite vastly different roles and missions, all these institutions have characteristics—and challenges—in common.

Few leaders will ever run the CIA, the U.S. military, or a huge university (or, fortunately for most, deal with Congress). Even so, I will make clear in these pages how the lessons I learned in those institutions are broadly applicable for, and useful to, leaders in nearly all bureaucracies. In external appearance, people are infinitely diverse, yet beneath the skin our anatomy and the way the body works are pretty much the same. So it is with bureaucracies. Each shares a lot of DNA with its kin, even distant cousins. You will see that despite the vast variety of bureaucracies in both the public and the private sectors, their cultures, organizational structures, and both internal and outside influences on their operations and behavior are remarkably similar. And thus the strategies and techniques for changing them—reforming them—are remarkably similar.

In the pages to come, I will dwell often on my experiences in government. Mainly, that is a manifestation of my belief that they offer considerable insight into what works well or badly. Partly, though, I hope that recounting those experiences will provide—as a bonus, if you will—information about our government that is worth the reader knowing as a citizen.

––––––––

Despite the many frustrations and very real shortcomings associated with government, I believe Americans have, at every level, the most dedicated, capable, and honest public servants anywhere. In my long career in government, I saw in U.S. political appointees and career civil servants, university faculty and staff, men and women in uniform, and intelligence officers in mufti—public officials all—an extraordinary number of people of the highest quality serving with steadfast integrity and love of this country and what it stands for. They want to be proud of the organizations they work for; they want the admiration and esteem of the citizens they serve. They, too, are often frustrated by the shortcomings of their institutions.

So, what gets in the way of reform? Why is reform of public institutions particularly difficult?

For openers, virtually all public bureaucracies report directly or indirectly to elected officials, whether Congress, state legislatures, presidents, governors, mayors, or city and county governing boards. Their political interests (getting reelected usually foremost among them) are often in direct conflict with efforts to streamline or reform the institutions they oversee. For example, despite all the congressional rhetoric about waste and inefficiency in the Department of Defense, any effort to cut unneeded programs or facilities (and the related jobs) in members' home districts or states invariably provokes howls of outrage and adamant opposition. Despite congressional demands for greater integration of American intelligence agencies, members deny intelligence executives (and the president) the authority to actually make that happen. At the same time state legislators rail against tuition increases at public universities, they slash state funding for those same institutions—and continue to impose inefficient state bureaucratic procedures that waste taxpayer (and student) dollars and inhibit cost cutting at those same universities. They don't want to relinquish political control even as state funding levels plummet to 10–20 percent of operating budgets. In short, politics—both local and national—is a significant obstacle to reform and adaptive change.

But it's not just politics that is the problem. Elective bodies with oversight responsibilities also are unreliable, unpredictable, and even irresponsible when it comes to the lifeblood of public institutions—funding. How can any organization do long-range planning when it never knows from one year to the next how much money will be available or, in the case of federal agencies, when the money will actually be approved and can be spent? Not once when I was secretary of defense did Congress approve our Defense appropriations before the beginning of the fiscal year in which the money was supposed to be spent. In a couple of instances, we didn't know how much funding would be available until midway through the year, and once (and several times since I retired) Congress never did approve our annual appropriation. And when you toss in mindless acts of congressional misgovernance—such as shutdowns, furloughs, and sequestration—and micromanagement masquerading as oversight, just keeping the doors open is a challenge. Even on the state level, funding levels from one legislative session to the next are usually crapshoots.

To draw a vivid contrast between leadership in business and that in government, imagine a company with a board of 535 directors, each of whom has as his or her principal objective personal self-interest and political self-preservation as opposed to a responsibility to the institution he or she oversees. Further, unlike a corporate board, Congress draws no distinction between strategic direction—providing big-picture guidance on operations and long-range priorities—and trying to manage the day-to-day affairs of the institution despite its proven incompetence to do so. Leaders in business by law are supposed to focus narrowly on what is in the best interest of the company and its shareholders. In the public sector, broader considerations—especially political—come into play in ways that make reform or change more difficult.

Another unpredictable factor in the oversight of institutions—mainly public ones but a lot of businesses as well—is the uneven quality of the individuals elected or appointed to fulfill the role. Members of Congress, state legislators, and (especially for business) regulators, for example, vary dramatically in expertise, diligence, understanding, and just plain smarts. Too often, it is the members who fall short in one or more of those categories who create the most problems, block reforms and appointments, oppose constructive change, and try to impose unworkable or costly policies, rules, or programs. In universities, too many individuals elected or appointed to oversight boards (regents, for example) know virtually nothing about higher education in general or the issues facing a given institution. The quality and qualifications of individual regents vary widely, from micromanaging, ill-informed, arrogant, self-serving cronies of a governor to independent, thoughtful, and open-minded appointees who add value and work hard (and selflessly) to make an institution better. Similarly, to a much lesser degree but in still too many businesses, one can find a wide range of quality in leaders, both in the boardroom and in the executive suite. Such wide variation in the quality of those charged with oversight is well-known to every public servant at every level of government—and to employees in more than a few companies. This, too, is an obstacle to bureaucratic reform and change.

Another big problem is that, at least at the most senior levels, many bosses in public institutions (again, at all levels of government) lack managerial or leadership experience. Even when the appointments process is working well in terms of focusing on qualifications rather than political loyalty or persuasion, too often senior government positions are filled with people—academics, lawyers, financiers, consultants, contributors, members of legislatures or their staffs—who may have reputations for expertise in a particular function or field but who haven't got a clue about how to run anything. Moreover, many appointees hope or expect to be in the position for a relatively short time, and a significant number see the public sector executive job as a stepping-stone to something more exalted. As a short-term steward, a boss who is a political appointee too often thinks short term and primarily in terms of how his personal performance will be perceived externally—including by the person who appointed him. Thus, he avoids controversial moves, fails to prioritize, and underinvests, especially in areas that only matter in the longer term. In short, most political appointees measure success by a yardstick other than effective management or successful institutional reform. Indeed, too many of these folks view change and reform as bad risk-reward trade-offs because such steps can create internal as well as external opposition and often bad press.

When a businessperson appointed to lead a government department falls on her face, it's often because nothing in her corporate experience has prepared her for the complexities of running an organization with the "help" of the president or governor, Congress or state legislature—much less a raft of lower-ranking political appointees in her organization whose loyalty as often as not is primarily to the political operatives and politicians who got them their jobs and not their day-to-day boss.

Another reality would-be reformers face in the public sector is that almost every career employee has some form of job security. While most think of tenure as lifetime job security for university faculty, in truth, except in dire budgetary circumstances, the uniformed military and civil servants have significant job protection as well. While firing people has become more difficult in the private sector, it is still relatively easy (especially if incompetence, mistakes, or misbehavior have been documented) compared with the public sector. Unlike in business, those opposed to an agenda for change or reform cannot easily be fired or even moved out of the way to another job. As a result, most civil servants who are opposed to change or reform can simply outwait the reformer. They were there when he arrived; they will still be there when he leaves.

In contrast, there is usually no job security at or near the top of public bureaucracies. In the executive branch of the federal government, about the only senior officials who have a term of office specified in law are the president, the vice president, and the director of the FBI (ten years). Every cabinet officer and all political appointees serve "during the pleasure of the President of the United States for the time being," as their commissions read. That is not exactly reassuring or conducive to pursuing risky and difficult change. There is significant turnover among such officials, and anyone coming in with a mandate to make changes has no idea how much time he or she may have to do so. The average tenure of an assistant secretary in a cabinet department is about twenty-one months, and it takes most people six to twelve months to get their feet wet. Officials' uncertainty about how long they will be in office is yet another impediment to reform and change.

In my very limited experience with unions in the public sector, at the federal level, they were not a particular obstacle to change. Most of the sclerosis that impedes change in terms of hiring, firing, work rules, pay, and personnel is generally hardwired into law or regulations. Union activity or leverage is usually aimed at legislators, not within the bureaucratic institution itself. This was certainly the case at the Department of Defense, where part of the civilian workforce is unionized. The unions there were an obstacle to only one change I wanted to make—an attempt to alter the pay structure and, in particular, to provide incentive pay for civilians. The unions did play a part in killing that reform, but it was through powerful allies in Congress rather than through direct action internally. Their influence is, I imagine, more pronounced at the local level. Still, I believe that when it comes to reforming the *way* business is done and the *organizational structures* for doing so—in contrast to pay and benefits—with the right approach, unions can be partners, not obstacles.

If you think removing *people* in a government bureaucracy is difficult, just try eliminating an agency or office once created. Talk about nine lives! In the Pentagon, if you stamp out an organization one day, it will likely spring up in another form and under another name—sort of like crabgrass—somewhere else. Senior Defense officials have eliminated organizations to reduce costs, only to discover later that no one lost his or her job—people just got shuffled elsewhere. It's the old "find the pea under the walnut" scam, and the boss is the sucker. I was the yokel more than once.

Business also does not have to take seriously the influence of retirees or alumni as do a number of public institutions, including virtually every university and college, the military, and at least some civilian organizations (for example, charities and foundations, police and fire departments). I found it ironic that students or employees who bellyached constantly about the shortcomings of an organization while they were still there, upon graduation or retirement decided the place was, in fact, nearly perfect. And thus they opposed any change as undermining the foundations, culture, and traditions of the organization. Perhaps an exception to this is in the uniformed military, where, upon retirement, some senior officers suddenly become much smarter and strong advocates for change, coming up with ideas for reform that somehow eluded them while they were in positions of responsibility and had the authority to make those changes themselves (or at least push for them). At the same time, most military retirees continue to advocate for their own service (army, navy, marines, air force) and for programs near and dear to them and their service.

Pro-reform or against, military or civil servant, spy or student, the voices of the departed demand to be heard by the leaders of many public institutions—and are.

Bureaucratic reform, ironically, must also overcome the growing demand for transparency in decision making. Imagine corporate executives having to devise strategy, internal restructuring, personnel policies, and marketing plans entirely in public. Or a chief executive officer of a company meeting with his or her board of directors on future strategy in a town hall. What is unthinkable in the business world is everyday practice in the public sector. Granted, some businesses—especially very large ones in politically sensitive arenas such as finance and banking, aerospace and defense, communications and social media, the Internet, pharmaceuticals—are subject to intense public scrutiny and their own form of congressional or other oversight. But the number subjected to unrelenting public attention and exposure is relatively small compared with the entire universe of companies.

However, for the would-be reformer in a public institution, plans for change are publicly aired by leaks, regulation, or state law—no matter how preliminary or immature—making her a rich, inviting target for advocates of the status quo. While the reformer is still developing a battle plan, opponents of change have ample time to deploy their forces and counterattack. Public scrutiny is constant, and the willingness of subordinates to create bold or controversial plans for change is undermined by the likelihood those plans and the identity of the author will be leaked, publicized, and meanly criticized. In states where legislation mandates open meetings, like Texas, almost nothing can be kept confidential. As an example, a university president there cannot meet privately with the board of regents to discuss strategic plans or direction; a gathering of more than three regents is considered a public meeting and must be announced in advance and opened to the public. While the CIA and the Defense Department operate under very different rules of confidentiality, the reality is that a culture of pervasive leaking of information in Washington, D.C., has nearly the same effect as open records and meetings laws. Without draconian measures by the CIA director, defense secretary, or other senior officials, any and all plans for institutional or budgetary reform soon find their way to Congress and the media. The reform leader of any public institution—even in the areas of intelligence and defense—must assume that everything she does or says will quickly be in the public domain, making the development and execution of reforms difficult in the extreme.

The culture of public bureaucracies and all too many private sector organizations is also a serious obstacle to change and reform. Fundamental to bureaucratic culture is risk avoidance: It is almost always safer for the public bureaucrat—and too often the business bureaucrat as well—to say no than yes. In a public environment of exposés, recrimination, faultfinding, and investigations both by officials and by the media, not acting is usually safer than acting—especially if the action involves something new or different. Common sense, and sometimes even doing the humane thing for someone, are set to one side out of fear of incurring a cautious supervisor's displeasure or being disciplined—or even fired—for not going "by the book."

This problem has been mightily aggravated by the more intrusive role of new forms of media that provide detailed coverage of what used to be minutiae below the threshold of major media interest. Blogs now specialize in widely distributing what was once office gossip and watercooler talk about officials under pressure or programs facing challenges, often even before senior management is aware or has had a chance to act. All this affects behavior and makes everyone more cautious. Further, the proliferation of investigative bodies, inspectors general, quasi-independent evaluation entities within traditional bureaucracies, together with the steadily growing propensity among politicians over the years to look for someone to hang for every single problem or hiccup, has contributed not just to risk aversion but to inaction. This is replicated to one degree or another at every level of government. Fear of making a mistake and being placed in the public dock keeps already cautious bureaucrats—and their political appointee overseers—looking over their shoulders.

Also fundamental to bureaucratic culture both in business and in the public sector is the "not invented here" defense mechanism. Almost any idea for improvement or reform or just doing something more efficiently that originates outside the affected organization automatically generates antibodies of opposition to repel the invading idea, especially if it comes from a known critic. Even more personally, a supervisor all too often rejects his own employees' ideas for improvement simply because they were not his ideas. Further, it is in the nature of bureaucracy for the boss at each level to want more people and more resources: each often measures her personal success not by customer satisfaction but by the size of her "empire." The idea of willfully shrinking one's empire to make the overall enterprise more successful and more efficient borders on heresy. And there is no financial incentive, personally or institutionally, to do so in a public bureaucracy.

Public institutions are often not served well by their culture of insularity—the conviction that no one outside the institution can possibly understand what those in it do, how they do it, or why they do it. In the private sector, the marketplace demands a far greater openness to new ideas. The near-total absence of competition to public bureaucracies enables and strengthens a fortress mentality. There is, in many bureaucracies, a pervasive sense of uniqueness and, implicitly, superiority. This is best captured by the mantra at Texas A&M about being an Aggie: "If you're on the outside looking in, you can't understand it. If you're on the inside looking out, you can't explain it." That sentiment is widely shared among the military and intelligence officers and, I'm sure, by law enforcement and many others. A sergeant in Afghanistan once told me in a town hall meeting that the values and character of those in uniform were far superior to those of the American public. The strong belief in the "oneness" of those inside and a common defensiveness against those on the outside are both great strengths and great weaknesses. They are strengths in that traditions and the feeling of being part of a special family are central to the success of such institutions. They are weaknesses because such a spirit is an intangible but powerful barrier to change and to outside ideas. In all cases, they make the job of reformer or "change agent" much more difficult.

The formidable barrier to reform represented by institutional culture and traditions was well captured by the great historian Jacques Barzun in his book *From Dawn to Decadence*. After spending nearly half a century at Columbia University and the University of Cambridge, he wrote, "Institutional self-reform is rare; the conscience is willing, but the culture is tough." Amen.

Business and public bureaucracies have in common many obstacles to change, but the final obstacle to reform unique to public institutions is simply the absence of any economic incentive to do so. If a public sector organization is pretty much guaranteed some basic level of funding year in, year out, what is its economic incentive to change or reform? More narrowly, unlike business, the public sector cannot use compensation as either reward or punishment of employees at any level. Management has almost no authority to affect the pay of those working for them, except through promotions and even those are governed largely by minimum "time in grade" (normally, a certain number of years must elapse for someone even to be eligible for promotion), the availability of positions at the higher grade, and institutionalized promotion processes. At the federal level, the 1978 Civil Service Reform Act provided for performance bonuses at senior levels (up to $20,000), but the number of recipients has always been severely limited, and only a small number of civil servants are even eligible. At times, even those bonuses have been suspended for budgetary reasons. Small, onetime performance awards are available (usually a few hundred to a thousand dollars or so), but not much used by supervisors. How, then, to motivate people to work harder or smarter?

———

When I was interviewed to be president of Texas A&M, I told the search committee that if they were looking for someone to maintain the status quo, they had the wrong guy. "I don't do maintenance," I told them. My interest, I continued, was taking on the challenge of making a good institution better. I would be "an agent of change" while preserving the core values and traditions of the university. This was, I had discovered, my "core competency." I loved all three institutions I led, but part of that love was the conviction that each could be better.

My first (probably presumptuous) essay on how to improve the CIA—specifically, its analysis of the Soviet Union—was published in 1970, just two years after I finished training and reported for work. A little over a decade later, in late 1981, the CIA director, William Casey, and deputy director, Admiral Bob Inman, advanced me over many more senior officers to head all of the CIA's analytical effort—several thousand people—because I had specific plans (based in part on nearly six years on the National Security Council, or NSC, staff at the White House) on how to improve the quality of that analysis. (More on that later.) And when I became director of central intelligence (DCI) a decade after that, I faced the need to completely reorient the CIA and the U.S. intelligence community away from their decades-long preoccupation with the Soviet Union, which was collapsing. With the help of a talented team and some two dozen task forces, that reorientation was well under way by the time I stepped down in 1993.

Texas A&M University is, as I often described it, "a unique American institution." An all-male military college of a few thousand students until the 1960s, it now has more than fifty thousand students on its main campus. Regents, alumni, faculty, staff, and students in 1999 joined together in setting the university on a path to even greater excellence, producing a report—*Vision 2020*—with a dozen major aspirational goals. It fell to me to lead implementation of that effort beginning in 2002.

President George W. Bush asked me to become secretary of defense in November 2006. The wars in both Iraq and Afghanistan were going badly; troops and commanders weren't getting the equipment they needed; outpatient care of our wounded was a scandal waiting to break; the Pentagon bureaucracy in all the military services remained focused on planning for future wars while seemingly incapable of fighting the two we were already in (or preparing for those we would be most likely to fight in the future); dozens of major equipment and weapons programs were overdue, overcost, and, often, no longer relevant; and bureaucratic overhead had swollen dramatically in the years since 9/11. Stewardship of our strategic nuclear forces had deteriorated, as repeated crises would demonstrate. I dealt with all these—and many other—problems.

Drawing on my experience leading transformational change in diverse organizations over many years, I aim in this book to offer leaders in bureaucracies—public and private and at all levels of leadership—specific ideas and techniques that can enable them to successfully reform and improve their organizations. Rather than create endless hypothetical situations and offer step-by-step action plans for those situations, I believe the principles of leading reform and examples from my experience are easily customized for and applicable to extraordinarily diverse situations. Some of what I have to say is just plain common sense, but you probably would not be surprised by what a rare commodity that is in bureaucracies. While my focus is primarily on public institutions, what I have written about leading reform of bureaucracies is broadly applicable to organizations of every size and kind: business for sure, and volunteer organizations, civic and service groups, schools, and churches as well. We need leaders up and down the organizational ladder with vision and purpose who can mobilize the willing and bring productive change.

———

At a time when so many Americans are frustrated and angered by government gridlock, political paralysis, and expanding government bureaucracies that intrude ever more into our daily lives, I am an optimist. I believe that with the right strategies and the right skills leaders can—whatever direction politics takes us—reform and change these institutions. Reform is not a luxury but a necessity. Failure to fix our institutions, and to do so urgently, can have catastrophic consequences for our way of life, our financial security, our national security, our freedoms, and, at times, our very lives. By showing that things *can* change, *can* get better, I hope in some small but significant way to convince Americans that the institutions that too often fail us can be reformed and to show that leaders at all levels can be involved in making that change come to pass. With skilled leadership, things can be made to work so much better.

This book is about people and how to lead them where they often don't want to go. It is about how a leader can make an institution better, both for those who work there and for those they serve. It is about improving people's lives.

I have an ulterior motive as well in writing this book. It is a sad truth that, broadly speaking, public service as a calling has been in disrepute for a number of years. The tone has been set from the top as, for decades, successive presidential and congressional candidates in both parties have run for office campaigning against the very government and public servants they hope to lead. Year after year, it becomes more difficult to persuade capable young people to enter the public arena. According to *The Wall Street Journal,* the percentage of federal employees under thirty was just 7 percent in 2013. It was nearly three times that percentage in 1975. Political paralysis and its consequences—government shutdown, bitter partisanship that blocks commonsense solutions to important national problems, and other irresponsible actions, not to mention the government's long-standing reputation for red tape and hierarchy—discourage young citizens with desirable and needed talents from entering public service. If, through this book, I can demonstrate that despite the politicians public institutions and other organizations can be reformed, made more efficient and more responsive to the needs of our people, perhaps more young people will be encouraged to consider devoting some portion of their lives to their fellow citizens.

I hope that this book will be of value to young people who aspire to become leaders: first, by demonstrating to them that public service organizations can be worthy of their talents; second, should they choose that path, by offering them, early in their careers, some of the tools and personal attributes for leading change that they can begin to develop and strengthen. After all, today's new recruits will be tomorrow's senior leaders.

John Adams, our second president, wrote to his son Thomas, "Public business my son, must always be done by somebody—it will be done by somebody or other—If wise men decline it others will not: if honest men refuse it, others will not." My fervent hope is that this book will encourage the wise and honest among us, especially young people, to consider serving our fellow Americans—with confidence that public institutions can be reformed and shaped to succeed.

2

Where You Want to Go: "The Vision Thing"

My dictionary lists fifty-four definitions of the word "leader." One is "a pipe for conducting hot air"—an apt definition perhaps for Washington, D.C., but not suitable for my purposes here. No, the definition that best fits what I have in mind is "one who guides, one who shows the way." The implication is that what lies ahead is new territory and the guide knows how to reach the destination. It is a good analogy for organizations and change. The problem is that too many leaders start on the path of change without deciding or knowing where they are headed. Sort of like Moses and the forty years spent wandering in the wilderness.

One of my favorite bumper stickers is "I don't know where I'm going, but I'm making good time." Sadly, that describes too many organizations today: once-great institutions that are losing (or have lost) their edge and don't know how to regain it; good institutions that want to be great but can't move beyond the rhetoric; organizations that are failing to adapt to new circumstances and problems, are floundering, and don't know what to do; self-satisfied and smug institutions running on the momentum of past achievements and moving obliviously headlong toward mediocrity and irrelevance; and bureaucracies seemingly "too big to fail" but also apparently too big to change and too resistant to reform. And then there are the many public entities mired in mediocrity, disinterested in and currently incapable of providing quality, efficient services to their customers, the taxpayers.

All such institutions have one thing in common: the need for bold, visionary leaders at all levels who can discern a different and better future for the organization, no matter its size, and who can map a realistic path to attaining that future. If there is to be transformation, it must start at the top. But the person at the top cannot succeed alone: leaders are needed throughout an organization. They are often there; they just need someone to liberate and mobilize them.

To be successful agents of change—of reform—leaders not only must be able to envision a new way forward but also must be practical, with the skill to build broad support for and implement their vision.

Recent history has examples of political leaders who were pragmatic visionaries: Margaret Thatcher revitalizing the United Kingdom; Ronald Reagan restoring America's confidence after the disastrous 1970s and believing the Cold War could be won; the West German chancellor Helmut Kohl and his vision of a unified Germany; Deng Xiaoping and economic reforms that transformed China; Anwar Sadat and Menachem Begin visualizing real peace between Egypt and Israel; F. W. de Klerk and Nelson Mandela, jailer and jailed, reconciling and envisioning a South Africa without apartheid. None of these figures were uncontroversial, but each had a vision of a better future. There are also failed reformers and visionaries, men such as Mikhail Gorbachev, who destroyed the Stalinist structure that propped up the Soviet Union but had no idea what to put in its place. Or the leaders of the "Arab Spring" who sought economic and political freedom but lacked the practical skills to overcome both Islamists and authoritarians.

Of course, business has its own successful pragmatic visionaries, people such as Alan Mulally (Ford), Bill Gates (Microsoft), Sheryl Sandberg (Facebook), Steve Jobs (Apple), Anne Mulcahy (Xerox), Howard Schultz (Starbucks),* Jeff Bezos (Amazon), and Marillyn Hewson (Lockheed Martin). And it also has its big strategic failures such as those who drove two of the big American automotive companies off a cliff, the CEOs of multiple failed financial institutions, and those big bosses who took a wrong strategic turn in manufacturing and retailing and wrecked their companies in the process.

To again quote Jacques Barzun in *From Dawn to Decadence*:

> To govern well requires two distinct kinds of ability: political skill and the administrative mind. Both are very rare, either in combination or separately. The former depends on sensing what can be done, at what moment, and how to move others to want it. . . . But one can be a true politico and be at the same time incapable of administration. To administer is to keep order in a situation that continually tends toward disorder. In running any organization, both people and things have to be kept straight from day to day.

If a single person with these two skills cannot be found, the boss must be the visionary, and she had damn well better have a deputy or chief operating officer who can deliver the practical goods.

––––––––

So, you are the new leader, appointed with the expectation that you can reform and improve the organization. You may be a middle manager with a dozen people working for you, or you may be

* Disclaimer: I serve on the Starbucks board of directors; Schultz's qualities of leadership are a big reason why I wanted to.

the big boss with thousands of employees. It is your first day in charge. What do you do?

Those who would be agents of change must first conceive and articulate where they believe an organization has to go and rally support for that vision. They need to diagnose what is wrong and needs to be changed, why reform is necessary. That is essential in order to persuade employees to get on board. How does a leader establish concrete goals, an agenda for action? Is the problem an immediate crisis, a near-term challenge requiring prompt action, or is it longer term, allowing for a more gradual approach?

To answer those questions, the most critical thing a new leader at any level should do is listen.

Too many new bosses arrive confident they have all the answers—the solutions to an organization's problems—and on day one begin firing off e-mails and giving orders to "light a fire" under people, to demonstrate a new sheriff is in town ready to kick ass and take names, and to show dynamism (and control). Too many openly disdain their predecessors and all that was done before: "Things are going to be different around here now that I'm in charge!"

We all have worked for such "conquering heroes," who see themselves as riding in on a white horse to save the day. What they do, mainly, is scare the hell out of people, who then focus on keeping out of the way—lying low—and keeping their jobs. Employees quickly come to resent the arrogant know-it-all who has just condemned the work they had been doing and either resolve to do all they can to thwart the new leader's agenda or passively stand to one side waiting for him to fail. The conquering hero (or hostile-takeover approach) is, in my view, all wrong. I learned this firsthand when I took this approach in one of my first senior jobs at the CIA, as I will describe later.

Before issuing a single directive or making a single decision, a leader should talk to people at every level of her organization, from the front office to the mail room. Career employees often have startlingly insightful views about the strengths and weaknesses of their organization, which of course they know well; as a result, they often have well-informed ideas for practical ways to improve it. If appropriate to her position, the new leader should talk to stakeholders, governing boards, directors, retirees, alumni, legislators, other elected officials, and, critically, the "customers." She should ask all of them about the organization's strengths and weaknesses and what they think the priorities for change should be.

Most of those the leader engages will have their pet peeves or projects, their axes to grind, or their own agendas. That's okay. Taken together, these conversations will make her far more knowledgeable about the organization, with a richer understanding of the dynamics and culture of the place. Getting out of the office and listening to employees on their turf allows the leader to learn much more than enduring countless PowerPoint presentations in her conference room and will help inform her agenda for change—her vision. Even if she is an insider promoted to leadership, she will learn a lot from people who will talk to her differently now that she is the boss.

If a leader listens during her first days or weeks—as I did as both CIA director and president of Texas A&M—she also will gain insight about the team she has inherited and the health of the organization itself.

Through listening, the leader will quickly learn who is willing to be candid with her about problems and shortcomings (including who cynically trashes colleagues and who does not). She will likely be able to spot early on those self-promoters who are suck-ups and untrustworthy. In her "listening tour," she will be able to make some preliminary assessments of who will be her allies in the effort to bring change and who will not. (A wise leader will not lock herself too firmly into these early judgments about people: there will be surprises along the way.)

Listening before making decisions on the agenda for change

has another significant benefit. It will allow the leader to put early points on the board in the eyes of the employees by sending the important message that their opinions matter, that she values candor, that she doesn't pretend to have all the answers, and that she didn't arrive with her mind completely made up or closed. But she mustn't let the initial listening tour go on too long. That risks conveying the sense that she doesn't have a clue about what to do, is simply a blank page waiting to be imprinted by the career folks, or is indecisive.

A new leader should make clear from the outset that she intends to establish goals early. She should seek out reactions to her own ideas and working agenda. In short, she should communicate clearly that she has ideas and is prepared to act decisively but wants to test those ideas with those who will actually be responsible for implementation—and also get their advice, suggestions, and criticism.

Whenever someone persuades the new woman in charge to alter her thinking or change her mind, she should make a point of saying so publicly, naming names. She may well convert the skeptic who challenged her into an ally, and she will reinforce the message that candor is truly welcome, has impact, and is career enhancing, not career destroying.

It is especially important in the public sector for the leader to establish goals early because she has no idea how long she or her principal lieutenants will have to implement their vision. As I've said, this uncertainty about the length of tenure in a position is a disincentive for many to take on serious reform at all, to invest the necessary time and political capital required. Too many political appointees, accordingly, will make some superficial decisions that sound good, get some positive press for taking on a problem, and then move on without having accomplished much (except to make their employees even more cynical).

When I became director of central intelligence, I knew that a presidential election fourteen months later might end my tenure (as it did). Thus, I moved very fast in launching virtually all my initiatives. At A&M, I was pretty confident I would be president for at least five years, and so I was able to sequence my initiatives and proceed more gradually. Even though I ended up with less time at the university because of being selected as secretary of defense, I still had nearly four and a half years to make progress on my goals. Arriving at Defense at the end of 2006, I assumed I would have only two years in office and focused almost entirely on overseeing the wars in Iraq and Afghanistan, by far the most urgent priorities. It was only when I was unexpectedly asked to stay on by President Obama that I turned my attention to internal and budgetary reform. Still anticipating I would stay on for only a year or two, I wasted no time in moving ahead quickly, particularly with regard to major cuts or caps on dozens of large programs that were unaffordable, unworkable, or unnecessary.

Even after a leader has established her goals and launched actions to implement them, she should keep reaching out and listening to people at every level for as long as she is in the job. By listening, she can learn whether her agenda for change is creating new opponents or allies and who they are. That, in turn, will give her the information she needs to assess whether to adjust her approach; at a minimum, at each step she will know the internal atmosphere as she moves forward.

––––––––

Right away, the leader developing a vision—an agenda—needs to accurately assess the kind of situation he faces. What does the bureaucratic battlefield look like? If he confronts an urgent problem or crisis, the agenda is obvious: it's settling on an action plan—a strategy—to accomplish it that can be tough. That was the case for me at Defense. If the challenges are long-term, as I encountered at A&M, the new boss, as I said earlier, has the leisure of taking more time to establish goals and a strategy to achieve them. In some instances, though, he will need to address an urgent problem *and* simultaneously develop goals for long-term reforms and restructuring, as I did at the CIA. So, let me describe in a little detail the very different situations I faced at those three institutions when I arrived and then explain their relevance to leaders across a wide spectrum of bureaucracies.

When I became director of central intelligence in November 1991, the Soviet Union was collapsing (it would, in fact, cease to exist in seven weeks). My most urgent task, therefore, was to provide the president and his senior advisers with the CIA's best assessment of the likely consequences of that collapse. Would there be chaos? Famine? Millions of refugees? Civil war? Ethnic cleansing? Economic ruin? Would Russia itself disintegrate? What would happen to the nearly forty thousand nuclear weapons in the Soviet arsenal or nuclear-armed intercontinental ballistic missiles—and the nuclear weapons and missiles deployed not in Russia itself but in newly independent successor states themselves in chaos? The stakes could not have been higher. There was no precedent in history for a major empire to collapse without a major war. And so, in an extraordinary effort, we produced nearly a dozen National Intelligence Estimates on these momentous questions within a few weeks to help inform the president's decisions during a critical time.

Even as I dealt with the immediate crisis, there was the equally obvious need for a broad, long-term vision of how to reorient the massive resources of the CIA and other American intelligence agencies from their decades-long preoccupation with the Soviet Union to a post–Cold War world. The collapse of the Soviet Union created a unique window of opportunity to make dramatic structural and operational changes at the CIA and in the intelligence community that would likely have been difficult if not impossible in normal times. While the agenda for change was long-term, I needed to take immediate advantage of the drama of Soviet collapse before its galvanizing impact on everyone dissipated.

Identifying my immediate goals for change as secretary of defense under President Bush was easy. As he, Congress, and the press reminded me daily, in December 2006 we were losing the wars in Iraq and Afghanistan. The need for immediate action to rectify that situation subsumed all other agenda items. My primary and urgent mission was to turn the wars around. In Iraq, the president made the courageous strategic decision to surge nearly thirty thousand additional troops in order to regain the initiative and put us on a path to establishing security and stability. My job was getting the troops there, getting them the equipment they needed, empowering the commanders to do what was necessary to accomplish their mission, and holding Congress at bay long enough for the strategy to have time to work. I was responsible for developing the necessary management priorities and strategies at the Pentagon. In Afghanistan, because we had few additional resources available during 2007–8, the agenda was to do whatever we could to prevent additional Taliban success until we and our allies could provide significant new assets. That involved modest reinforcements, better equipment, new commanders, and efforts inside the U.S. government to narrow our objectives in Afghanistan to those we could realistically achieve.

When I was unexpectedly asked by President-elect Obama to remain as secretary, there was still much to do in terms of the wars, both in the Department of Defense and on the battlefield. But I decided my vision for change at Defense had to expand dramatically beyond simply a successful conclusion to the wars we were in. I had been secretary for two years, and I had realized early that two very big, very ambitious reforms were needed, changes I would now have the opportunity to get under way. As my staff put it, "Gates 2.0."

The first was to begin changing the way the Pentagon thought about the future and how to plan, train, and equip our forces for what I believed would be a very diverse range of potential conflicts in the coming decades. While we needed to retain our capability to deter—and, if necessary, defeat—other powerful countries with modern militaries, we had to abandon our long-standing single-minded focus on so-called conventional conflict and strengthen our capabilities for unconventional non-state foes, such as those we had encountered in the Balkans, Somalia, Lebanon, Panama, and Libya, and non-state enemies such as al-Qaeda, Hezbollah, the Islamic State of Iraq and Syria, and other terrorist groups. Those are the sort of adversaries we had actually fought over the previous forty years—with the sole exception of the brief first Gulf War in 1991, when we expelled the Iraqi army from Kuwait. This mix of unconventional and irregular conflict—with the lesser likelihood, but hugely consequential possibility, of a major military confrontation with Russia or China—was the world the U.S. military was most likely to encounter in the future. I knew the changes in approach I felt necessary would be a heavy lift with the military services and the defense establishment.

The second big reform was prompted both by political reality and by the 2008 economic crisis. I concluded we had to pre-emptively and dramatically begin to restructure the Pentagon budget—to cut overdue, overcost, and underperforming weapons and other acquisition programs and to take far-reaching steps to reduce bureaucratic overhead costs. We needed to tackle inefficiency and waste on the merits but also in anticipation of future significant budgetary pressures on us from both the president and Congress. I thought we'd be foolish moving forward if we didn't anticipate some financial belt-tightening. I hoped that if we credibly showed we could change the way we did business internally, we might just preempt others from making draconian and strategically dangerous cuts. This would be, I knew, a long-term undertaking. But this vision—or goal—of beginning to change the Pentagon's approach to budgeting and fiscal management would dominate my internal agenda throughout the time I served President Obama.

With regard to our approach to future conflicts, I had few allies among the military top brass. As for the budget, nearly everyone saw a train wreck shaping up, but no one was much interested in cutting *his* budget or organization.

Another bumper sticker I like reads, "Lead, follow, or get the hell out of the way." I felt it was my responsibility to take on these two big challenges under Obama. No one else was in a position to do so—in either rank, experience, credibility, or political independence. I believed the change in course to address both was critical to the future of the department and to America's national security. (The importance of such changes is why I am taking you inside the institutions I served—to make clear just how important the matters dealt with by bureaucracies are and therefore why it is so important to improve them.) I had talked about both reform agendas throughout 2008 in a series of major speeches and in an article published in *Foreign Affairs*. I had also listened to the concerns and views of both civilian and military leaders. But moving the Defense Department forward was my responsibility, and I was confident of the direction we needed to go, so I acted despite the reservations of others.

I encountered a completely different situation from the CIA and Defense at Texas A&M. Five years before I became its president, my predecessor, Dr. Ray Bowen, proposed that A&M strive to be recognized as one of the ten best public universities in the United States by 2020 while at the same time maintaining and enhancing the distinctiveness of the institution. He mobilized a broad effort involving more than 250 people on and off campus to assess the current strengths and weaknesses of the school and how to achieve his goal. As mentioned earlier, the nearly two-year-long study was called *Vision 2020*. The conclusion was honest and stark: "We are good but not good enough." The report expressed "steadfast determination to build on strengths, eliminate weaknesses, seek opportunities, and face threats creatively and energetically." The report had broad support from the board of regents, the faculty, and administrators.

The recommendations were presented as twelve overarching ideas called "Imperatives." In brief, they included strengthening the faculty both in excellence and in size, enhancing both the graduate and the undergraduate academic experiences, emphasizing the liberal arts, increasing ethnic and geographic diversity, expanding and enhancing the physical plant and landscape, developing more "enlightened" governance, attracting more financial resources, and building closer ties with the local community and the state of Texas.

Just six months after the board of regents approved the *Vision 2020* report in 1999, a huge bonfire fifty-nine feet high and consisting of some five thousand logs—built by students before the annual football game with the University of Texas—collapsed, killing twelve students and seriously injuring twenty-seven more. The bonfire had been one of A&M's most cherished and popular traditions for ninety years. The entire campus was devastated, and the university leadership would be preoccupied with the tragedy and aftermath for the remainder of Bowen's tenure as president. When I arrived on campus as the new president in August 2002, little progress had been made in implementing *Vision 2020*.

I had made clear during the interview process that I would consider the study a blueprint for change if I became president. As I said earlier, I had no interest in the job if maintaining the status quo was expected. I wanted no illusions about my intentions.

Shortly after arriving at A&M, I appointed Dr. David Prior, dean of the College of Geosciences, executive vice president and provost—my second-in-command. We immediately undertook a rigorous schedule of visiting each of the colleges in the university (engineering, agriculture, science, liberal arts, veterinary medicine, and all the rest) to meet with the dean, department heads, and faculty—a listening tour. I had already concluded that addressing all twelve imperatives in *Vision 2020* was impossible. To tackle change on so many fronts at once would be a formula for paralysis if not disaster. So at each college we asked which three or four of the imperatives we should tackle that would give us disproportionate leverage and momentum—and a fast start—while advancing the other imperatives as well.

In less than a month, by early September, I was able to report our findings to the faculty senate. I told them that there was an emerging consensus on the top four priorities: We needed more faculty, and we needed to increase salaries. We needed significantly more graduate fellowships and other financial assistance.

We needed to confront the critical shortages of classroom and laboratory space. We had to vastly improve our record in recruiting and retaining minority faculty and students, which was lamentable.

I made two other points. First, we would not diminish strong academic programs to strengthen weak ones. Second, I made clear that *Vision 2020* was a set of aspirations, not a plan. I wanted each college to develop specific objectives looking out one year and five years, with clear milestones and metrics by which we could measure progress. I said I expected the plans for each college to be unique, reflecting its particular strengths and weaknesses. I left no doubt that "change has come to Texas A&M and more is on the way. This university is ready to move to the next level of excellence."

In just three weeks of listening and of dialogue, we had moved from twelve broad statements of intent in *Vision 2020* to a prioritized set of four goals with broad support across campus.

Universities are often held up as examples of the most difficult institutions in which to make changes. I inherited an aspirational set of goals and ideas with broad faculty support. By involving the faculty and staff in establishing priorities for change from among those goals and ideas, I made the professionals my allies and strongest supporters for moving ahead. That is key in any public institution. While faculty are, by nature, independent actors who are rarely motivated en masse, there are faculty organizations that can play an important and constructive role. I worked hard to develop close, cooperative relationships with each of these groups, and the effort paid off with the faculty as a whole in gaining their support for what I was trying to accomplish.

———

Leaders of public institutions often cannot avoid politics, as I mentioned earlier. In this case, before becoming president of A&M, I would have to face off with the governor of Texas, Rick Perry, an A&M graduate who, I was told, had promised the president's job to Senator Phil Gramm, who had taught economics there for some years. After the search committee had settled on me, I received a call from Perry, who pressured me to withdraw my candidacy. He said he did not want me at A&M, neither did many Aggies, and he would be appointing *all* the members of the board of regents in the future—hinting I would face very rough going as president. The last thing I wanted was to get mixed up in Texas politics, but I also wasn't about to let the governor intimidate me into pulling out. As I later told my wife, I had been confronting—in person— the leadership of the KGB while this guy was a freshman member of the Texas House of Representatives. I told Perry I would just let the board of regents decide. All three of his appointees then on the board voted against me (including Gramm's wife, who did not recuse herself, as is normally done when there is a personal conflict of interest), while of the other six, appointed by the previous governor, George W. Bush, five voted for me and one "courageously" abstained. (Behind the scenes, Perry and I would have an adversarial relationship the entire time I was at Texas A&M, though we managed to maintain public civility. I contacted him on several occasions with private, handwritten notes, but there was never a response. He was not an advocate of *Vision 2020*.)

If a leader is not making at least a few enemies along the way, he must not be doing much. Still, in public or private institutions, overt hostility to elected officials or one's bosses—or disloyalty to them—is an unaffordable luxury. If the leader can't persuade them, accommodate them, or reconcile with them, if he cannot do his job in good conscience, then he must quit. No job is worth selling one's soul for. The governor was a pain in the neck, but I could still do my job the way I thought best.

————

So, what is the relevance of my experiences as a new leader to others in government or business when developing an agenda for change—a vision for future action? After all, almost no one will be faced with a challenge like the collapse of the Soviet Union or how to redirect American intelligence after the end of the Cold War, leading the military in wartime, or repositioning a large university.

One takeaway for a new leader is that external circumstances and challenges must take center stage in developing her agenda for change. At times, those circumstances will dictate the agenda. The leader should proceed accordingly. Ignoring the realities of the bureaucratic battlefield makes no sense: a leader must not fight reality just because she arrived with a preconceived plan or goals that pointed in another direction. Her plans must accommodate the situation as it is in creating an agenda for present and future change.

Another lesson is simply this: in developing an agenda, as change agents, all leaders *will* have to decide the relative importance of urgent problems versus long-term challenges and, in the process, figure out how to allocate time and effort among them. If a new leader faces an immediate crisis, dealing with that must take precedence over, while not totally eclipsing, long-term goals. A leader placed in charge of an organization facing a firestorm should reach for a hose, not a PowerPoint. In consultation with her professional staff, she must ascertain what should be done to address the immediate crisis—and then act. Her success in dealing with immediate problems also will pay dividends as she deals with longer-term challenges.

Finally, when challenging the status quo, even after listening to everyone, the leader must sometimes be prepared to act alone, to boldly go where no one else wants to go. Many leadership training and management programs, in business and in government, focus a great deal on teamwork, team building, group dynamics, and building consensus. Such skills are important, but when establishing an agenda for reform, for transformational change, a leader will almost always be going against the consensus and conventional wisdom in much of what she does. People will think she is wrong and will tell her so. The change agent must be an oak, not a daisy.

Successfully leading reform in bureaucracies, large and small, is not for the fainthearted or for the egomaniacal. As a leader develops her goals, hearing the ideas, assessments, and thoughts of others in the organization about what change is needed will make a critical contribution on many levels. Still, also taking into account the realities of the organization's situation, the leader alone must decide the path forward. The important thing to remember is that in any public or private sector organization, whether it has three million employees or three, having a clearly defined and achievable vision—or set of goals—and getting the priorities right in moving forward are the preconditions for successfully leading change. After all, as Yogi Berra said, "If you don't know where you're going, you will wind up somewhere else."

3
———

Formulating a Strategy

Armed with clearly defined goals for change, a new leader will be tempted to plunge ahead and let the chips fall where they may. He shouldn't. Too often, especially in the public sector, a leader comes in with a bold agenda for change, gives a powerful speech, and then ... Nothing. There is no plan, no strategy for implementation.

A good example of this was the speech President Obama gave in Cairo in his first months in office. It was a terrific speech, candidly acknowledging U.S. missteps in the Middle East and describing the new directions he intended to take. Arab audiences were excited by what he had to say. But over the following weeks, their enthusiasm turned to bitterness when it soon became clear there was no follow-up plan or strategy to implement his vision. This happens too often both in the public sector and in business.

Carefully considered strategies for implementation are critical in reforming bureaucracies. On every matter I thought important, small or large, I always took time to devise a specific strategy to achieve my goal and to identify milestones and deadlines to measure progress. You can't depend just on luck or goodwill to make things happen. Begin with a concerted effort to win the support of internal and external constituencies for the reform agenda. Decide on the sequence in which you will pursue your objectives and the managerial tools and techniques to be used for each. And then carefully choose your lieutenants.

For successful change at every kind of institution in both the private and the public sectors, a leader must win the support of those in the trenches who deliver the mission of the organization. Recognition of their critical role and respect for them go a long way.

It is imperative early on for a leader to reassure (or disarm) those who will be apprehensive about his intentions—that is, probably nearly everyone in the organization. At minimum, opposition needs to be preempted or defanged; at best, allies can be won. Taking the time and making the effort to prepare various constituencies for change are steps often omitted by new leaders, dismissed as "stagecraft" or "getting warm and fuzzy."

I know such an approach to be important because early in my career I failed to take it, with profound consequences. In 1981, the CIA director, William Casey, was unhappy with the quality of analysis produced at the CIA, as were a number of appointees of the newly elected Ronald Reagan. Indeed, I knew from having spent five and a half years on the National Security Council staff at the White House under Presidents Nixon, Ford, and Carter that they too had been disappointed by the CIA's analytical work. I had long felt there was room for improvement. By late 1981, I was a senior CIA officer running the offices of both the director, Casey, and the deputy director, Bob Inman. I wrote a long paper for them laying out a number of specific measures I felt if implemented could significantly improve the quality of CIA analysis. When the job of deputy director for intelligence (analysis) came open, they jumped me over a number of more senior managers to become its head and to implement the recommendations I had given them. I had little experience running a large line organization. (I was thirty-eight.)

I proceeded immediately to prove it. In retrospect, it was clear that a number of senior officers in the directorate also believed far-reaching change was needed, that our analytical work for the president and his senior advisers had become intellectually lazy, lacking sufficient rigor. But confident I had all the answers, I hardly consulted with my colleagues. Instead, I filled the agency auditorium with managers and analysts and proceeded to deliver a jeremiad about past failures and shortcomings (with little reference to successes) and announced nearly a dozen measures that would upend the way the directorate had been doing business. In the space of an hour, as a brand-new boss, I managed to anger nearly everyone who worked for me and to antagonize even those who agreed with me on both the diagnosis and the remedies. It was the worst possible start.

I held that job for more than four years, and over time many of the changes I imposed by fiat were accepted as necessary. The analytical product improved substantially in the eyes of most policy makers. But, internally, resentment smoldered for a long time over my early, mistaken approach to bringing change.

I learned my lesson and applied what I learned in every subsequent job. From the first days I took charge, wherever I was, I targeted the career employees whose roles and attitudes would determine whether any initiative for change would succeed or fail. Gaining the respect and cooperation of the professional cadre—or at least getting them to keep an open mind—should have very high priority on every new leader's to-do list.

Both real and symbolic actions and gestures of respect early can have significant impact in softening resistance to change and persuading people to be receptive to what a new leader is trying to do. The following actions I describe are peculiar to the three institutions I led but are easily adaptable to any public or private bureaucracy.

Faculty are deeply suspicious of university administrators and their often empty promises of "shared governance." To paraphrase Mark Twain, for an administrator to deliver on such promises "will gratify some [faculty] and astonish the rest." But making the elevation of the faculty the first item on the broadly agreed agenda for change at A&M addressed that problem quickly.

Texas A&M has commencement ceremonies in May, August, and December. Before I arrived, the entering procession at the ceremonies was led by the vice presidents with the deans and faculty following. On the stage, the vice presidents sat in the front row, with the deans relegated to the back rows. The faculty in attendance were seated on the arena floor next to the stage, nearly invisible to everyone. At my first commencement in August, just days after I arrived on campus, I placed the deans in the front row onstage (some were a little miffed they now had to pay attention and not read *Sports Illustrated* or check their e-mails during the ceremonies), the vice presidents behind them; and the faculty were seated together on the expanded stage at the side of the official party. At the next commencement, the faculty led the procession. These were little things, symbolic to be sure, but the faculty noticed.

The administrative vice presidents at A&M essentially ran the university when I arrived. Decisions on budgets, space allocation, and spending priorities were made by them and the university president with little input from deans and faculty. I resolved to subordinate administration to the academic mission of the university. (You would be surprised to know how often it is the other way around at colleges and universities.) The head of academic programs at Texas A&M, the provost, also carried the title of executive vice president, a hollow honorific. I made it real by requiring the administrative vice presidents to report to me through the executive vice president/provost, again sending the message that academic needs would drive administrative decisions. The person in charge of the academic program would be the chief operating officer of the university.

Less than a month after assuming my position, I went before the faculty senate to inform them of these reforms—and more. I would, I told them, create four councils of eight to ten people to advise the provost and me, three of the councils to be chaired by deans with both faculty and administrators as members. A finance council, chaired by the dean of the business school, would participate in creating the university budget and make recommendations for how better to align academic needs and budgetary allocations. A research council would be chaired by the dean of the College of Science, and an education council would be chaired by the dean of the College of Education. The "built environment" council would be chaired by the vice-provost and would make recommendations on the allocation of existing space and new buildings.

I also told the members of the faculty senate that I understood past administrative practices had created skepticism, even cynicism. I invited them to ignore my rhetoric and just watch what we did—but also to work with me as I tried to build a form of governance that recognized the primacy of the colleges and the faculty in accomplishing the mission of the university.

There were other gestures toward the faculty. I invited the speaker of the faculty senate to be a regular attendee at my staff meetings. I said we would have no secrets from the faculty—"After all, this isn't the CIA." I met routinely with the senate's executive committee and consistently sought its recommendations for faculty members to sit on search committees and task forces. I created a new award, the Presidential Professor for Teaching Excellence, two of which would be given out each year with a stipend of $25,000. That award had great appeal to the faculty but also scratched the itch of those who felt research universities like Texas A&M did not sufficiently value superb teaching.

Nothing makes an impression on a constituency accustomed to being ignored, in this case faculty, than for them to make a suggestion and have the boss simply say on the spot, "That's a hell of a good idea. Let's do it." I went out of my way to find such opportunities from my earliest days at A&M.

Midway through my first year, I announced that we would hire 450 new faculty, with the deans and faculty working with the provost to decide how to allocate the positions. That would be transformational, having substantial impact both on teacher-student ratios in the classroom and on research.

Through the actions I have mentioned and others—outreach efforts, symbolic moves, and more—by the end of my first semester I had gained the important allies I sought among faculty and deans. Without their support, there was little I could have accomplished. Collectively, the blitz to win friends and allies took a lot of time, but the investment paid off handsomely when I started to change things. A consistent message to all was the need to preserve and strengthen those traditions at A&M that were core to who we were and made us unique and to shed those that were holding us back.

When I became secretary of defense, I had the same strategy for winning allies early through gestures of respect and recognition. When I was nominated to be secretary, rumors were rife that I would purge most of the senior civilians who had worked for my predecessor, Don Rumsfeld, and name new people to take their places. But I had learned a lesson about that. Many years earlier, I had worked for a director of the CIA who, when he assumed the job, had brought with him dozens of his own acolytes from outside the agency. He never recovered from the hostile reaction. Before I began my job, I resolved not to change a single senior official at the Pentagon at the outset and to walk in the door alone, entirely alone, without bringing even a personal secretary. It was a message of both confidence in and respect for the incumbents. It was also recognition that in the midst of two wars, both going badly, trying to find (and get confirmed) new people would be a waste of precious time. This was in stark contrast to my approach at A&M, where I was far more willing to replace senior administrators because, as I've said, I had plenty of time and no pressing crises.

There were gestures toward the military leadership. Rumsfeld nearly always met with the Joint Chiefs of Staff in his conference room. When I met with them as a group, I would go to their conference room, "the Tank." I would try to meet there with them once a week just to hear what was on their minds, even if there was no other reason to get together. Similarly, rather than summon the ten or so major commanders from around the country and the world to brief me when I took over, I visited their headquarters; I went to them. Aside from the gesture, that gave me a chance to see them in their "native" habitat, where they were comfortable, but also to meet a number of the men and women in uniform who worked for them—from whom I would always learn something. I also would try to attend as many change-of-command ceremonies for these major commands as possible. I believe that the respectful way I treated senior military leaders made a huge contribution to their support of what I was trying to do or, when they disagreed with me, their willingness to refrain from undercutting me or running to Congress to sabotage my efforts. That had been a common practice under many of my predecessors.

Until 2004, the DCI not only headed the Central Intelligence Agency but also was the nominal head of the "intelligence community," with considerable control over the budgets of the other fifteen or so major intelligence agencies and authority in establishing priorities both for collection of information and for assessments. As deputy DCI from 1986 to 1989, I put into practice what I had learned from my earlier managerial mistakes, so my relationships with most senior people in the CIA were pretty good. When I became DCI in 1991—I had been gone less than three years—that paid off.

As for the leaders of other intelligence agencies I did not know, I quickly began to establish a close working relationship. Unlike a number of my predecessors and successors as DCI (and later director of national intelligence), I realized the limits of my direct authority to manage the other agencies. I had real influence—partly statutory, partly because of my close relationship with President George H. W. Bush—but knew I couldn't boss the others around. I used regular get-togethers as vehicles for gaining their support for my ambitious agenda for adapting the intelligence community to the new, post-Soviet world. Treating them as colleagues and not subordinates, listening and using their ideas, I forged a strong team with them that made historic changes in American intelligence—restructuring agencies, reorienting our activities and budgets away from the Soviet Union to myriad other global problems, and changing the way we collected and analyzed information for the nation's leaders. I think these lessons can be successfully applied wherever change is sought.

There is another important constituency to cultivate in every organization: those low in the institutional pecking order—line workers, staff, troops, or students. The only way for a leader to persuade them he has their interests at heart is through consistent actions over a period of time. Rhetoric cuts no ice. But knowing the person at the top cares matters a lot, regardless of the kind of institution or its size.

Most new bosses—both in business and in the public sector—who want to change things don't make much of an effort to reach out to these folks. Especially in very large organizations, the leader is usually a remote figure seen at ceremonies or special occasions. One summer at the CIA, an upper-echelon boss who rarely visited our office was spotted in the vicinity. One office wag loudly commented that because the boss was visiting us, "it must be Christmas." College students, like their contemporaries in the military, are especially skeptical about the intentions of older people and cynical about authority figures.

At A&M, I became a sort of ombudsman for students, lending my personal support to individuals when I believed the bureaucracy was being unfair or too inflexible (with grades, fees, and university rules, among other issues). One August, I voided three thousand parking tickets given out on freshman move-in day by overly zealous campus police. I was persuaded by a group of students not to convert their small residence hall into offices, and I agreed to student pleas to delay for a year a similar move involving another dorm. There were numerous other such actions.

I gave student leaders a lot of my time at A&M. I invited the president of the student body to attend all my regular staff meetings—like the speaker of the faculty senate—and I routinely went before the student senate to answer any and all questions. I showed up at virtually any event student leaders suggested. I appointed students to every university search committee, task force, and council. They became strong advocates for a number of my initiatives for change, including especially the push for greater diversity.

I think my approach to winning the confidence of students worked, because when I left the university to become secretary of defense, ten thousand of them turned out to say good-bye.

My chief of staff at Texas A&M was a young lawyer, Rodney McClendon. Rodney brought many skills to the position, but one special asset was that he knew—by name—nearly every staff person at A&M, whether secretaries, members of the grounds crew, people in food services, or custodians. When I would walk across campus with him, he would make sure to introduce every one of these folks to me when our paths crossed. Perhaps more important, he made sure I was aware of issues that affected them, their concerns, and their complaints. He arranged for their leaders to meet with me to discuss problems. Rodney also kept me informed about key events in the community in which many of these employees participated, and I would often attend them. Through his efforts, I was able to establish a connection to those who played a critical role in the life of the university even if they were on the lowest rungs of the rank ladder.

On every visit to a military post or base around the world, and on every visit to the front lines, I would have breakfast or lunch with enlisted troops, noncommissioned officers, and junior- and middle-grade officers. In these get-togethers, too, I learned a lot,

but they—like the other actions I have described—were also cal-
culated gestures of respect. From my actions to help wounded
warriors and their families, to get needed lifesaving equipment
to the war zones, and more, the troops came to have confidence I
had their backs—that I was truly there for them.

I also would regularly visit offices in the bowels of the Pentagon that no previous secretary of defense had ever seen. I visited
workers in the mail room, the loading dock, the communications
center. I attended the morning briefing for the Pentagon police. I
visited offices of professionals many links down the chain who did
critical work but never saw the boss. They were always forewarned
of my visit to ensure that most who worked there were present. I
stayed just long enough for each person to tell me briefly about
his or her job, to have a photograph taken with each employee, to
shake hands, and to thank them for their work. Such visits have
an impact.

My efforts as director to reach out to lower-ranking employees
at the CIA included eating lunch most of the time in the cafeteria
and inviting myself to join several of them at their tables. On one
occasion, this led to an embarrassing situation. I had engaged a
group of young spies in a lengthy conversation, and during the
course of it I dismissed my security detail, telling them I would
just return to the office on my own. I had forgotten that there was
a security guard post between the cafeteria and the main building
and, as director, I had no identification badge. The young guard
on duty properly refused to let me pass. He did agree to let me use
his phone, and I called my office to arrange a rescue. The senior
officers on my detail rushed to the guard station and escorted me
through. As they did so, I overheard one of them talking about
reporting the guard to his superiors for treating me disrespect-
fully. I turned on the man, telling him in no uncertain terms the
guard had done exactly the right thing, and if anybody called his
superior, it would be me to commend him for doing his duty.

The thinking behind the steps I took to meet and cultivate
support among employees at every level is universally applicable,

even if my exact steps aren't. Other organizations offer different opportunities to gain the support of the people in them. These gestures are all a part of leadership, a means of connecting with those you seek—and need—as partners.

The wise leader's strategy for change must include a concentrated campaign to make as many friends and allies as possible as early as possible before he starts taking actions that will inevitably make enemies. To be an effective leader, one must demonstrate from the start an understanding of and respect for the role and views of the career employees in an organization and be clear that the new boss intends to make them participants and partners in reforming the place. This is the best possible preparation of the bureaucratic battlefield.

———

As mundane as it might seem, another important aspect of a new leader's strategy from her first days should be to quickly seize control of her calendar. No matter the size of an organization, a boss's time is her most precious commodity. It is her "capital," and she only has a finite amount to spend. Every day there will be innumerable demands on a leader's time that have nothing to do with her agenda for change. Indeed, be warned: the most effective defense of every bureaucracy to keep the boss from meddling, interfering, or changing the status quo is to fill up her calendar with meetings.

A leader must make time to think and to plan—to strategize.

Leading reform of bureaucracies requires constant attention and effort. A leader attempting transformational change must dedicate herself to the endeavor wholeheartedly. During the waking hours, a leader must always be thinking about what she is trying to do and how to do it. Nothing must be left to chance, and hardly anything is unimportant. For every problem and every challenge that arises, the leader needs to formulate a strategy on how to deal with it, eliminate it, or use it. Before any meeting, press conference or public presentation, I was always calculating how I could advance the reform agenda. Reforming bureaucracies is so complex and support for change often so tentative that loose ends have the potential to unravel the entire effort.

All this strategizing takes time, and it is a common failing of leaders of big institutions that they get so trapped in day-to-day issues, meetings, and travel, they neglect their own agenda—change. I always tried to set aside an hour or so every day to work on *my* agenda. In the normal course of affairs, the demands of others filled up most of my day. If I wasn't careful, routine matters would consume the entire day. But during that daily "quiet time," I could think about what progress was being made, what the problems were and how to tackle them, how various individuals were performing and whether that was good enough, and think through strategies for implementing the change agenda.

I mentioned earlier that a new leader's strategy needs to include carefully choosing his lieutenants. This is important because he must delegate leadership and implementation of specific initiatives on his agenda for change whenever possible. Those surrogates must be chosen carefully to ensure that they can deliver results that accomplish the established goals on time and then can lead the effort to gain acceptance and, where necessary, approval.

However, on some initiatives, a leader must lead the effort personally, must be seen doing it—and must take the time to do so. Most of the challenges I faced at the Defense Department were rooted in a structure so complex, cutting across so many organizations, that no one person or entity below the secretary had the authority or resources to solve most problems, including getting the right equipment to the front lines and canceling major programs. Accordingly, more than at either the CIA or A&M, I had to be personally and routinely involved in virtually every consequential initiative and change on my agenda. As an example, in selecting the thirty-odd major acquisition programs to cut in early 2009, I chaired forty meetings over a period of just two months. I met with the task force charged with overseeing the production of the mine-resistant, ambush-protected (MRAP) armored vehicles every two weeks; the same was true of most other initiatives related to the wars in Iraq and Afghanistan. While the chairs of the task forces were exceptionally able, it routinely required my personal involvement to keep the bureaucracy from smothering their efforts. When we set out in 2010 to reduce projected Pentagon overhead spending—by $180 billion, as I mentioned earlier—between mid-May and mid-December I chaired sixty meetings ranging in length from one to eight hours.

The situation was completely different at A&M and the CIA. In both places, I made wide use of task forces and councils, but other than periodic updates I spent little time with them until their work was complete. The important thing in these circumstances is to prepare a strong and detailed charter for the work of such groups and then to choose men and women to lead them who not only agree with the overall agenda for change (if not the particulars; after all, you do want creativity and give-and-take) but also by virtue of their institutional role and personal reputation can win wide support for those changes. Also, in both places, I assigned my special assistant at the CIA and my chief of staff at A&M responsibility for monitoring the task forces and reporting to me whether they were on track and coming to conclusions compatible with my agenda.

A transformational leader needs to set priorities in his reform agenda, decide how to sequence his initiatives, and develop creative strategies for change well suited to the specific institution he heads. One size does not fit all. In doing these things, a leader is able to shape the bureaucratic battlefield in ways that significantly enhance the chances for success.

The greatest American presidents have three or four major accomplishments for which they are remembered. If a leader is too ambitious, he will dissipate his energy and focus, lose momentum, and fail. Within the broader agenda for change, a leader must choose his priorities with great care.

Too many leaders give too little thought to which change initiatives ought to be launched early and which should wait. When a leader initially surveys the bureaucratic battlefield, he needs to determine which of his initiatives for change are going to be greeted with enthusiasm and broad support and which are going to provoke the greatest opposition. Whenever possible, the popular changes should be made first and the tougher ones later. By successfully effecting changes that are broadly welcome, a leader creates a positive climate for further change. In doing so, he generates political capital and credibility for when he takes on the controversial or more difficult issues.

This worked especially well for me at A&M. I felt strongly about creating a new undergraduate degree that would reflect twenty-first-century reality by allowing a student, with a faculty adviser's oversight and approval, to design a degree program that cut across multiple colleges and disciplines. Because this kind of degree was new and nontraditional in that it involved several colleges and no specific major, there was substantial faculty skepticism. So I waited nearly three years to launch it, until I had built up considerable capital with the faculty by, among other things, implementing the program to hire hundreds more faculty and beginning construction of several hundred million dollars' worth of new academic facilities. I named Elsa Murano, dean of the agriculture school, and Jerry Strawser, dean of the business school, to lead the task force studying the proposal and added as members several former speakers of the faculty senate who I knew would be supportive. It was still a tough slog, but ultimately the degree program was approved.

To achieve especially challenging goals, a leader should always be prepared to tailor his reform strategy to the culture of the institution. This requires investing much thought in tactical creativity—as well as unorthodox approaches and the element of surprise—in developing strategies for implementation.

My determination to increase diversity at A&M required just such a tailored, unorthodox strategy. While the number of minority students there had grown over the years, the percentages significantly lagged the changing demography of the state. I was determined to change this, but I knew I had to shape the initiative carefully to win broad support among conservative former (and current) students, the board of regents, and others important to the university. More than a few among them saw no value in greater on-campus diversity and certainly no value in spending money to achieve it. So, my strategy had to be designed specifically for Texas A&M and its culture.

In December 2003, a few months after the Supreme Court approved limited use of affirmative action in college admissions, I announced a number of measures we would take to increase minority recruitment and enrollment. We would establish a statewide network of "prospective student centers"—permanent recruitment, admissions, and financial offices (with bilingual staff) in predominantly minority areas of major Texas cities and along the border with Mexico. I announced twenty-four hundred new four-year scholarships (six hundred per year) of $5,000 per year for first-generation college students who came from homes with $40,000 or less in family income. For families at that income level, we could stack other scholarships and grants so those students could go to A&M virtually free. Demographically, about two-thirds of those scholarships would go to minorities, the remainder to poor whites.

At the same time, I announced A&M would not use affirmative action in the way it was being used at most universities, that is, assigning students extra "points" in the application score if they were of a certain ethnicity. Everyone would be admitted purely on the basis of individual merit. Most A&M students and alumni applauded the merit-only approach—until I announced a couple of days later that we would no longer use legacy (previous family attendance at A&M) as a factor in admissions. As I told the Aggies, we couldn't have it both ways: purely merit-based admissions *and* legacy. The shit that hit the fan as a result of these combined admissions initiatives came from the media, minority leaders in Texas already deeply skeptical of the university's commitment to greater diversity, some alumni, and a number of faculty. With respect to race-blind admissions, most minority leaders figured the new approach was just a dodge to avoid increasing the number of minority kids and evidence of hostility at A&M to minorities.

Within days of my public announcement, I was summoned to the state capitol to meet with a dozen or so legislators who came from racial minorities. They lambasted me in the most graphic terms for the better part of two hours. Years of testifying before Congress had inured me to this kind of treatment, so I just sat and took it, repeatedly and politely reaffirming my commitment to bring more minorities to Texas A&M. I didn't make much of a dent in their anger. One very powerful African-American state senator, Royce West of Dallas, who had been impressed with how I had quickly responded to his criticism of A&M's poor record in using minority-owned businesses, berated me publicly and stated his disagreement with my decision. Privately, however, he said he wanted to help and told other minority leaders around the state that I should be given a chance to succeed. He invited me to Dallas to talk with minority community activists and the editorial board of *The Dallas Morning News,* in both cases accompanying me and introducing me. He repeatedly avowed that I had delivered on what I had promised in the past and he had confidence I would do so again. I will never forget his confidence and his willingness to take a risk by supporting me. He helped buy me the time I needed to make my strategy work.

Sixteen months after arriving on campus, I implemented a

tailored strategy for increasing diversity at A&M: rejecting the use of both affirmative action and legacy, and allocating millions of dollars to a unique and aggressive recruitment effort. The strategy was controversial among both external and internal audiences. But sometimes a leader must decide what is in the best long-term interest of the institution, suck it up, make a tough decision, put his head down, and plunge ahead—even if alone. I was convinced that if I was to meaningfully increase minority representation at A&M, I had to have an unorthodox strategy consistent with the institution's culture. I was determined to convince Hispanics and African-Americans that I was dead serious about increasing their numbers in both the student body and the faculty and equally determined to persuade the university community that greater diversity was essential for Texas A&M's stature and its future.

I spent the next three years implementing that tailored strategy. It worked. By fall semester 2006, African-American freshman enrollment was up 77 percent from the fall of 2003; Hispanic freshman enrollment was up 59 percent. Our success in enrolling minorities, especially compared with a number of other major public universities nationwide where minority enrollment was declining in absolute terms, was recognized in a front-page article of *The Chronicle of Higher Education* and by the editorial board of the *Houston Chronicle*. (Between 2002, before I launched my initiative, and 2012, African-American and Hispanic undergraduates at Texas A&M increased from 10.6 percent of the student body to 23.6 percent, a major step forward, though there is room for continued improvement.)

––––––

My priorities when I became secretary of defense—getting more troops into the war zones, getting them the equipment they needed to succeed in the missions they had been given, getting them home safely, and, if wounded, getting the best possible care for them—were not the priorities of the senior leaders in the Pentagon. They were preoccupied not with waging the wars in Iraq and Afghanistan but with planning and procuring equipment for future wars against major nation-states. I had to shape my strategy accordingly. The most immediate change I had to make, shocking to me, was to get the senior leadership focused on Iraq and Afghanistan.

President Obama's onetime White House chief of staff Rahm Emanuel said you should never let a crisis go to waste, an important lesson for all leaders. Further, I would add, if a new leader manages a crisis effectively, it can have an enormous ripple effect, enhancing his authority and his ability to address other problems.

My first management crisis as secretary was the result of a series in *The Washington Post* in February 2007 detailing the squalid living conditions and bureaucratic morass that troops recovering from their combat wounds had to deal with at Walter Reed Army Medical Center in Washington, D.C. The Walter Reed scandal demonstrated that while the medical care was superb, outpatient wounded soldiers undergoing further treatment and rehabilitation were being neglected; they had to fight the military's health bureaucracy at every step on their difficult paths. Both Walter Reed and the defense establishment more broadly presumed—hoped, really—from 2003 on that the war in Iraq would be wrapped up relatively quickly, we could begin withdrawing our troops, and we could get back to "business as usual." There wasn't much interest in disrupting established organizations, routines, and programs, much less creating and funding new ones aimed at meeting the immediate war-related needs of troops and commanders.

Walter Reed provided me with an opportunity to address this mentality—and related shortcomings—in ways that also tackled the broader issues affecting the war effort. I declared that helping our wounded warriors and their families would be our highest priority "after the wars themselves." Because so many different elements of the Pentagon were involved, I created the Wounded Warrior Task Force, which reported to me every two weeks on our progress. The task force was just the first of several I created to accomplish other priority tasks associated with turning the wars around. They would become an essential instrument for me not just on matters relating to the wars but on other problems in the department as well.

I knew I personally would have to shape the Pentagon battle-fields and devise strategies for winning the internal fights over providing better support for the troops. And the fights came fast and furious, including those over better armored vehicles (mine-resistant, ambush-protected vehicles) to provide significantly better protection for troops on the move—a program opposed by virtually all of the senior civilian and military leaders; improved intelligence, surveillance, and reconnaissance and better detection of, and defenses against, roadside bombs (bureaucratic paralysis and air force opposition complicated solutions); reduced medevac times in Afghanistan—again opposed by nearly all the top brass. One action that certainly helped shape the internal battlefield for the years ahead was my firing of the Walter Reed hospital commander, the surgeon general of the army, and the secretary of the army less than three months after I took office. I made clear that when it came to getting the troops what they needed and taking care of them, I would not tolerate neglect, obstacles, or halfhearted commitment.

———

When I became DCI in November 1991, my strategy for change was to blitz the CIA and the other intelligence agencies with multiple initiatives for change, all with short deadlines. Unlike the Defense Department and A&M, where the need for change was questioned by more than a few, virtually everyone in the CIA and other intelligence agencies recognized that we had entered a new and very different world. Thus, there was little opposition to the overall effort, though there would be to specific proposals.

In intelligence organizations, secrecy and "need to know" are integral elements of the culture, but I decided that there was nothing particularly sensitive about the structural and procedural changes I was contemplating or, for the most part, changes in the way we did our business. Thus, at the very beginning, I made clear that reports of the two dozen or so task forces would be widely circulated for comment and reaction, as would the drafts of any decision memo I prepared to implement the recommendations of the task force. I wanted the most inclusive process possible, with the widest possible number of intelligence professionals invited to participate.

Of course, sometimes the best of intentions go awry. One of the task forces I established was to examine how the CIA, in particular, could be more open in its relationships with the media and the public. Many good ideas surfaced, including declassifying decades' worth of analytical papers dealing with the former Soviet Union, providing greater availability of senior agency officials for media interviews, facilitating access to already declassified documents, and easing access to classified files for scholars. Unfortunately, we were subjected to considerable—deserved—criticism and mockery when it was revealed in the press that the task force report on "openness" had been classified "secret." I immediately declassified it, but the damage was done, thus proving, yet again, that old habits die hard and bureaucracies are often their own worst enemies.

––––––––

One strategy new leaders often use in reform initiatives is reorganizing the bureaucracy. But all too often, they confuse organizational and name changes with real change. They believe that moving the boxes around on the organization chart, changing the lines for who reports to whom, making dotted lines into solid lines, and the like will fix problems and represent real change. They are nearly always wrong. When you get a new boss who is bent on changing things by changing the boxes, it usually means he isn't really serious about change or he doesn't understand how to lead it.

If a leader wants real change, he must realize the main target is *how* people do their work, not *where*. How you make people more efficient and productive, more effective, more responsive, more open-minded, better at their jobs, is little affected by the placement of their organization on the chart. There is one exception to this general proposition: getting rid of boxes on the chart—reducing layering—is almost always a good thing.

Rearranging the organizational boxes, especially if it involves physical relocations, also is enormously distracting to an organization. Employees will be preoccupied with whether their personal and office status has improved or declined in the reorganization—as well as whether in the game of bureaucratic musical chairs they might find themselves without a job. The large CIA office analyzing Soviet foreign and domestic affairs was moved to a building distant from the agency's headquarters in the early 1980s; I believe it affected the quality of its work for up to two years. Whether in the public or the private sector, try to leave the boxes, both actual and organizational, alone unless absolutely necessary.

———

Finally, how a leader informs her organization and external constituencies about her strategy for reform and how she intends to proceed is an important decision. She needs to decide whether to be low-key and simply announce each initiative or make a big splash.

If you have done the proper preparatory work in terms of consulting with a broad array of your constituencies and shaping the battlefield, my preference is to go with the big splash. A strategy I used again and again wherever I was in charge was to blitz the organization with multiple actions simultaneously, the totality of the measures communicating seriousness of purpose, heft, and the reality of change. For anyone bent on change, one individual gesture or action will often not be persuasive; a dozen or more announced simultaneously are hard to ignore or dismiss. Laying out the full breadth of what you plan to do has dramatic effect, gets people's attention, and can build enthusiasm and excitement. Announcing initiatives all at once reduces uncertainty about hidden agendas or future surprises. Whatever apprehension employees feel can be mitigated by making clear that they all will have the opportunity to help shape the actual implementation.

Less than a month after I was confirmed as DCI, I gave a speech to leaders of the intelligence community about their future:

> Now it is time to look ahead to needed changes in priorities, mission and structure.
>
> I have been around too long to underestimate the difficulty of changing longstanding structural arrangements, old habits, and vested bureaucratic interests. Yet, I believe everyone agrees that change must come to the Intelligence Community and that it must come now. I hope and believe that through a cooperative, inter-agency and intra-agency effort in which all points of view are represented and have a hearing, and where people and institutions have a say in shaping the future structure, we can in fact bring about real change.

I then described in detail the potential areas for change we would examine, laying out ideas for what needed to change, where we were headed, but without prejudging the conclusions of the two dozen task forces I would establish. Because of my preparatory work, and my reassurances, this speech was greeted with enthusiasm, in stark contrast with the disastrous speech I had made as the CIA's deputy director for intelligence almost exactly ten years earlier.

I had a similar experience at A&M. In remarks to the faculty senate a month after my arrival on campus, I laid out the priorities for change that would dominate my tenure as president of the university. I said that in each case, the issues would be addressed by deans, faculty, and administrators working together. I described the provost's and my listening sessions during the preceding weeks with the deans of the colleges, department heads, and faculty and the conclusions I had drawn from those sessions in terms of the four areas of change that would be our focus. The response was quite positive. I covered much of the same ground in a university-wide convocation three weeks later, with all the various constituencies of the university community in attendance.

Because the changes I had to make as secretary of defense in the Bush administration would take time, they did not lend themselves to a single dramatic announcement. But under President Obama, I gave a long press conference announcing thirty-three major programs I was cutting and why. In this case, while all these decisions had been discussed and debated intensively inside the Pentagon, and the civilian and military leaders of all the services had played a big part in identifying the options and making recommendations, for maximum political effect I had kept what we were up to secret from all external constituencies (the defense industry, the media, and, most important, Congress). I think this can be an effective tool for a leader if used selectively. Of course, I kept the president informed and, at the last moment, briefed the leaders of the two Armed Services Committees. The announcement was a bombshell, just what I wanted. When, a year later, I announced that long list of "efficiencies" cutting nearly $180 billion in overhead costs from the Pentagon budget, I used the same approach of extensive internal consultation and collaboration while keeping external audiences in the dark. The result was another bombshell. This approach, in both cases, yielded significant political and public opinion advantage and went a long way toward assuring success in making the changes.

A lengthy and carefully prepared public statement was necessary in both cases because all of the changes—and the reasoning behind them—were in many cases interrelated and held together by a common strategy. Announcing the decisions and reforms piecemeal—or worse, allowing them to leak, as so often had happened in the past—would have lost this cohesive rationale and thus been far less persuasive and politically effective. The results upended the conventional wisdom on defense spending that the secretary would always get rolled by Congress or the military services on specific programs. Of the thirty-three changes I announced in April 2009, thirty-one would be enacted in the next defense budget. The other two came a year later.

———

By this point, an effective leader will have reached out to all the important constituencies to listen to their views and to win their support; established priorities; decided which initiatives she must lead and which can be delegated; developed strategies to shape the bureaucratic battlefield to maximize chances for success; and announced what she plans to do. Now it is time for the hardest part of reform: implementation, the part of the process where all too often good intentions go to die.

4

———

Techniques for Implementing Change

When it comes to implementation, what you are after is the same outcome for every change you seek: practical policies, meaningful and workable structural and cultural changes, achievable plans, and outcomes that are affordable and have the broadest possible support within (and outside) the institution. Over the years, I have used several techniques to achieve those results. They can work at all levels of leadership and in all kinds of organizations.

———

In bureaucracies, the *process* of bringing change is critically important to getting lasting results, including acceptance or even enthusiastic embrace. Any fool can (and all too often does) dictate change from the top in a public or private sector bureaucracy. Fundamental to success, though, as I think I've made clear by now, is *inclusiveness*—getting as many people involved as possible, especially among the career professionals.

In every senior position I held, I made extensive use of task forces to develop options, recommendations, and specific plans for implementation. I relied on such ad hoc groups to effect change instead of using existing bureaucratic structures because asking the regular bureaucratic hierarchy (as opposed to individuals within it) if the organization needs to change consistently yields the same response: it almost never provides bold options or recommendations that do more than nibble at the status quo. At the beginning of most presidential administrations, the White House (either the president or the national security adviser) asks the State and Defense Departments to propose areas for significant changes in national security policy—bold departures reflecting changed priorities or circumstances. Such efforts have historically produced pap. In recent decades, significant changes in policy almost without exception have been driven by the White House (or forced by external factors such as foreign crises or congressionally mandated budget cuts).

It is a rare company where the head of a line unit—an operating division—will offer the CEO a dramatic proposal for transforming (or eliminating) his own organization. I never had a line of executives outside my office anywhere I worked who were there on their own initiative to tell me what was wrong with their outfit and how they intended to fix it. I am confident the same is true of most CEOs. Leaders have to understand that a bureaucracy is incapable of reforming itself.

Asking established organizations to come up with ways to restructure or change what they do implicitly suggests that what has been done before was inadequate, has failed, or can no longer meet the need. Many people in middle and senior positions have gotten where they are by offending as few people as possible and disrupting as little as possible. So, a leader focused on bringing significant change must find a way to break up the bureaucratic concrete and create the opportunity to develop new thinking and approaches. Involving employees in forging the path forward mitigates the implied criticism. The talent and ideas are often available inside the institution; ad hoc structures offer the best chance for them to emerge.

The best way to get access to, and use, internal talent and ideas for specific steps to implement reform is to get people from different parts of the organization working together outside their normal bureaucratic environment.

Task forces and similar ad hoc groups are silo busters. Most bureaucracies—both private and public—are rigid, pyramid-like structures in which information is shared with those in ever-higher boxes in the structure but rarely laterally. Properly designed task forces make diverse elements within an institution communicate and coordinate with one another at a level not achievable within the daily routine. New relationships get established that often endure long after the task at hand has been completed.

I fully understand the inherent limitations of committees. Sir Barnett Cocks, a former clerk of the British House of Commons, wrote acidly, "A committee is a cul-de-sac down which ideas are lured and then quietly strangled." Yet committees, task forces, councils, and review groups that cut across bureaucratic boundaries—properly used and directed—can be an exceptionally useful tool in leading change. However, committees in any organization must never be allowed to roam unleashed, undisciplined, uncontrolled, and without a specific date for extinction. Otherwise, they are a menace. An effective leader must structure the groups, be involved in the selection of members, give them their agenda, closely monitor their behavior and actions, and then, except in rare cases, disband them.

In naming the chair and the members, a leader has the opportunity to ensure that all elements of the organization most likely to be affected by the task force's recommendations—and his decisions—are represented and have the opportunity to have their ideas considered, to be involved. Having people on the task force who must eventually implement the change will contribute mightily to its recommendations being practicable and workable. With only a couple of exceptions, virtually every task force I appointed improved on and enriched my ideas and often expanded the scope of the change.

The chair of a task force is the most important appointment, and all leaders, from middle managers to the top dog, must choose that individual with great care and always with the end goal in mind. The chair must know the general outcome sought and be in full agreement with it. A leader must be able to count on the chair to provide the freedom for members to offer options and ideas, incorporate what is helpful, and then gently but firmly—Socratically, if you will—guide the majority to the desired change, even if they come up with a different way of implementing it. The chair of a task force must also be a person respected by all those involved and have real influence throughout the bureaucracy, because part of his job is to sell the recommendations.

That was the role I was given as deputy national security adviser and chairman of the NSC deputies' committee at the White House in the first Bush administration. Nearly every day, on countless issues, I chaired meetings of the committee of senior officials charged with providing policy options and recommendations from State, Defense, and other departments to the president. Each morning, the national security adviser, Brent Scowcroft (and sometimes President Bush 41), and I would decide what we wanted the interagency committee to recommend to the president. It was my job to deliver.

I had been DCI for less than a month when, on December 4, 1991, I announced the formation of fourteen task forces with a deadline for all of March 20, 1992. Ten additional task forces would be added in the ensuing weeks, with similarly short deadlines. There was not a single task force I appointed at the CIA or in the intelligence community that did not have a deadline of just a few months, no matter how complex the subject. Nearly all of the task forces comprised intelligence professionals, but at least one was made up entirely of experts from outside the intelligence community. The task forces addressed nearly every aspect of U.S. intelligence activity, including creating a single organization to manage both national and tactical photo reconnaissance; creating a new mechanism for coordinating and managing human intelligence collection, whether the CIA, military attachés, embassy officers, or others; restructuring the DCI management and budget function; changing the way National Intelligence Estimates are prepared; figuring out how to better collect and exploit unclassified information, including from the Internet (sounds elementary, but this was nearly twenty-five years ago); working out better coordination of the overseas activities of multiple U.S. intelligence agencies; coming up with new approaches for increasing our human intelligence collection capabilities; improving CIA support for military operations; devising options for providing intelligence assessments to decision makers electronically, in real time; improving reporting of possible criminal activities to appropriate law enforcement agencies; and developing initiatives for enhancing public understanding of what intelligence agencies do.

I offer this level of detail to give you a concrete sense of the massive scale of the changes we were undertaking; we were going to the guts of the entire U.S. intelligence enterprise. The issues we engaged also underscore the importance of what those bureaucracies do and the concomitant need for the best possible leadership. What they were—and are—doing is critical for our national security. As with so many other public sector bureaucracies, what they do really matters. And when they don't do it well, as we have seen repeatedly, there can be devastating consequences.

A number of the subjects the task forces tackled were quite controversial. Nearly all cut across jealously guarded bureaucratic turf boundaries and upended long-standing roles and responsibilities. More than a few professionals in the CIA were critical of my willingness to move parts of the agency into new "joint" organizations that better integrated overall government intelligence efforts. Indeed, hardly any part of U.S. intelligence was unaffected. But I believed the imminent collapse of the Soviet Union—which occurred less than four weeks after my December 4 announcement—provided just the kind of jolt needed to kick-start a far-reaching reappraisal of how U.S. intelligence agencies had been doing business for decades and to make broad and significant changes. Everyone recognized the world was transforming dramatically, creating a unique opportunity for change.

Speed of change, as I said earlier, is important to a leader if he doesn't know how much time he has. As DCI, with a U.S. presidential election coming in less than a year, I didn't know whether I had one year or five years to implement change, so that uncertainty was part of my need for speed. There also was growing pressure in Congress to concoct legislation reorganizing U.S. intelligence and the way it did its business. I was convinced—correctly, as congressional action along these lines a dozen years later would prove—that if Congress tried to pass legislation, it would just screw up everything. So I argued to senior intelligence officials in the CIA and other agencies that if we didn't move fast, Congress might take the action out of our hands with disastrous consequences. The strategy worked.

———

As president of Texas A&M, I largely followed the same approach. I spelled out my philosophy with respect to both change and governance at the university at an academic convocation shortly before I was asked to become secretary of defense:

> Giving those responsible for carrying out the mission of this university an assured opportunity and assured venues to offer advice and to influence decisions on the management and direction of this institution is just plain common sense—at the department, college and university level. Department heads, deans and the president and provost must, and will, continue to make the final decisions. But those decisions will be better, and better understood and supported, if transparency, discussion and debate, communication and collaboration precede them.

Shared governance based on those principles—transparency, open communication and discussion, and mutual respect—establishes the healthy and open environment for creating a culture of excellence in all we do and for our further enduring improvement as a university.

To create that environment and give it content, from the time I arrived at A&M, I used a mix of task forces, councils, and advisory committees in leading change. Some were issue-specific and had relatively short life spans, as at the CIA.

On occasion, though, the leader of an organization—public or private—with multiple, traditionally independent units must create a wholly new, permanent structure to effect institutional change and alter long-standing ways of doing business. As I mentioned earlier, the four university-wide councils of deans, faculty, administrators, and students I created were intended to be permanent. I saw the councils as a long-term mechanism for ensuring university-wide collaboration in the development of policies that cut across every college and administrative unit, a necessary and enduring collaboration not possible through any other means. The councils were a wholly new idea, at least at A&M.

The councils had a central role in implementing my agenda for change and, in all cases, expanded and improved on my ideas. Each council, in its turn, appointed task forces to examine ideas and make recommendations, first to the council and then to me. The role of these councils provides insight into the challenges of leading an academic or research organization and, in particular, leading change in institutions where there are many independent fiefdoms unaccustomed to working together. Each council was created to establish a venue in which all the elements of the university could be involved productively in setting priorities and policy for the entire institution.

The Finance Council, chaired by the dean of the business school, played an active role in establishing priorities in the budget process, restructuring campus business operations, and reallocating existing funds to help pay for new initiatives such as the faculty hiring program, pay raises for faculty and staff, and programs to increase diversity.

The Research Council, chaired by the dean of science, improved procedures by which the university could help faculty secure research grants, worked with others to increase graduate student stipends, and helped faculty obtain licenses, patents, and even commercialization of their discoveries.

The Council on the Built Environment, chaired by the vice-provost, allocated existing space (especially important as we hired several hundred additional faculty) and oversaw the distribution of classroom and lab space in new academic buildings. Space, almost as much as parking, is a very sensitive subject on campuses, and having this kind of forum and mechanism took a lot of the turf fighting and jockeying off the table.

Finally, the Council on the Educational Environment (academics), chaired by the dean of education, took on a wide array of controversial issues and, in virtually every case, brought productive, broadly supported recommendations to me. Its task force on improving the undergraduate experience would ultimately have ten working groups and make eighty-six recommendations. The task force on academic integrity recommended, and the university established, an honor system and honor council made up of elected faculty and students to deal with student cheating and plagiarism. Other task forces made recommendations relating, among other things, to online learning, an academic program in leadership development, enhancing the contribution of summer school to improving four-year-graduation rates (many students took longer), and expanding the academic honors program. And, important to my agenda, a task force led by the dean of business recommended establishment of the earlier-mentioned University Studies degree that would allow undergraduates—with approval of a faculty adviser—to design their own degree programs more in tune with the twenty-first-century economy than the traditional curriculum.

I dwell on these councils to highlight that I used the process of change and new structures at A&M to create a permanent institutional framework for policy making and shared governance. Sometimes radical action is required to tackle a tough structural and cultural problem.

Did all these councils, task forces, and working groups slow down the implementation of change? Probably. However, as I told the university community as I began my fifth year, "The results speak for themselves. During a period of dramatic changes at Texas A&M, a remarkably tranquil and productive partnership between faculty and senior administrators has emerged on the basis of mutual respect and open communication."

There was hardly a facet of university life regarding which I did not initiate some kind of change, and the pace was breathtaking (at least by the standards of academia). Because I included so many faculty, administrators, students, and former students in the process, the changes were accepted with surprisingly little resistance and mostly endured after I left. The faculty and staff, in particular, felt the outcomes reflected their ideas, their suggestions, and their influence, and thus to a great extent they supported the changes and made them their own. Amid a whirlwind of change, broad participation in these efforts generated a sense of purpose, stability, and esprit.

At Defense, I used task forces quite differently, mainly as operational instruments to monitor implementation of my decisions on measures to support commanders and their troops in Iraq and Afghanistan, especially where I felt speed was critical and lives were at stake. They identified problems and logjams and brought them to me for resolution. In each of those cases, the bureaucracy either had been unwilling to move forward or was unable to do so.

When it came to budgetary and programmatic issues, I created senior-level, department-wide working groups to discuss and evaluate proposals prepared by my staff and the Office of Cost

Assessment and Program Evaluation—led by Christine Fox, a savvy leader—a group of very smart folks who serve as the secretary's personal number crunchers and bullshit detectors. Those groups, which I chaired, afforded the senior military and civilian officers frequent opportunity to debate specific ideas and make recommendations.

One option open to a leader is to form a task force made up entirely of people from outside the organization to examine a problem. Such groups can provide a different perspective, more easily propose out-of-the-box solutions, and provide credibility and independence an internal group cannot. One drawback of such panels, though, is that inside the bureaucracy they can create antibodies of resistance to their recommendations. And it is rare for an outside group to get organized, do its work, and report in a timely manner. But sometimes external credibility and the need to mollify public critics must override the drawbacks of such panels.

That was the case when I appointed an outside task force in the aftermath of the Walter Reed hospital scandal. I asked President Reagan's secretary of the army, Jack Marsh, and President Clinton's secretary of the army and veterans affairs, Togo West, to lead an examination of outpatient care for wounded warriors at Walter Reed and at other hospitals. I turned to an outside panel mainly because I thought such a group would have more credibility with the troops, the families of the wounded, Congress, and the media than a group of insiders.

When the group completed its work and I had approved virtually all of its recommendations, I appointed a follow-on internal task force to monitor implementation of my decisions—implementation, as I've made clear, being essential to leading change. Over time, the group identified other areas for improvement in the treatment of wounded warriors. Indeed, as new problems cropped up or old ones took on new forms, I decided to keep the task force in place. I had my own issues with how effectively the wounded and their families were being helped, and my regular meetings with the task force—meetings that included most of the senior military and civilian brass in the department—provided an opportunity to keep the heat on people and to ensure the problem would continue to have high-level visibility. Direct participation by any leader keeps his colleagues focused.

Similarly, after making decisions to provide the aforementioned MRAP vehicles to troops in Iraq and Afghanistan, as well as dramatically expanded intelligence, surveillance, and reconnaissance (ISR) support, I kept active the task forces that had made the original recommendations. In the case of the MRAPs, it was to ensure quick resolution of production, funding, transport, and deployment issues—and, ultimately, to oversee development of an all-terrain variant for Afghanistan. In the case of ISR, it was to keep the pressure on elements of the Pentagon that were not as energetic in procuring these assets as I wanted. I disbanded the MRAP task force about three years after my original decision, but the ISR task force was still doing its job when I retired. Prior to that, I was briefed on a number of new ideas for detecting, disarming, or destroying improvised explosive devices (IEDs), which were being used increasingly frequently by the Taliban to attack our soldiers and marines on foot patrols. In response, I created the Counter-IED task force to identify new capabilities. It, too, was still working when I left the department.

While the ISR task force made a significant contribution in getting needed capabilities to commanders in the field, it also illustrated some of the potential problems a leader can face with such ad hoc groups. Over time, I had to change its leadership several times in search of the right chemistry. More troublesome, this task force I created to identify short-term responses to battlefield needs—delivery within a few weeks or months—spent more and more energy trying to broaden its mandate to get into long-range (multiyear) research and development projects, hired massive consultant support, and even paid to have its own "challenge coin" (a token used by military leaders to build esprit de corps and recognize superior performance, but a practice entirely inappropriate for such an ad hoc group). The task force kept fighting to become a permanent fixture with a long-term perspective in defiance of my direction to remain narrowly focused on short-term needs. It is a case study in the challenges inherent in managing ad hoc task forces. At a certain point, they need to close up shop and have their functions integrated into regular organizations and processes. I probably let that one go on too long.

Unlike the multitude of short-term task forces I created at the CIA and Texas A&M, most of those I established at Defense endured through much of my tenure as secretary, mainly because there was no other entity within the department through which I could continuously exert direct pressure on the entire bureaucracy to quickly meet the needs of the commanders and troops. I typically followed the recommendations of the task forces. One exception was whether to open to families and the media the ceremonies at Dover Air Force Base when the remains of service members killed in action were returned to the United States. That task force recommended a cautious approach, with extended outreach to veterans' groups, families, and service members. I disagreed but went along with a weeklong outreach effort, after which I simply directed opening the "dignified transfer" ceremonies to families and, with their permission, to the press.

One problem I tried to address using the normal bureaucratic process—not a task force—to assess the issue and come up with a new approach was whether to try to reduce the average medevac time in Afghanistan from two hours to one hour. The Joint Staff and others gathered numerous statistics on survival rates, medevac times, and related issues and recommended making no change in the existing standards. They concluded that changing the timeline would not materially affect survival rates, but I think underpinning their recommendation for no change was the cost and disruption associated with putting more medevac helicopters, field hospitals, and medical personnel into the country, which would be necessary steps. I responded that if I were a soldier or marine who had just been blown up, I'd want a helicopter on the way as soon as possible. I overruled the group and directed additional assets into Afghanistan to ensure medevac in an hour or less.

This issue vividly illustrates my comments earlier about what happens when you ask the normal bureaucratic structure to evaluate the need for change—in effect, to reform itself. Even if the issue at hand is elevated to a very senior level and is literally a matter of life and death, the answer is almost always that things are just fine as they are. That is what the task force led by the Joint Staff—a standing Pentagon organization of more than a thousand mostly mid- and senior-level officers from all the services working for the chairman of the Joint Chiefs of Staff—did regarding medevac timing. I rejected the bureaucracy's recommendations outright. Opponents of the change were arguing the statistics; for me, it was a matter of morale and moral obligation.

Business leaders, in my opinion, do not use task forces and other such silo busters often enough. Divisions of big companies are often too much like our military services: they work together only when they must (or are forced to do so by their boss). Whether engineering, marketing, human resources, finance, different product lines or divisions, research and development, or other functions, different business units usually need to work together better than they do. As well, they can learn from one another. I have served on the board of directors of more than one company where the engineers, the financial gurus, and the marketing or sales folks didn't talk much to each other. (I'm no expert, but I think that was a problem with some of our automotive companies in the United States.) Especially in larger companies, significant change in one division or component will have consequences— usually unintended—on others. Too often, the same pyramidal, hierarchical structures, and lack of lateral communication, that pervade the public sector also negatively affect the private sector. Task forces are a tool in the leader's kit to address such problems.

Also, as in the public sector, such groups are immensely useful in building personal relationships across a big organization that can only be beneficial in the long run.

———————

So far, I have been talking about the value of task forces, councils, and working and review groups as a mechanism to develop specific measures for implementing change and increasing the odds of support within the organization—an offensive instrument for a leader. But there is another valuable purpose, particularly when a leader is confronted by an unexpected demand for change—one not on her agenda—that may involve real institutional risk. That purpose is defensive, to buy time to let passions cool and to gather information for smart decision making.

At A&M, a faculty-generated storm rose up in the fall of 2004 over the issue of a living wage for the lowest-paid university staff. While a job at the university was locally coveted because of pay, benefits, and security, there was no question those on the bottom rungs of the ladder had a real challenge making ends meet. Some eight hundred workers on campus made $9.00 an hour or less, or just shy of $19,000.00 a year. A&M's faculty was usually not broadly engaged with community issues, but this one generated quite a bit of heat. The faculty senate passed a resolution endorsing implementation of a living wage for all Texas A&M employees, a "living wage" defined as "meeting or exceeding 130% of the federal poverty level guidelines for a family of three, or $9.76 an hour plus benefits." The faculty's concerns were legitimate, but the university was—as always—under financial pressure as our health care, energy, and other costs were rising.

To complicate the matter, there was little support for the initiative among local elected politicians, much less the governor-appointed, entirely Republican board of regents, who did not like being publicly pressured, especially on a "liberal," faculty-driven issue. There was, as well, a considerable backlash among students, alumni, and others, who evinced little sympathy and opposed any action on the wage issue. "Screw the living wage, and too bad for the janitors if they don't like their jobs" was a representative e-mail I received.

Such sentiments notwithstanding, I wanted to show the faculty and the staff that I took the problem seriously, and I needed to cool the situation so we could look at the wage issue with facts in hand. A good leader is not going to be able to solve certain controversial problems until he can examine the issue without pressure being applied relentlessly. A leader sometimes needs to slow things down. I met with the Living Wage Coalition of the Brazos Valley, representatives from the community and faculty who were leading the effort to raise wages. Later the same day, I announced the creation of the Task Force on Wages and Benefits to review wages and benefits of lower-paid university employees and evaluate such compensation in comparison with local and statewide data, as well as with governmental guidelines and cost-of-living information. I appointed the retired dean of the business school Dr. Benton Cocanougher to chair the group, which included faculty members, administrators, a student, and representatives from both the custodial and the food services staffs.

The task force did its work while tensions abated, and with its recommendations in hand I found the money to provide a modest increase in the wages of our lowest-paid employees—not as much as the faculty senate had asked, but still a meaningful increase. This issue was not on my original agenda, but it would have been a mistake, both on the merits and in terms of my larger agenda, to politely listen to the concerns of the faculty and then do nothing. Creating the task force and appointing my closest adviser as chair demonstrated I was serious and responsive to faculty concerns but also that I intended to remain in control of handling the matter.

Similar, but far more significant, was my use of a review group as a means to win support for overturning the "Don't Ask, Don't Tell" (DADT) law, which banned openly gay people from serving in the military. The review group provided the time and means to gather information crucial to effective implementation of repeal, paving the way for gays to serve openly. It also bought time for a first-ever dialogue within the military about gays in the services and time for the vast majority of service members simply to get used to the idea that change was upon them.

As I described elsewhere, President Obama and I were caught between two seemingly unmovable forces—on one side, gay activist groups, which were important members of his core liberal constituency and who were demanding immediate repeal of DADT, and, on the other side, most senior military leaders and, it was assumed, most service members, all concerned, among other things, about the impact on military readiness, unit cohesion, and troop retention. A number of Republican senators and congressmen also were against a change in the law, even as the courts were moving toward overturning it. Admiral Mike Mullen, chairman of the Joint Chiefs of Staff, and I testified together to lawmakers that we supported changing the law but wanted to take the time to survey our military forces to get a better sense of how much opposition there would be, to gauge the difficulty of implementing change, to identify areas of particular concern to the troops, and to properly prepare for change by revising regulations and training our forces. We said we thought it would take up to a year. Proponents of repeal thought the idea of forming a review group was a stalling tactic; opponents, especially in Congress, thought it was a sham because the president had already decided to move forward.

The review, co-chaired by the department's general counsel, Jeh Johnson, and army general Carter Ham, was a thoroughly professional job. They surveyed 400,000 service members and 150,000 service spouses about their attitudes and concerns with respect to having openly gay individuals serve in the military. There were countless focus group meetings and even a confidential channel through which gays in the military anonymously made known their views, problems, and concerns.

The outcome of the review—completed in just over seven months—surprised nearly everyone, including me. Two-thirds of those surveyed thought having gays serve openly would cause no significant problems or might even be better for the military. The review process identified those Department of Defense policies that would need to be revised and prepared training materials to be used at every level of the military. The outcome of the review, I believe, changed enough Republican votes to allow repeal of DADT, with the proviso that the new rules would not come into effect until all training had been completed and the president, secretary of defense, and chairman of the Joint Chiefs certified that the change could be made without any serious problems. There is no doubt in my mind that eliminating DADT by presidential executive order would have had a much more divisive and disruptive result, harming those with the most at stake, including military commanders dealing with readiness and discipline issues and gay and lesbian troops seeking to "come out" in a more tolerant environment. As of this writing, I have heard of no significant problems associated with repeal of DADT and gays openly serving in the ranks.

The salient points about the DADT task force for any aspiring leader are that establishing the review group demonstrated that action was being taken and that all points of view would be heard, it provided time to temper emotions (somewhat) and gather facts (as opposed to previously only anecdotal speculation), and it presented a detailed action plan for implementation. I will always be convinced that the review group paved the way for successful incorporation of the biggest personnel policy change in the U.S. military since women were brought into the ranks in significant numbers a generation earlier. As in every other example, the keys to success were the broadest possible inclusiveness, transparency, and open internal debate and dialogue; especially important here was the need to buy some time.

I want to emphasize one last time that I found task forces and other ad hoc groups immensely useful, indeed crucial, for developing specific proposals for implementation of reforms and for tracking progress. Any leader can use them effectively. They break down the bureaucratic barricades to change and, drawn from different parts of an organization, can also help build collaboration and relationships that will result in long-term benefits.

A leader bent on transformational reform will benefit greatly from demanding—and demonstrating—transparency and sharing of information about implementation, both internally and externally.

I spent nearly all of my professional life in a secret world—a world of secret, top secret, and above top secret documents; secret operations; secret procedures; secret budgets; secret identities; secret congressional hearings. Often, even my personal calendar was secret. At the CIA, the National Security Council staff, and the Defense Department, everything was secret (including information that could easily be obtained by searching the Internet or reading the newspaper). But layered on top of "secret" were countless "compartmented" programs requiring special security clearances—intelligence collection programs, covert operations, military plans, new weapons, and more. I had clearances I could not remember for programs I had forgotten existed. And people were always showing up in my office or at home—usually at odd hours—with colored canvas bags with strange locks and seals that could only be opened or broken in front of me.

What troubled me increasingly with each passing year was the realization that too much was being kept secret because of habit, culture, internal power politics, and a desire to avoid embarrassment or accountability rather than any risk to national security. Issues from budgets to bureaucratic turf wars were unnecessarily shrouded in secrecy internally, and the public could—and should—have been told more about how and why we did what we did without compromising sensitive information and operations. I became convinced that excessive secrecy was an obstacle to needed changes inside government organizations. Equally important, at least at the CIA, I felt that with the end of the Cold War and collapse of the Soviet Union, the agency had to be more open about what it did and why or risk losing the public and political support that had been taken for granted during the Cold War.

And so, despite a professional lifetime spent in an ocean of secrecy, I became an ardent advocate of far greater transparency both internally and externally in organizations I ran.

Especially in bureaucracies, people are suspicious of change and always suspect hidden agendas. For too many leaders, the monopoly on information is deemed a source of power: "If you only knew what I know." But it is an ego trip to dole out little bits of information to subordinates and career professionals, keeping them in the dark. This is, I believe, the sign of either a weak, insecure leader or an arrogant know-it-all. Whichever it may be, it is fatal to successfully implementing lasting reform. Transparency has some costs in terms of premature disclosures of options or leaks intended to influence outcomes, but overall the benefits of being open far outweigh the downsides for the reformer.

This applies equally to business. Too often leaders don't trouble to share—routinely—with their employees the reasons for various changes, the direction of the company, and its goals or even to talk about the company culture. This isn't about handing out to everyone a small laminated card imprinted with the company's mission and values. I've seen those, and employees mainly ignore or discard them. This is about a leader's effort to reach out in his own voice—not something prepared by human resources or by the vice president for communications—to offer his personal perspective on company strategy and aims, and his hopes. To talk about the company's culture. It's not a onetime rah-rah speech but regular and personal outreach to the entire workforce, updating it on company performance, changes under way, and other developments affecting the business. Through serving on ten corporate boards and many encounters with business leaders, I have met a number of superb and successful CEOs. Some have regular sessions between executives and rank-and-file employees during which the company culture is highlighted, a lot of information is shared, and enthusiasm is generated. But I have come across only one CEO who communicates with *all* his employees routinely in the way I am describing—Howard Schultz, CEO of Starbucks. Other business leaders should emulate his example.

As mentioned earlier, as director of central intelligence I made it a priority to increase transparency, appointing a task force on "openness," with a view to giving the public a greater window into what intelligence agencies did and the contribution they made to national security. I made significantly more senior CIA officials available to talk to the press routinely, created a new historical declassification staff, gave scholars clearances allowing them access—with restrictions—to classified files, and opened our decades-old archive of satellite photographs of the Arctic region of the Soviet Union to scientists studying global warming. We declassified the forty-year file of analytical assessments of the Soviet Union, and I pledged to declassify our files on selected covert actions from the 1950s. I agreed representatives from the CIA would testify before Congress in hearings open to the public and the media whenever possible. I was convinced we could do all this—and more—without compromising intelligence sources and methods or national security.

But greater internal transparency was also core to successfully implementing my agenda for change in the U.S. intelligence community. Accordingly, with only one or two exceptions, each of my memos setting up a task force was widely circulated in draft with comments from the entire workforce invited: Were there additional issues the task force should examine? Were some issues I had proposed not worth the effort? When each task force completed its report and made its recommendations, copies were made available throughout the CIA and the intelligence community for comment, criticism, and additional suggestions. The resulting comments were appended to the reports when they came to me. Finally, my decision memos were circulated in draft so intelligence officers could let me know their thoughts on whether my decisions could be implemented effectively or whether they could be better stated to facilitate action. Never before had the entire professional cadre at the CIA or in the intelligence community been repeatedly asked their views on such sweeping changes. I insisted on the transparency. Any good leader should.

In addition, I regularly circulated updates (which I personally wrote) on all the changes that were going on, which were provided to everyone in all the intelligence agencies. In those technological dark ages before e-mail, these missives—to tens of thousands of people—were circulated in paper copies and also posted on bulletin boards. Today, the ubiquity of social media and e-mail makes ridiculously easy the kind of communication between the leader and her employees that I believe is so important. Failure of leaders to take advantage is a big mistake.

I spoke to the value of transparency and information sharing (and task forces) in promoting change in remarks to both the CIA and the intelligence community managers and employees in January 1993:

> Taken together, I think it is no exaggeration to say that CIA and the Community have not seen so much change in decades—especially in so short a time. And the best part is that every single measure has been a team effort—all of us working together to improve the way we do our work, not just because the Cold War is over, but also because of wide recognition top to bottom that we can do better. The task forces, the many comments that helped shape decisions on their reports, the cooperative spirit among CIA and Community managers—all this was critical to so much being accomplished. All this reflected the value of the broadest possible involvement of our people at every level.

I could at least understand the culture of holding information close, even internally, at the CIA. I couldn't understand it at all in a big university. As a dean for nearly two years, I was surprised and appalled at how little information on budgets, administrative decisions, and day-to-day operations was shared with deans and faculty. When I talked with counterparts at other universities, it was clear that what went on at A&M was the norm, not the exception, in higher education. In no small part because of my experience with transparency as DCI, when I became president of A&M, I resolved to be as transparent about choices and decision making as possible—most especially with respect to implementing my agenda for change. But even on routine matters, I saw no reason not to provide the faculty senate and its leaders, the council of deans, and student government leaders with detailed briefings on development of the budget, financial options, trade-offs, administrative issues, and problems we were facing. Apart from sensitive personnel matters, there was very little information about university affairs that I was unwilling to share in the broadest possible manner. I not only shared information on specific issues; I regularly sent e-mails to all faculty, staff, and students about progress in implementing the many different change initiatives under way. Ironically, the more information I was willing to share, the more people were inclined to trust me—and support what I was trying to do. I think that is almost always the case in leadership positions.

———

I had a different problem at Defense. Despite its penchant for classifying just about everything, the place leaked like a sieve; no internal issue or dispute was too trivial or too sensitive for someone to share with the press and congressional staff. The challenge, then, was how to tighten up the decision-making process to reduce leaks at the same time I made that process more inclusive and more transparent.

The Pentagon is actually quite disciplined when it comes to keeping military plans and operations secret; after all, lives are at stake. But any budgetary, personnel, administrative, or policy matter was fair game for leakers. I had been furious when it leaked that I was going to extend tours of duty in Iraq and Afghanistan from twelve to fifteen months, mainly because the leak denied us the chance to explain it first to the troops and their families. I disliked leaks about the senior military's preferences regarding troop surges and timetables, which also infuriated both Presidents Bush and Obama. In the real world of Washington, however, regardless of a secretary of defense's fulminations, such leaks are nearly impossible to stop altogether. (And presidents or secretaries—or leaders in business—who obsess over leaks and use every means available to stamp them out rarely come to a good end.)

I felt strongly, though, that leaks about major budget decisions, and especially the need to cut or cap major programs, would be fatal to real reform. Any leader has to decide where the line must be drawn. In preceding decades, decisions by a secretary to cut unneeded programs had often been compromised when word got out prematurely to members of Congress or interest groups. Based on my reading of history, one of the main reasons many of Robert McNamara's efforts failed was that decisions were made with a small group of his civilian "whiz kids" and without significant participation of the senior military leaders. Feeling excluded (and opposed to the changes), the generals and admirals did not hesitate to go around McNamara to friendly members of Congress to thwart the secretary's intentions.

When I decided to aggressively winnow dozens of major defense programs that were failing or no longer affordable (or relevant to our needs), I led an intensive consultative process that involved all of the senior leadership of the military services as well as senior Pentagon civilians. I keep returning to this point of inclusion; leaders who exclude others from decision making run a high risk of failure. I asked all participants to sign a nondisclosure agreement (basically giving their word they wouldn't share our deliberations with others, even their staffs). The number of lower-level staff who had access to any information about options under consideration was dramatically reduced.

I believe that because officers had given their word and because of the transparency of the process to senior leaders—and multiple opportunities for their views to be heard in the larger group or just with me—there was not a single leak. An important reason why Congress ultimately accepted—or acquiesced in—all of the decisions was that no senior civilian or military officials went around me to complain to their supporters on the Hill. Some almost certainly did not agree with my final decisions, but they "supported" them in the Pentagon sense of the word, which meant carrying them out.

Be wary of consensus. When it comes to implementing reform, you must look very closely at any recommendation for action characterized as the consensus of a group. Does it advance your agenda? Is it as bold as you want or need?

The erudite Israeli foreign minister Abba Eban insightfully observed that a consensus means that "everyone agrees to say collectively what no one believes individually." I cannot begin to calculate the time I have wasted in meetings—and task forces—as the person in the chair strives to get all participants to agree to a single recommendation or point of view, instead of presenting several options to their higher-up. This process inevitably yields the lowest common denominator, the most bland of initiatives, which everyone can agree to. Pap.

A leader who seeks true reform will never get bold ideas or recommendations from task forces or working groups if consensus is the priority objective. Instead, a leader must instruct her task force chairs or subordinates leading other groups that consensus will only be valued if it represents agreement on something bold. The Supreme Court justice Oliver Wendell Holmes Jr. described this process graphically. He wrote that one of his Court opinions as originally written "had a tiny pair of testicles but the scruples of my brethren have caused their removal and it sings in a very soft voice now." Recommendations that come to a leader of reform must not sing in a very soft voice.

When I was chairing the deputies committee at the White House under President George H. W. Bush, my responsibility was to clear away the bureaucratic underbrush on issues so the president would only have before him the bare-bones substantive differences of view among his principal advisers that he could weigh before making a decision. Sometimes opposition from one organization or another will, when fully exposed, be nothing more than old bureaucratic rivalries hiding behind purportedly substantive differences of opinion. It is the job of a leader at any level to choose chief lieutenants who will use a flamethrower to burn away the bureaucratic weeds so the options that remain are real and significant.

When Henry Kissinger was national security adviser, he would only half jokingly comment that every policy paper had three options: Option A was essentially to do nothing; Option C was so radical as to be automatically rejected; and thus Option B, a middling and therefore very modest course of action, was the only sensible approach—the bureaucracy's preference. In effect, it avoided the appearance of inaction or any serious opposition but accomplished little. A leader can't allow her task forces, councils, or reviews to trap her into accepting Option B. A leader must insist upon real options. If they aren't forthcoming, if the choice among them isn't difficult, she must send people back to the drawing board. The bureaucracy can't be allowed to dictate terms.

A process effective in bringing forward significant proposals for reform and their implementation, noting who is for and who is against each and why, is important. In many instances, there will be a majority opinion. The leader needs to know why the minority objected, and those objections may influence the decision or lead to adjustments, but differences of opinion must not deter decisions and implementation.

A leader implementing reform, within the confines of law and regulation, must decide how much analysis is needed before making a decision and acting. Analysis must not be an excuse for paralysis.
The man in charge must decide when further study is war-

ranted in order to gather more information, to build support for what he wants to accomplish, or to improve the measures for implementation. When to stop studying and start acting is a judgment call, and a leader has to rely on trusted advisers as well as his own experience and political instincts in making that call.

As beneficial as inclusiveness, transparency, and patience are, they cannot turn into an excuse for putting off tough or unpopular decisions. Particularly when you are trying to pursue bold initiatives that change the status quo, there will be those who insist that not enough analysis has been done to properly evaluate the options, support a decision, or proceed with implementation; it always seems that just a little more work needs to be done. Sometimes, the concern is legitimate and intended to keep the person in charge from rushing pell-mell into hasty and ill-thought-out actions. Sometimes, complaints over insufficient analysis are born of timidity and risk aversion. But as often as not, the demand for more analysis is simply a stalling maneuver to avoid change or to wait until a more sympathetic leader takes over.

Calling for further study is an especially favorite tactic of the U.S. Congress when a senior executive branch official makes a commonsense decision based on judgment and experience. This is the usual recourse when the secretary of defense decides to take some action that will cost jobs in a representative's home district. Congress demanded copies of all the backup documentation supporting my decisions to close Joint Forces Command and to cancel a number of weapons and equipment programs. The whole point of the exercise was to allow congressional staff time to find holes in the analysis, require further study, hold hearings, and pursue other such tactics to forestall unwelcome decisions.

In another example, over the years the air force had conducted multiple "Air Mobility Studies" to determine just how many cargo aircraft the U.S. military needed. The studies repeatedly concluded that even with the Iraq and Afghan campaigns under way the military had more cargo planes than were needed. Congress's response was always to send the military back to the drawing board to study the issue one more time. Too many members had a vested interest in the cargo plane production line and in keeping open bases where they were stationed. Paralysis by analysis.

Congress is far from alone in using the need for further analysis as a way to prevent action. It happens every day at the local and state levels as interest groups of all kinds insist on yet another study to block, among other things, new highways, pipelines, or hospitals or to change school district boundaries. Environmental impact reviews, however necessary, have become an especially effective tool of delay at the state and local levels; imagine trying to build the transcontinental railroad, the Hoover Dam, or the Golden Gate Bridge today. The demand for further study can be the bane of CEOs in business as well. I have seen their frustration when subordinates ask for "just a little more time" to study an initiative.

The proliferation of investigative bodies in government, especially at the federal level, is becoming a serious impediment to managing—and changing—bureaucracies. The increasingly intrusive role of outside commissions and audit agencies such as the General Accounting Office, inspectors general, and the Congressional Budget Office and their ability to delay or overturn decisions by insisting on further analysis or study are unwelcome realities, especially if the leader has limited time in office. Indeed, I would argue that the actions of Congress, congressional staffs, and these investigative bodies—even if they are supposed to oversee bureaucracies and hold them accountable, and sometimes do—invariably embolden and strengthen bureaucratic resistance to change.

Deadlines for implementation are important in every initiative for change in every organization.

Everybody hates a deadline. The acerbic American writer Dorothy Parker was on her honeymoon when she received a telegram from her editor complaining she had missed a deadline. She wired back, "Too fucking busy and vice versa." On the other hand, everyone knows they are necessary. Duke Ellington was quoted as saying, "I don't need time. I need a deadline." Bureaucracies look at deadlines much as did Parker. If you want to get anything accomplished, though, Ellington is your man.

Deadlines need to be short. A distant deadline is an invitation to lethargy and delay. A leader should set realistic but short deadlines on each initiative she undertakes. Every task force or effort I commissioned while DCI had a deadline of less than three months. When I was secretary of defense, the deadlines ranged from a week to ten months. A university operates on a different time frame from virtually any other enterprise in the universe, but even at Texas A&M my deadlines were short, ranging from one to several months.

Short deadlines focus attention on an effort and signal its importance, creating momentum. They usually generate a new level of energy (or panic) and even enthusiasm; short deadlines sustain the electric charge. They also limit the time available for the opposition to coalesce and develop blocking strategies. Finally, short deadlines demonstrate a leader's seriousness of purpose: that she is determined to implement change as soon as practicable, understands the dynamics of bureaucracies, and is using time limits as a means to counter an organization's naturally cautious instincts and resistance to change. If I were limited to just one suggestion for implementing change in a bureaucracy, it would be to impose short deadlines on virtually every endeavor, deadlines that are enforced. Sometimes brief extensions are justifiable, but a leader should make them rare and make sure there is ample justification.

Implementing reform, a leader must master the available information, make decisions, assign responsibility for action, have a regular reporting mechanism that allows her to monitor progress and performance, and hold people accountable. And then she must get

out of the way. "Micro-knowledge" is necessary; micromanagement is not.
A leader cannot reform a bureaucracy while flying at thirty thousand feet. Leading change is hard work. The leader must do her homework to understand what change is needed, what change will work, who is a reliable source of information and who is not, whether recommendations will lead to the changes she wants, and whether her decisions are being effectively implemented. Broad perspective is always important, but a leader must get into the weeds as well. She must pore over and understand endless briefing books, know the innermost parts of the organization, get a sense of everyday life on the job from employees at every level. She must constantly be learning, listening, and asking questions. A leader must have sufficient detailed knowledge so she can recognize when someone is bullshitting her, when people are giving her inaccurate information (and whether it's because they don't know the facts themselves or are trying to mislead or steer her), whether options or recommendations are based on sound data.

In the military and in corporate America, there is great emphasis on delegation and not being a micromanager. All things being equal, that is good advice. But subordinate managers must know the person in charge knows what she is talking about. An effective leader must master much of what others in the organization know so she can integrate it into her decisions. A leader who can say that the proposals presented to her in one briefing contradict those presented in an earlier briefing is a leader to whom attention will be paid. A leader who can point out that numbers that should have remained constant have changed from one meeting to the next is a leader to be reckoned with. (In my first meeting with the Pentagon comptroller, I pointed out that a number in one massive budget binder—I had taken home several to study over the weekend—didn't agree with what should have been the same number in another binder. In another instance, I noticed that budgetary numbers on the same matter from two different components disagreed. People quickly realized I actually read the briefing books I was provided, and they took note.) It is also important to be aware when common sense has somehow fallen by the wayside.

When a leader is aware of the nitty-gritty, it doesn't take long for people to realize they had better double-check their work and that different organizations involved in the same briefing had better cross-check with each other before marching into a meeting. Such displays of micro-knowledge also send the message that it will be very hard to bamboozle the leader and the consequences of that or trying to bluff will be unpleasant. Moreover, micro-knowledge often allows a leader to better understand what she is being told, to place it in context, ask penetrating questions, and make smarter, better-informed decisions.

Too often, leaders think that knowing all these details is somehow unnecessary or "beneath" them, that their time is better spent on the "big picture." Such leaders will find themselves "kept" men and women of the organizations they purport to lead, dependent on others who may not have the same agenda or priorities to tell them what they need to know. For a leader to get the big things right depends a great deal on knowing the little things, especially when implementing difficult and controversial change. Whether I was restructuring reconnaissance programs at the CIA, pushing diversity at A&M, or cutting wasteful programs at Defense, knowing the details enabled me to make informed decisions—and also to defend those decisions in public. As President Obama told me on more than one occasion, "If I don't understand it, I can't defend it."

The point of a leader having micro-knowledge is neither to embarrass someone nor to nitpick. Both will make a leader look small and should be avoided. Everyone comes into a meeting with the boss with some measure of apprehension. Increasing people's anxiety or fear by faultfinding is counterproductive. If an error is meaningless to the larger discussion, ignore it; dwelling on typos, format, or some trivial issue in a chart suggests to people that the leader is not just in the weeds but lost in them. A leader should signal her command of detail, but that's not where her focus should be. Remember that most briefings one gets as boss—from middle manager on up—will have been reviewed by several layers of supervisors and colleagues. Nearly always, if there is an error or problem, it is a problem that extends well beyond the briefer. My approach in such circumstances generally was to address my questions or concerns to the briefer's boss, in part to convey that I suspected the mistake was not the briefer's fault. I tried never to be nasty, condescending, or personal. I don't think I ever intentionally embarrassed anyone. The more junior the briefer, the gentler I tried to be. Employing humor, when appropriate, is a good idea. Having the boss point out an error is mortification enough. And after a particularly contentious briefing, I would try to remember to thank the briefer for his or her efforts.

The purpose of doing your homework—of micro-knowledge—is not to show off how much you know, for one-upmanship, or to play "gotcha," but to be able to make better decisions. Without micro-knowledge, you are the prisoner of your bureaucracy and your staff, and they will play you like a cheap fiddle.

Where too many leaders of change fail is in not understanding the difference between micro-knowledge and micromanagement. As head of the CIA, I wanted to know if a case officer was having a particularly sensitive meeting with an agent, but I sure as hell was not going to try to tell him or his boss how to conduct the clandestine rendezvous. A university president is going to care a lot about the quality of teaching but is not going to tell deans or faculty how to teach. And the secretary of defense, in the midst of two wars, is going to pay close attention to strategy and even tactics insofar as the latter have political ramifications but is not going to be telling generals how to deploy their troops tactically.

In trying to change any bureaucracy, especially a large one, the leader must decide on the proper course of action and then assign responsibility for implementation to his subordinates—and empower them to carry out the task. Give them space to show what they can do. Stay out of their hair. There were bosses at the

CIA who were so constantly reaching down to see if their instructions were being followed we accused them of "pulling us up by the roots to see if we were growing." A leader at any level who tries to oversee the daily efforts of his subordinates is doomed to fail. Besides which, if a leader doesn't trust his lieutenants to carry out his strategy, he has chosen the wrong people.

Lasting change in a bureaucracy depends, above all, on those below you embracing the change and taking ownership, making it their own. The more frequently you intrude, implicitly reminding them it is *your* change, the less they will believe it is *theirs*. Successful implementation, in short, depends upon them. The leader cannot hold individuals accountable for driving change if he refuses to let go of the steering wheel. He must trust his subordinates, replace them if necessary. But he mustn't micromanage them.

If you don't have the guts as the leader to make tough and timely decisions, for God's sake, don't take the job.

Nothing crushes momentum for implementing change, for reform, like an indecisive leader. And nothing takes the air out of a campaign for change—for transformation—quite like sending bold options to the boss and then waiting, and waiting, and waiting for a decision. I can't count the times over my career when I saw truly dramatic proposals for change land in a boss's in-box only to be slowly asphyxiated as they lay there gasping at the bottom of the growing stack of incoming paper because he didn't want to make a decision—or couldn't.

I witnessed this repeatedly at the CIA and heard plenty about it at both A&M and the Defense Department, where, in both cases, stories were legion about major efforts for change that languished in the front office, gathering dust because the person in charge shrank from the challenge. No wonder professors and generals alike—anyone charged with coming up with proposals for reform—become cynical. They are asked to invest huge amounts of time and energy (and sometimes personal reputation) in a project and then left to wonder whether their work was valued or appreciated—or even read. A firm no would be better. In some cases, inaction is due to sheer laziness or lack of courtesy. Whatever the reason the leader fails to make a decision, the result is that not only does he leave his own people in the lurch but he also has made it all the harder for his successor to engage the professionals' enthusiasm the next time around.

Of course there is risk in making decisions. Rarely are there obvious answers, and few are easy. Sometimes, a leader will have to choose the least bad option because there are no "good" ones. Planning, organizing, and implementing change put a leader, by definition, in uncharted territory. They are, after all, about the future. But remember the definition of a leader I cited earlier in these pages: "one who guides, one who shows the way." A leader is in his position precisely because people had confidence in his judgment and believed he was the person for the job. There are no guarantees of success, but if he doesn't lead, who will?

As a leader confronts difficult decisions regarding implementation, as with every other part of the reform process it is important to discuss with people she respects and trusts the pros and cons of the different options before her. She shouldn't be afraid to test-drive her decisions with them and listen closely to their reactions. If they're worth their salt, they will give voice to objections, concerns, and problems, and even if the leader opts to proceed, she will have been forewarned of likely criticisms so she can either adjust her decisions or be better prepared to counter critics. Still, she, and she alone, must make the decision.

As the leader goes through the decision process, she must not send the bureaucracy signals that she is anguishing over a decision or is having a hard time making up her mind. She should be willing to take time to hear last-minute appeals from subordinates if necessary, take time to review all the considerations, but then decide decisively and unambiguously, with no vacillation, caveats, caviling, or hesitation. And she must avoid those "middling" options. As Justice Holmes said, they sing in a very soft voice.

A final, and critical, technique for implementing change is ensuring follow-through.

There must be some law of bureaucratic physics about how initial energy slowly degrades into inertia. The leader has to be the variable in that formula. Great ideas, great internal support, great decisions, are all for naught if the actions she has directed are not implemented. Contrary to what most bureaucrats believe, a good process is not an end in itself: Outcomes are the only things that ultimately matter. Decisions are really only the starting point. Just think of the number of big ideas that became troublesome because of lack of attention to implementation—like the Obama-Care Web site.

Being a visible presence during implementation is mandatory. A leader cannot delegate that. The bureaucracy needs to know its leader is personally involved in the implementation of his initiatives and monitoring their progress. Those techniques used in formulating the agenda and making decisions—transparency, inclusiveness, decisiveness, micro-knowledge (but not micro-management), and accountability—all will continue to be essential in implementation.

At the Defense Department, I met with each task force every two weeks for status and progress reports. My immediate staff was monitoring the efforts even more closely. When problems and obstacles cropped up, as they inevitably do, we knew about them quickly and were able to act just as quickly to overcome them. My chief of staff at A&M and my special assistant at the CIA operated similarly, closely tracking initiatives under way in each of those organizations to ensure they were proceeding as I wanted and on the timelines I had set.

At A&M, when I was fighting to increase diversity, I made frequent recruiting trips to predominantly Hispanic and African-American high schools all over the state. I regularly went before both the faculty and the student senates to report on the agenda for change and take questions. As DCI, I spoke out frequently in public about the changes we were making. I've already mentioned my engagement at Defense, to which I added innumerable public statements about the changes under way internally.

————

Winston Churchill attached to important decision papers red tabs that read, "Action This Day." That must be the mantra of the agent of change. Even when lives are not at stake, a sense of urgency must accompany implementation of a leader's decisions regarding change. It sustains energy, momentum, and the conviction that what is being done is vital to the future of the organization.

5

It's Always About People

This chapter, and the two that follow, are about intangible aspects of leading change in every circumstance and every organization. I have observed many presidents, cabinet officers, generals, admirals, and CEOs over many years. Some in their actions are superb examples of how to treat subordinates and motivate them; others were from the "fear and loathing" school of leadership, treating those below them with contempt and disrespect. What follows is distilled from my observations of others and my personal experience over some four decades of leading very different kinds of organizations, often under the most trying conditions. For a young person just starting a career, a middle manager, or someone in a more senior position, I believe the lessons are equally applicable.

People, not systems, implement an agenda for change.

As a leader pursues her reform agenda, she can't get so enamored of flowcharts and PowerPoint slides that she overlooks a critically important factor that will determine her success or failure: the attitudes and commitment of the people who work for her. A leader who can win their support and loyalty will be well on her way to successful reform. Whatever a leader's place on the public or private bureaucratic ladder, she must provide the people working for her with the tools and opportunities for professional success and satisfaction. She must empower them and provide them with respect, motivation, job satisfaction, upward mobility, personal dignity, esteem, and, finally, the confidence that, as leader, she genuinely cares about them collectively and as individuals. If a leader convinces them of that, employees will forgive a lot of the little mistakes that are inevitable.

People at every level in every organization need to know their work is considered important by the higher-ups. At every level, a leader should strive to make his employees proud to be where they are and doing what they do. It doesn't matter whether you are president of the United States, CEO of a huge company, or a supervisor far down in the organization.

As a senior CIA official, especially when we were in the middle of one of our fairly regular political uproars and scandals, I would often be asked, "How is morale at the agency?" No CIA officer wants to face friends and neighbors (or his own teenage kids) when the agency is being accused of nefarious deeds. But I always believed morale there depended, more than anything else, on whether the CIA professionals thought their work was valued. If they did, that would carry them through troubled times.

Belief in the importance of what one does is of course vital in any job. Bureaucrats, wherever they work, want to believe that what they do every day has real value for their company, community, or country. It is up to leaders—at every level—to explain why their work is important. Even if the organization is a little one tucked away in an obscure part of the enterprise, part of a leader's responsibility is to ensure that employees know how their work fits into the bigger picture, how it makes a contribution, a difference. Taking time on a regular basis to explain to employees the organization's mission and why they matter is an important leadership obligation on its own merits, but also because it is both motivational and builds the individual esteem of every member of the team.

More than thirty years ago, Thomas J. Peters and Robert H. Waterman Jr. wrote *In Search of Excellence: Lessons from America's Best-Run Companies.* A key theme was the importance of leaders communicating with employees (in their own work space), both to listen and to provide a sense of organizational purpose. I did this at all three places I led. At Defense, I also would travel to factories—such as the Oshkosh plant in Wisconsin where an MRAP-variant was being built—to tell the workers how their efforts fit into the larger war effort and to thank them for saving lives. Far from the battlefield, it was important for them to know their jobs were important and why.

Of course this kind of effort gets a bit complicated if an organization's mission isn't clear, the purpose of a time-consuming project is unfathomable, or there is no positive reinforcement from above; or if a task force report that required enormous effort simply ends up on a dusty shelf; or, as everyone in a bureaucracy has experienced at one time or another, if an employee realizes he has been assigned a pointless task. (Perhaps worst of all is a military unit exposed to danger at an outpost or sent on a risky mission that soon after was deemed unnecessary.)

It's unfortunate when the big boss's intentions are unclear, no one is encouraged to ask for clarification, and people proceed blindly to try to be responsive to what they imagine or guess is the real issue or question. A leader must encourage clarifying questions, and his answers must be direct and convincing.

There is a famous story of the FBI director J. Edgar Hoover writing in the margin of a memo, "Watch the borders." As a result, a number of agents were dispatched to the Mexican and Canadian borders. When this was reported to Hoover, he furiously informed the briefer that his note had been referring to the size of the margins on the original memo—not the country's geographic boundaries. As President Reagan's DCI, William Casey was a notorious mumbler and often hard to understand. He also had trouble using his telephone, which had a couple dozen direct phone lines to various senior agency officials. He would jab a button at random, shout an order into the receiver, and then hang up. As his chief of staff, I spent a lot of time each day interpreting what he had said to people and sorting out who should have gotten the call directing a specific action. My chiefs of staff at both A&M and Defense knew one of their principal responsibilities was to ensure my directions were clearly understood. Often they would come back into the office to determine what the hell I had been talking about on a given topic or to ask if I really meant to have someone perform a given task that seemed questionable.

Unintended miscues, though, pale in significance to the frustration of people assigned major tasks that are principally make-work. This was the case at the State Department and the CIA in the early 1970s, when the national security adviser Henry Kissinger assigned massive projects to the bureaucracy on both the Soviet Union and China, mainly to keep us busy and distracted while he and President Nixon pursued secret diplomacy with both countries. The success of their policies was only partial consolation for our wasted time and effort.

Government bureaucrats tasked with writing reports that end up in limbo enter the first circle of Dante's hell. And, of course, this happens in private sector bureaucracies as well. In fact, the bigger the company, the more such useless work seems to flourish. When it comes to major projects, limbo and dead ends crush morale and feed cynicism. Both are dangerous for organizations with aspirations for excellence.

A leader must not only explain to and reassure employees that their jobs are important to the overall mission of the organization; he must ensure that their work really does contribute, that it is not pointless make-work or wheel spinning.

A leader should be very sparing in publicly criticizing those beneath her on the organizational ladder.

In recent decades, most candidates for U.S. president—both Democrats and Republicans—have blamed the very government professionals they aspire to lead for many of the problems Americans face. In my adult lifetime, only two presidents have consistently and publicly praised federal public servants—John F. Kennedy and George H. W. Bush. Never mind that many of the challenges Americans face in dealing with federal bureaucrats are the result of poorly drafted or compromise congressional legislation that is itself ambiguous, unclear, or even contradictory—leaving it to the bureaucrats to interpret what Congress or the president intended or to figure out how to make convoluted laws or decisions work.

Senior elected or appointed officials are the worst when it comes to blaming "bureaucrats" for problems, usually because the alternative is to assume personal responsibility for failure. And nameless, faceless bureaucrats are an easy target for demagoguery. I've previously mentioned my anger when the secretary of the army blamed the problems at Walter Reed Army Medical Center on unnamed noncommissioned officers not doing their jobs. I was similarly disturbed when the air force disciplined some colonels and NCOs for problems in that service's nuclear mission that were systemic and had resulted from earlier decisions made at much higher levels. But business leaders often do the same when facing a disaster, whether it's a product recall, financial disaster, or any other failure or scandal. Very rarely do the big boys take a hit or show themselves to be self-critical. These leaders don't understand the long-term negative impact on their employees of broad criticism of those lower down in the ranks—criticism usually more deservedly aimed elsewhere. It is the antithesis of how they should be treated.

There are many ways of reinforcing for employees their importance to an organization. The tools depend on where a leader sits in the chain of command.

Those at or near the top should do the following:

- Remind employees often that what they do is important to a task or organization and to successful accomplishment of a mission.
- Criticize in private and focus on a specific problem.
- Make clear to their own subordinates that if they don't understand the boss's guidance or decisions, they have a responsibility to seek clarification.
- Avoid setting up task forces or committees unless there is a reasonable certainty they will come up with useful recommendations. Too many of these efforts are about kicking the can down the road, an excuse for inaction. People's time and energy should not be misdirected for feckless purposes.
- Establish specific goals and milestones for any task. A good leader must accept responsibility if it proves a dead end or a mistake.
- Listen to practical concerns from below.
- Publicly praise employees at every level as often as possible when it is deserved. Specific individuals must be acknowledged and rewarded, the further down the food chain the better. Whether through monetary, purely psychological, or symbolic means, excellence and achievement must be recognized in front of peers.

A leader further down the management ladder has fewer options. Explaining to people why their work is worthwhile is important, but without exaggeration or blowing smoke. Individuals and the team should always be praised publicly with sincerity and credibility. (Keep the bullshit quotient to a minimum; phony overstatement is worse than saying nothing.) It is essential that any middle manager understand what is going on if she is to be able to explain it to subordinates. A leader at any level should be receptive to suggestions and ideas from her subordinates. She should be careful about complaining downward about problems up the chain: there is a fine line between being seen by subordinates as a toady to your superiors and being insubordinate or disloyal to those who put you in your job. I think the best way for any leader to find the balance is to make sure she is prepared to question directions from above and also willing to go to bat for the team if given dumb orders. But be ready to salute and get on with the job, or quit. (More about that later.)

A successful leader, and especially one leading change, treats each member of his team with respect and dignity. It seems obvious, but in far too many bureaucracies bosses at all levels fail to do so.

Nearly everyone has worked for a "toxic" boss, someone who bullies, belittles, humiliates, or embarrasses subordinates. A shouter. A desk pounder. They can be found at every level. As I told midshipmen at the United States Naval Academy and cadets at West Point, "You will all surely work for a jackass at some point in your career. We all have."

Early in my career at the CIA, I worked for such a supervisor. When one of my colleagues went to see him one day about serious morale problems in our division, the boss's reply was "They should be glad they have jobs." Later, I worked in the White House for a deputy national security adviser with a formidable temper. He would scream and shout and carry on, routinely lacing his comments with loud and truly foul obscenities. On one occasion, his shouting and swearing on the phone was so bad that the vice president of the United States strode down the West Wing hall from his office and, without a word, slammed my boss's office door shut. Another time, this same person got so angry while on the telephone that he jumped up from his desk chair without pushing his chair back from under the desk, thus badly cracking his knees on the underside of the desk and then landing on his butt on the floor, breaking the Plexiglas mat under his chair. I witnessed this entire tantrum-induced workplace injury and nearly fell out of my own chair I was laughing so hard. He was not pleased by my reaction. The man was very smart and I actually liked him, but he had one hell of a temper.

Such poisonous pills may be smart, charismatic, decisive, and able mostly to get the job done—traits that can get you pretty far in most organizations. But the cost in morale, employee dissatisfaction, and creating a toxic environment is very high. People whose day-to-day job life is miserable are not going to feel motivated to excel, make change work, or better serve a customer or policy maker. And it doesn't matter whether they are CIA spies or retail clerks.

I have long called these kinds of bosses "little Stalins." They choose to demonstrate they are in charge by using their authority—their power—mainly to make people miserable. Someone needs to take off for a couple of hours to take a child to the doctor? Denied. Time off to attend a kid's baseball game or tend a sick spouse? Denied. My training officer in U.S. Air Force Officer Training School—a first lieutenant—in San Antonio in 1966 was a little Stalin. Our training period included two days off at Christmas, and one member of our group planned to travel to Dallas to see his newborn daughter. The lieutenant found a way to give him just enough demerits to prevent his trip. That happened nearly fifty years ago, and I still have not forgotten what I considered a wanton act of cruelty or the name of the officer who perpetrated it.

Little Stalins can do untold harm to an organization. I once thought they were primarily individuals appointed to their first supervisory position who, lacking training and experience, thought the best way to demonstrate their newfound authority over other men and women was by being tough on people. Only later did I discover that there are little Stalins at every level of every organization.

The trouble is that little Stalins are often hard for superiors to spot because they usually relate well to those up the bureaucratic and corporate ladder and are considered by their bosses to be polite, reasonable, and effective. There seems to be a direct correlation between the meanness of a little Stalin downward and his or her talent for sucking up to superiors—the "kiss up, kick down" syndrome. Given the dangerously corrosive effect such people can have within an organization, it is important to ferret them out and either move them to a nonsupervisory position where their individual skills might still be of value or, if necessary and possible, fire them.

A senior official who exhibits such behavior is especially problematic. If such a person is not the highest ranking in an organization, the only option—as at lower levels—is to get word to the top boss, often through a chief of staff or someone else close to the head honcho. I had this happen everyplace I worked. My chief of staff in each case would learn about abusive behavior at a lower level and either informed the little Stalin's boss about it (telling him to handle it), spoke to the individual directly, or, as a last resort, got me involved. If I had to talk to someone, I made it clear mine was a final warning: if there were a recurrence, the offender would be leaving permanently.

If the guilty party is the CEO, sad to say, the organization will just have to grin and bear it, waiting for the person to depart or for his ugly behavior to find its way into the media (hint, hint) and—with luck—force a change in behavior or resignation.

I pounded the desk just once in my career. It was in 1982 during my early days as deputy CIA director for analysis (the same position where I mistakenly began my tenure with the scorchingly critical speech). I called someone to my office to chew him out for some fairly egregious blunder. For dramatic effect, at one point I noisily slammed my hand down on my desk. I brusquely told the person to get out of my office immediately. I threw him out in haste mainly because I thought I had broken my hand. I hopped around the office holding my hand, alternately crying and laughing. Crying because my hand hurt so badly, laughing because I realized how ridiculous I looked and felt. Not only did I never pound my desk again, but I don't think I ever again raised my voice or threw someone out of my office. It was a lesson painfully learned.

A leader who treats his team members with respect and dignity can win the loyalty of subordinates literally for life. Throughout his entire career, George H. W. Bush was consistently kind to all those who worked with and for him. Most memorable were the countless little notes he would send to people who had gone out of their way for him, had received recognition of some sort for an accomplishment, had just done a good job, or had suffered some kind of personal tragedy or setback. He treated everyone—from White House groundskeepers to cabinet officers—the same way, asking about their families and their children (usually by name), asking how things were going for them generally, talking about the latest sports event of note. Virtually all who worked for him were considered part of a larger family, and no one ever forgot it.

An equally respectful boss was Zbigniew Brzezinski, President Carter's national security adviser. At one point, I was traveling with him to Cairo in 1978 during the final stages of negotiating the Camp David peace accords between Israel and Egypt. When he met with the Egyptian president, Anwar Sadat, I accompanied him as his note taker. I will never forget Brzezinski introducing me to Sadat not as his aide or staff assistant but as his "colleague." It was a tiny gesture of respect, but one I remember vividly nearly forty years later. Zbig was a demanding boss but unfailingly polite to those who worked for him. I was lucky to work for several such bosses, including the national security adviser Brent Scowcroft and the DCI William Webster.

The gangster Al Capone allegedly once said, "You can get a lot more done with a kind word and a gun than with a kind word alone." Still, never underestimate the power of a kind word. Treating subordinates properly always pays dividends—and others notice. It doesn't mean being a soft touch.

Leaders can—and, when necessary, must—level tough criticism at individuals, but due regard for their dignity requires doing it in private, not adding embarrassment and humiliation to the equation. Criticism, done privately, is far more likely to bring about constructive change. "Praise in public, criticize in private," as the saying goes.

Even firing people can be done in a way that preserves that dignity—such as offering to let them resign. At A&M, when I fired vice presidents, in nearly every case I gave each a year or so to step down. I had the time to do that because, in academia, searches for replacements are long and drawn-out affairs—although jobs with special requirements often take a long time to fill in both the private and the public sectors. In my case, before acting at A&M, I had my chief of staff look into where the departing employee stood in terms of eligibility for retirement, potential loss of benefits, and so on; I needed to remove such employees, but I did not want to punish or hurt them. In one or two cases, I delayed acting for a few months to ensure there was no loss of retirement or other benefits. Leaders should never lose their humanity. And when I told those employees it was time to go, I said I would go along with any story they wanted to concoct; if they wanted to tell people they quit because they couldn't work for that son of a bitch Gates, I wouldn't contradict them.

At Defense, when I told senior officers they had to go, I let them resign. I also tried to be gracious in any public statements I made, pointing to their long record of public service. On at least two occasions, I spoke at the farewell or retirement ceremony for senior leaders—our top Afghan commander and the secretary of the air force—whom I had let go in a very public and abrupt way (given the urgency, I felt there was no alternative). Each was classy enough to invite me to attend his ceremony and I returned the gesture by paying tribute to his many real accomplishments without being patronizing or disingenuous. I think the two men appreciated it, although the friends and family present were probably of a different mind.

You can be the toughest, most demanding leader on the planet and still treat people with respect and dignity. Whether it's the lowest-level supervisory position or the very top job, a leader can and should treat people right. To quote President Harry Truman, "Always be nice to all the people who can't talk back to you. I can't stand a man or woman who bawls out underlings to satisfy an ego."

To lead reform successfully, a leader must empower subordinates.

Whether the changes a leader wants to make are sweeping, minor, or something in between, she cannot achieve them alone. She needs to trust those on the team below her who should have been involved from the outset in establishing goals and the plans to achieve them. A leader must be willing to delegate to them the authority to carry out plans. One person simply cannot effectively oversee implementation of significant change that affects multiple parts of an organization. It doesn't matter whether it's a government bureaucracy or a business.

At each affected layer of the organization, there needs to be a leader committed to the overall agenda, a leader who has the authority not only to implement but also to adjust or adapt plans as needed. Generals develop strategy; they don't hover over captains and lieutenants to see if they are doing their jobs on the front lines. There is a reason for the military chain of command: everyone knows his or her job but, within the realm of their specific responsibilities, can make tactical adjustments to achieve success. The same principle applies to bureaucracies, public and private.

In each of the large institutions in which I led change, I depended heavily on the officials who reported to me to carry out my directions. Once I made a decision, I counted on the CIA's deputy directors and the heads of other intelligence agencies, the deans and vice presidents at A&M, and the military leaders and senior civilians at Defense for implementation. I expected them—along with task force chairs and those heading other entities—to report on their progress to me on a regular basis. Equally important, I expected to be informed when someone ran into problems or obstructions to getting the job done so, as necessary, I could clear the blockage. I rarely had a problem when someone leading an effort or project proposed adjustments or changed a plan to make it work better. But the employees in each of those three very different organizations all knew that those leading the change efforts had my confidence and my backing and that I would support their actions and decisions.

While I was president of A&M, an explosion caused by a gas leak in an on-campus graduate student apartment killed one person and gravely burned several others. Both the provost and I were traveling. The vice-provost and my chief of staff convened a meeting of relevant officials to address the situation, during which they learned that exhausted A&M maintenance officials were inspecting only some of the other units in that complex for additional gas leaks. My chief of staff felt empowered to direct that every apartment be inspected even if it required contracting for external professionals from all over the state—regardless of the cost. He knew that was the action I would have taken, and he took it himself knowing I would support his decision. Any leader wants his subordinates to be able to act on their own if necessary.

That kind of empowerment is equally important in the private sector, as I saw time and again as a corporate board member. A CEO cannot successfully lead a company except as the head of a team.

Another benefit of empowerment is that a leader ends up with a broad cadre of senior career professionals committed to implementing the change agenda. While they are not necessarily "disciples," they do tend to believe in what a leader is trying to do. And in my experience, they will often support much of the reform agenda after the leader who initiated it leaves.

As I sought to persuade the army not to return to its pre-9/11 conventional warfare model subsequent to the wars in Iraq and Afghanistan, but to sustain a broad range of capabilities—based on lessons recently learned at great cost—for diverse kinds of conflict, I knew that appointing one reform-minded senior general wouldn't be enough: the institutional army could outlast and overwhelm one person. So I advanced more than half a dozen senior army generals (Martin Dempsey, Ray Odierno, David Rodriguez, Pete Chiarelli, and Lloyd Austin, among others) who I believed shared my point of view to positions where I knew they would dominate the army for perhaps a decade or more. I also supported the secretary of the army when he brought General David Petraeus back from Iraq to chair a selection board for new brigadier generals. I wanted to make sure the colonels who had distinguished themselves commanding troops in unconventional combat would be put in a position to shape their service in the future. Too often, the "Big Army" establishment used promotions to keep perceived iconoclasts from getting into a position where they could shake things up.

A leader empowering subordinates who believe in the desired agenda is going a long way toward ensuring reforms will endure after she is gone. Empowering subordinates also helps them develop their own leadership and decision-making styles, thereby advancing their careers and providing the institution with a strong bench of capable future senior leaders. Everybody wins.

As I told the graduating midshipmen at the United States Naval Academy in 2011, leadership includes "the ability to stand in the shadow and let others receive attention and accolades. A leader is able to make decisions but then delegate and trust others to make things happen. This doesn't mean turning your back after a decision and hoping for the best. It does mean trusting people at the same time you hold them accountable. The bottom line: a self-confident leader doesn't cast such a large shadow that no one else can grow."

A successful leader—and reformer—never misses an opportunity to give credit to those working for him as a group and as individuals. He also is willing to let excellent employees move on when they are offered new opportunities or a chance to ascend the ladder.

Too many bosses, when congratulated by higher-ups for some

accomplishment, are content to take all the credit for themselves. The real leader will give credit to those who did the hard work that made success possible. Every time I praised a commander in the field in Iraq and Afghanistan, he would immediately tell me—and everyone else—that it was all the doing of his soldiers or marines. No one likes a glory hog.

A good leader helps create opportunities for the members of his team. It is hard to let go of a superior performer; it is nearly always a genuine loss to the organization. But I know of too many instances where a boss has refused to let someone go (by weighing in with higher-ups, arguing that the loss would imperil overall performance) or has even actively sabotaged a move up by someone he wanted to keep. When I was first invited to join the NSC staff in 1974 on loan from the CIA, one of my senior bosses at the agency told me flat out there probably would not be a job for me when I wanted to return. Too many aspiring people at every level have had the experience of "leaders" putting obstacles in their career way forward.

After my personal experience at the CIA, I tried to be supportive of superb subordinates who had a chance to move up or on to better positions. As secretary of defense, I hated to lose my old friend and colleague Jim Clapper as undersecretary of defense for intelligence, but when President Obama asked him to become director of national intelligence, I knew it would be a step up for Jim and that it was the right move also for the country. Truth to tell, I even proposed Jim's name to the president. I relied heavily on all of my senior military assistants and, in every case, would have liked to keep them longer. But I would not stand in their way.

The chief of protocol at the Pentagon has myriad responsibilities including arranging visits by foreign leaders, a wide range of ceremonies, and presidential visits. Mary Claire Murphy held the position when I became secretary, and she was a genius at it—warm, welcoming, creative, and attentive to detail. She had been doing protocol work for years and was offered a job at a major corporation to oversee its foundation and charitable efforts. It was a rare opportunity to broaden her experience and get into a field far less dependent on the political fortunes of her bosses. And so, with great reluctance, I encouraged her to take the job. How good was she? Years later, she was still being called back into service for major events—including organizing the memorial ceremony (at which the president spoke) at Fort Hood for the thirteen soldiers who were killed there.

For any leader in any business or public sector bureaucracy, blocking the advancement of his people is short-term, shortsighted thinking. If a leader's organization is seen as high performing and a place where promising people have a chance to grow and to see their careers fostered and advanced, the highest-quality individuals will want to work there. Such an office will soon acquire a reputation as a launching pad for further career success rather than a dead-end job. Believe me, a leader's own superiors will notice when a disproportionate number of highfliers seem consistently to come from one place.

Empowerment means taking care of one's subordinates in other ways as well, including bringing to their attention opportunities for professional education or broadening, as well as for advancement. Little things can mean a lot, such as including junior professionals in meetings with senior officials so they have an opportunity to demonstrate their skills or giving them face time with other leaders in the organization so they get known. One of the many reasons I admired Michèle Flournoy, the undersecretary of defense for policy who worked for me during Obama's first term, was her determined effort to enhance the performance, career, and potential of all those who worked for her. She was a true leader in this regard.

As DCI, I relished sending a GS-13 analyst expert (an army major would be a military equivalent) to the Oval Office to brief the president. I had great confidence he or she would do well, whether I went along or not. I never had one let me down. As secretary of defense, on foreign trips sometimes I would have a young desk officer ride to the formal evening event in the limo with me and pass through the honor guard and welcoming ceremonies by my side. It was recognition of that person's hard work, but I also knew, from my own experience, he would never forget the occasion. It also had the ancillary benefit of making an impression on the senior foreign officials our desk officer would be dealing with long after my trip was over. It demonstrated that this mid-level American interlocutor had the ear of the boss, so those he'd be dealing with would pay better attention and show some respect.

From the vantage point of the corner office, whether you are a corporate CEO, the secretary of defense choosing the next generation of military leaders, or a middle manager, identifying talent and growing it are two of the primary responsibilities of a leader. Maybe one of the reasons I feel so strongly about these particular responsibilities of a leader is that I owe my career success to such an act of empowerment. The DCI Bill Casey and his deputy, Bob Inman, passed over dozens of more senior officers to appoint me as the CIA's deputy director for intelligence in January 1982 because they had the confidence I could succeed, and they were willing to let me go as chief of their executive staff to assume the new job.

A leader who looks out for his subordinates will almost always reap big dividends.

A successful leader must always be evaluating the people around and below her. She should empower the strong, try to help those who show promise despite shortcomings, and get rid of the deadwood.

One of the fundamental roles of a leader is to assess her people: Who is an asset, and who is a liability? In nearly all public bureaucracies, evaluating the performance of individuals and acting on that evaluation is a deeply flawed process. Determining someone's performance with some accuracy and fairness is often difficult. Telling someone in person about his shortcomings and weaknesses—areas for improvement—or even his strengths in a constructive way is even tougher. The result is often that a supervisor is so negative that the individual thinks he's about to be fired or, more commonly, the discussion is so anodyne that someone who is not performing up to snuff thinks he's doing just fine.

Written evaluations are even worse. In the military, individuals are scored on a number of different criteria, from worst possible performance (an X in the far-left-hand column) to best (an X in the far-right column). In practice, any mark not in the far-right column is disastrous and mostly a career ender. Similarly, if in the "comments" section the individual is not described as walking on water and able to leap tall buildings in a single bound, the chances of promotion are slim. Supervisors are reluctant to provide honest comments precisely because they have such disproportionate consequences. Thus, to take a worst-case example, several supervisors would later acknowledge they saw disturbing behavior on the part of Major Nidal Hasan, the Fort Hood soldier who killed thirteen people in a rampage, but they never recorded it in his evaluations. While that is obviously an extreme case, the failure to make an employee's problems and weaknesses part of the evaluation record is typical.

For subordinates, such an evaluation system encourages timidity and an unwillingness to challenge superiors or to be candid. If they just keep their heads down, they will be assured a good review and a shot at future promotions. Rocking the boat puts that future at risk.

Although the preparation of personal performance evaluations at the CIA was not quite as skewed as in the military, the same tendencies were prevalent. Indeed, when I was deputy DCI, from time to time I was asked by senior officials to approve early retirement for an individual based on poor performance. I would call for the individual's personnel folder, and, sure enough, the performance ratings for the preceding several years were always "strong" or "outstanding." After years of failing to establish a paper trail of inadequate performance, supervisors wanted me to push someone into retirement. In such cases, I usually refused in the hope of forcing more honest appraisals. It was a forlorn hope. I encountered much the same situation at A&M, although I did ask the vice president overseeing human resources to devise a process that gave supervisors freedom to provide more substantive feedback to employees.

The ability of a leader in a bureaucracy to move people or fire them because of poor performance is significantly limited by failures of the evaluation system. Exceptions are few and far between. And, increasingly in business, you had better have a record of warnings and counseling over time if you want to fire someone, or you will face a problematic lawsuit. (The director of the CIA probably has the most comprehensive unilateral authority to fire someone in either the public or the private sector, an authority upheld by the Supreme Court. But even that authority can be challenged if it is deemed "arbitrary and capricious." So, even at the CIA a paper trail is required.)

Early in my CIA career, after several successive positive annual evaluations, a new boss gave me a pretty crummy report. The good news was that he gave most others in our little unit crummy reports as well. We all objected up the chain of command, and, amazingly, some months later he was fired as our branch chief. The group of us, collectively and individually, had a strong performance record, and the powers that be apparently didn't want us transferring elsewhere because of a toxic boss. I would realize in later years what an extraordinarily rare action that was.

Evaluating performance is not only difficult but risky. A hard-ass boss who lacks objectivity can send talent flying away from an organization because of unfair appraisals. An easygoing boss can allow slackers and mediocrities to nest in a unit. And a boss who is careless with words can get you a lawsuit. I wish I could offer a way to evaluate people that isn't too hard or too easy but just right. But there isn't one. A leader probably can't do away with the formal review process, but there are several ways to mitigate its worst effects.

- Is a poor (or superb) evaluation an anomaly, and if so, is the reviewer new to the job? If not, what caused the abrupt change?
- As so often, my advice again is to listen. I learned an amazing amount of information about how people were performing just by keeping my ears open. Peers say things, subordinates gossip among themselves, and old colleagues often pass along what they hear. A leader's immediate staff often has insights into the behavior of subordinate leaders—or can find out about it easily. A leader shouldn't hesitate to listen to them and to make use of their access. Nearly all of the information you glean will be gossip, hearsay, impressionistic, or anecdotal. But put it all together and it can provide a feel for whether there is a problem with the boss of a unit and whether more questions or a deeper probe is warranted.
- Watching how people behave in meetings is useful: Is a subordinate afraid to speak up if his immediate boss is there? If the boss says something clearly incorrect, will subordinates pipe up with a correction? Or, vice versa: How does a boss treat a subordinate who speaks up or corrects someone? Is anyone bold enough to use humor or sarcasm? (I always found the use of humor—or lack of it—quite telling about the health of an organization and relationships within it.)

Evaluating subordinates in business has its own pitfalls, and judging intangible qualities such as people skills can be as fraught with difficulty as in the public sector. But many jobs in business at least have some unambiguous performance metrics. Did the employee make his numbers or not? Did he meet the sales or revenue target? Did he meet or beat his expense allocation? Did he receive fewer customer complaints? With additional effort, I think some of these kinds of metrics can and should be applied in the public sector. No evaluation should be entirely statistical, but neither should it be entirely subjective.

———

Candor is critical to a leader's success. Every boss needs to understand that creating a climate where people feel comfortable in being honest in their opinions is the cheapest possible job insurance for the person in charge.

Leaders who think they don't need frank, critical advice every day are usually doomed. I would never knowingly hire such a person. However, encouraging candor is one of those areas where rhetoric is meaningless; only actions over time have any impact in terms of persuading people a leader is serious and overcoming their concerns about the career risk of speaking up.

George Washington was pretty thin-skinned but recognized the importance of candor and criticism. He once wrote, "I can bear to hear of imputed or real errors. The man who wishes to stand well in the opinion of others must do this, because he is thereby enabled to correct his faults, or remove prejudices which are imbibed against him." Would that all leaders were as insightful. No one likes to be criticized or told of his or her shortcomings or errors, yet everyone needs to hear it—and welcome it.

One of the greatest American generals and statesmen was George C. Marshall, chief of staff of the army during World War II (considered "the architect of victory"), author of the Marshall Plan to save Europe after the war, and secretary of both state and defense. In September 1938, after the British prime minister, Neville Chamberlain, had signed the Munich agreement with Adolf Hitler, the then brigadier general Marshall attended one of his first meetings at the White House. A number of more senior officials were present. As described by the historian Eric Larrabee, in that meeting President Roosevelt proposed a program to build some ten thousand airplanes a year but with no supporting forces. At the end of the meeting, Roosevelt asked Marshall if he thought that was the correct path forward. Marshall replied, "I am sorry, Mr. President, but I don't agree with that at all." Nearly everyone at the meeting thought Marshall had just ended his career.

But less than a year later, Roosevelt named Marshall army chief of staff. Marshall had, in a phrase now famous, "spoken truth to power." Equally as important as Marshall's courage and candor, however, was Roosevelt's understanding of the value of having a person at his side who would tell him what he needed to hear, not just what he wanted to hear.

Virtually all leaders tell their subordinates that they want and expect candor. The problem is that most don't really mean it. They fall more into the camp of Samuel Goldwyn, one of the founders of MGM, who allegedly once told his people, "I don't want any yes-men around me. I want everybody to tell me the truth even if it costs them their jobs." No one, especially a person who has risen to the top of an organization, wants to be told he has just committed a huge blunder or is about to. Or that he just gave an awful speech. Or that his policies are failing. Or that he totally misjudged someone. More than a few professionals who have been assured candor was welcome have been sidelined or cast aside for offering unvarnished opinions on such matters. Just as the army general Eric Shinseki was sidelined by the secretary of defense after the general had the temerity to tell Congress that the occupation of Iraq might require several hundred thousand troops. And Richard Helms was fired as DCI for telling President Nixon candidly what he didn't want to hear—that the CIA would not take the fall for Watergate. Under more than a few modern presidents, candor and dissent such as Marshall demonstrated has resulted in the culprit being cast into the outer darkness— persona non grata in the Oval Office. (Although I must say that despite my disagreements, dissent, and candor with President Obama, he never once told me to back off or froze me out.)

No one makes the right decision every time or hits a home run with every interview, testimony, or speech. Yet nearly all leaders, especially at more senior levels of business and government, have sycophants who will always tell them how smart, how wonderful, how amazingly thoughtful and insightful they are. Every normal human being loves hearing how great he is, and therein lies the danger, because few really are. Most of us have flaws, blind spots, and biases we can't easily see. We often don't understand the consequences—both intended and unintended—of actions we are considering.

At home, if we're lucky, we have spouses who keep us grounded. (As an NSC staffer in the 1970s, I'd come home and brag to my wife about attending some meeting with the president that day, and the response would usually be along the lines of "That's nice, dear. Now take out the trash.") At work, we need people who do the same. Every leader needs people around him or her who will speak their minds freely.

All that said, getting candor, even when you want it—even when you make clear you welcome it—can be difficult. I worked hard at the CIA, A&M, and Defense to create an environment where candor was encouraged and welcome. I knew how much I needed it. Even so, when I was CIA director, I could get true candor only from my deputy, as well as my secretary, executive assistant, general counsel, head of congressional affairs, and the inspector general—but not from a single senior line officer. At Texas A&M, among administrators, I could count on only the executive vice president and provost, my chief of staff, secretary, director of special events, head of legislative affairs, and the senior vice president for finance. (On the other hand, a university president never has to worry about a lack of candor from the faculty.) Interestingly, at both institutions, I found women disproportionately more willing to be candid with me.

At Defense, much to my surprise, the number of people who would be candid was far larger than I expected: the chairmen of the Joint Chiefs Pete Pace and then Mike Mullen, and my chief of staff, senior military assistants, press spokesman, and a couple of assistants in my immediate office. I also found nearly all the military service chiefs and senior commanders to be quite open about their concerns and about decisions under consideration, especially those involving the wars in Iraq and Afghanistan, as well as on budgetary matters. Almost every junior officer and enlisted man and woman I encountered was candid as well. They were fantastic. Maybe they were just so far down the chain of command they thought, "What the hell?" Much to my surprise and delight, men and women in uniform—in the most rigidly hierarchical organization there is—were the most open and candid of any I worked with over four decades.

I've thought a lot about why those in the military were so different in this regard from the CIA and a big university. I'm sure senior officers pulled their punches and left certain things unsaid when disagreeing with me, not revealing just how much or how deeply they differed. But I always had a good idea where they stood on important issues. Clearly, this was due to more than something in the Pentagon drinking water and probably has to do with military training and culture—and perhaps because the stakes are so high on most Defense issues and the sense of responsibility to the troops so great.

Every time someone persuaded me to change my mind, urged me to revisit a decision or to acknowledge I had made a mistake, I would publicly highlight the episode, including the name of the person who had spoken up. For example, when the time came to nominate a new U.S. military commander in South Korea, I decided to appoint someone from a service other than the army for the first time. General George Casey, the army chief of staff, came to see me to contend that the circumstances in Korea at that time made it imperative for the army to hang on to the job for at least one more rotation. George made a persuasive case and I changed my mind. I was very open in telling people Casey had gotten me to reverse my decision. I wanted to do all I could to emphasize that candor was career enhancing and not career destroying.

Even so, as I've said, in two of the three organizations I led, the number of those willing to speak up and disagree with me or offer a contrary opinion—or warn me I was about to make a mistake—remained disappointingly small. I always wondered whether officials who were chary about being candid with me did not particularly welcome such candor from their own subordinates. Indeed, at A&M I was often approached by faculty members who would ask me why their department head or dean was not as open about matters as I was as university president.

I have served on the board of directors of ten corporations over the last two decades and found getting candid responses to questions—particularly from those below the CEO—often to be just as challenging as in the public sector. Executives are reluctant to acknowledge problems or mistakes or that an initiative has failed. In the boardroom, getting a lower-level executive just to admit he doesn't know the answer is all too often like pulling teeth. When a senior company official wasn't candid with the board, I always worried that he might not be candid with the CEO either—or that the CEO himself did not welcome candor. I served on one board where no idea ever surfaced that the CEO didn't make clear he had already thought of it—as though admitting he hadn't thought of something revealed some deep inadequacy. I always thought it was just bullshit. In contrast, I always thought the willingness of executives to express different points of view among themselves in the presence of the board reflected a healthy internal environment. The bottom line: the scarcity of candor afflicts public and business bureaucracies and is an impediment to effectiveness in both.

Despite the difficulty, though, the leader must make the effort because candid advice is so important to success. Every leader must encourage respectful, loyal dissent. Every leader must look for every possible opportunity to demonstrate that candor is welcome. A leader must have people around him who will speak truth to power. Even if a leader doesn't agree with the comments or criticism, he will be aware of points of view different from his own and be better prepared to respond to those concerns. Leaders need candor because none of us are as smart as we think we are.

Exhausted people make bad decisions and give bad advice.

President Reagan loved to say that while it was true hard work never killed anyone, he saw no reason to take any risk. While many people in bureaucracies share that view and watch eagerly for the clock to indicate it's quitting time, a substantial number in both the private and the public sectors put in extraordinarily long hours—often for no good reason. Indeed, particularly at the CIA, Defense, the NSC, and many other national security departments and agencies, there is an unspoken rule that if you don't put in twelve- or fourteen-hour days and work on weekends, you are a slacker. Sometimes subordinates stay in the office for long hours simply because the boss is still at his desk and might call. The advent of BlackBerrys and smart phones has only made the situation worse as bosses at home or on vacation can monitor what's going on at the office. While there are certainly times when long hours are needed to get the work done or to deal with a crisis, I think all too often it's more a matter of office culture, habit, and machismo. *My God, my job is so important that I'm working seventy hours a week.* And I'm afraid too many bosses force people to put in long hours just because they can demand it.

Similarly, I would frequently encounter people in the federal government and in companies who rarely took vacations. I always felt they either had a profoundly exaggerated view of their importance to the organization or were so lacking in self-confidence that they were afraid they wouldn't be missed and their job thus considered redundant: their desk might be gone when they returned. I always thought both of those excuses rather sad. When I was DCI, I took three weeks' vacation every August and, even as secretary, took two weeks each summer and another week at Christmas. At A&M, I took four weeks. We all need to recharge our batteries and spend time with our families. And in all three jobs, I always returned from vacation with a yellow tablet full of ideas and initiatives for further change and reform.

As both CIA director and secretary of defense, I arrived in the office about seven in the morning and, absent a meeting at the

White House, tried to leave for home by six. While an eleven-hour day is not exactly loafing, I was often one of the first people out of the building at night. I would always take a briefcase full of homework with me, but I thought it healthy to get out of the office, go home, see my wife (and, while I was at the CIA, my kids), relax with a drink, and have dinner. I also hoped that if I left the building at a reasonable hour, others who were staying only because I was there would also go home to spend the evening with their families. As secretary, while I often had to attend meetings at the White House on Saturday or Sunday, I never once in four and a half years went into the office on Saturday. I didn't want to go in personally, but I also didn't want a bunch of subordinates losing their weekend just because I decided to work on my in-box at the office instead of at home.

All that said, there will be times in both public and private organizations when the leader must demand extraordinary exertions from his or her subordinates, perhaps over an extended period. Just as a junior officer or NCO must look after the well-being of the young troops in his charge, the wise leader will take responsibility for husbanding the physical and mental strength of the team. This involves avoiding unnecessarily long hours expended for no significant purpose and encouraging people to take time off so that when the crisis strikes or a big new initiative is undertaken, the team has the stamina and reserve strength to put forward maximum effective effort when it really counts.

Accountability is essential to any successful reform effort.
The only way someone can achieve transformation in a bureaucracy is to empower individuals to complete specific tasks, establish milestones to measure progress, and hold those individuals accountable for success or failure—and then reward or penalize as appropriate and possible.

Because responsibility for everything in a big organization

is often so diffuse, when something goes wrong or isn't working properly it is tough to assign blame and hold individuals accountable. That is the conventional wisdom and all too often true. But it is neither necessary nor inevitable.

Failure to hold senior people in big organizations accountable for monumental screwups and disasters is common. Examples abound. To the newsworthy failures I have mentioned previously, one could add the veterans' health-care scandal in 2014, General Motors' giant recalls in 2014, the mismanagement of Fannie Mae and Freddie Mac, and so many more. In all but a few cases, no one was truly held accountable for incompetence, ineffectiveness, or failure to do the job right. If senior officials aren't held accountable for failing to prevent or respond adequately to major disasters, it's no surprise that no one gets held accountable for ordinary bureaucratic ineptitude.

It shouldn't be that way. If you truly want to implement lasting change in a bureaucracy, you have no choice but to hold people accountable for performance, especially at senior levels. I saw all too often in my decades of government service that when something went wrong, it was the lower-level or mid-level official who was assigned blame and had to walk the career plank while more senior officials, who should have known about the problem and acted, escaped reprimand altogether. Many years ago, I resolved that if and when I was in charge, "accountability" would reach much higher on the totem pole.

What was astonishing to me was the amazement in Washington when I did fire senior people, amazement that a senior government official *could* actually be fired for anything short of mass murder or getting caught red-handed with a sack of dirty money. When you think of the countless public and private organizational disasters and problems in recent years, when you think of the day-to-day ineptitude of so many bureaucracies, it is staggering how few senior officials responsible are replaced. All too often, this is because firing a senior official will reflect badly on his or her boss, or on the president or CEO who appointed the person, or on a political leader's policies more generally. So the cycle of unwarranted praise and deflection of responsibility continues.

It is just as true in local and state government bureaucracies, and in universities as well. And the private sector is just as flawed as the public sector when it comes to holding senior people accountable for failure—the bigger the company, the more likely the problem. In fact, the failure to hold people accountable for performance seems to be characteristic of virtually all bureaucracies. In the public sector, if you cheat on your expense account, travel and entertain too lavishly, or spend too much money redecorating your office, you're fired, but oversee a financial meltdown, a botched program rollout, a failing war effort, or steer a great institution or critical initiative into the ditch, and you have nothing to worry about. This is a failure of leadership.

By the same token, when legislative bodies or the media want someone held "accountable" for a disaster, failure to perform, or revelation of a long-ignored problem, they really mean they want to hang someone. "Accountability" has become synonymous with "blame." This is too bad because accountability is an invaluable tool for leaders and is really about empowerment: setting expectations and measuring performance, the results of which can be either positive or negative. The private sector is quite effective in holding people accountable for good financial results in the form of bonuses, stock options, pay raises, and the like—rewards not available in the public sector. The latter is dependent on small cash rewards, a letter of commendation, a promotion, or a medal. The upside of accountability in public bureaucracies is more symbolic and psychological than material.

There are a number of ways to enforce accountability. If someone is simply not up to his job, a leader should move him to another job he can do—or at least get him out of the way until a permanent solution can be found. Onetime lapses might earn an oral or written reprimand or, in the private sector, some financial consequence like loss of a bonus. But if a subordinate is purposely trying to undercut what you are doing or has allowed a major problem to develop without acting, then you must be willing to fire the individual. If rules and regulations prevent you from actually firing the culprit, then relegate that person to an empty office in the basement. While that may be extreme, the point is to send a message to the rest of the organization that negligence, incompetence, or obstructionism will not be tolerated. It is demoralizing to any organization when employees—especially younger ones—see there are no consequences for failure or mediocrity. Why work harder (or smarter) if everyone is treated the same, regardless of performance?

It is always easier to fire or discipline a low-level employee than a supervisor or senior manager, but for any leader it is those high-level folks who need to know they will be held accountable for performance because they are precisely the ones upon whom a leader must depend if his efforts are to be successful. If high-level employees are underperforming or resistant to change, they must go, and the leader must be the one to act. It is the price of being an agent of change.

Does holding people accountable and being willing to fire senior executives create fear? A veteran Washington journalist once told me that I was one of the few secretaries actually to run the Department of Defense. He went on to opine that was because I had people "scared to death." I certainly did not intend for that to happen, but I suppose that because almost no one in D.C. ever gets fired for anything, my willingness to do just that on several occasions probably did create apprehension and fear. Creating fear is not, in my view, a constructive leadership tool. But if it is the consequence of simply holding people accountable for unsatisfactory performance, then so be it.

I want to offer one cautionary note in that vein. Too many new bosses, especially at senior levels, arrive looking for someone to fire just to demonstrate they are in charge and willing "to hold people accountable." They *want* to create fear upon arrival. With just two exceptions, I never fired anyone in my early weeks in a new job. I gave everyone the opportunity to prove himself or herself under new leadership. Firing someone in one's first days as boss in a bureaucracy looks more like muscle flexing or showing off than leadership. There may be occasions when it is called for, but I'd be very careful about doing so.

I fired, moved out of the way, or reprimanded a number of senior people over the course of my career. In every case, I had to take action against someone I liked personally. Every time, it was hard. Only a few times had anyone done something I considered egregious. Most of the time, I simply concluded the individual was not up to the job to which he or she had been assigned or promoted. I think the toughest personnel decision a leader faces—in government or business—is when he realizes that someone who has given years, often decades, of faithful and competent service does not have the requisite skills to help take the organization to the next level of excellence or just does not have the right background to take on the tasks ahead.

The cost of leaving such people in place is just too high. Replacing them is a challenge peculiar to leaders charged with reform. Performance that might be tolerable in maintaining the status quo won't do in a time of transformative change.

This is where the leader must be held accountable: Is he prepared to tell a long-serving, hardworking, competent person that he does not have the ability to take his organization to the next level and therefore must retire (or take a nonsupervisory position)? This is, in some ways, the supreme test for the agent of change. It must be done, but done with as gentle a hand as possible. If the person is too young to retire or unwilling to do so, can a place be found as a senior adviser or counselor or some other role that allows a graceful transition out? During the first couple of years I led the analytical directorate of the CIA, I felt I had to replace a number of office directors. I found alternative positions for every single one; none had to leave the agency. Similarly, at A&M, as described earlier, I made departures as easy as possible in all but one or two cases where I felt an immediate change was needed. The entire organization and many stakeholders will be watching how a leader handles the removal of "old hands," an action most will probably agree must be done but with proper recognition and appreciation of past service rendered.

———

Historically, it has been characteristic of Americans—from the beginning of the Republic—to question authority and, when given direction or orders, to ask why. One of the greatest strengths of American soldiers throughout time has been the ability and willingness to think for themselves and to act independently when necessary. If anything, our modern culture has intensified skepticism of authority figures—bosses. Respect for authority, deference of any kind, is not automatic but earned. Cynicism is allayed only by deeds and proven integrity over time.

Experience with bosses who were arrogant and autocratic (or timid and indecisive), as well as with egotists, incompetents, fakers, and blowhards, has given most people in bureaucracies a very tough hide and a deeply skeptical attitude toward their leaders. Yet these are the very people a leader must persuade to believe in the importance of and need for reform and to follow wholeheartedly. The suggestions in the foregoing chapters—and this one in particular—are intended to provide ways to break through that skepticism and bring those career professionals to support what a reform leader seeks to accomplish.

To change bureaucracies effectively, a leader must first make his people proud and eager to excel. Particularly in public bureaucracies, where financial reward for performance is rare and difficult, a leader must rely primarily on intangible incentives to motivate. A leader must believe the task before her—the reforms she seeks—is important before she can persuade others to believe it. She must manifest pride in the organization before she can inculcate it in others. She must have a positive, eager attitude if she expects the same from her subordinates. If people are to be transferred or let go, it must be done as humanely as possible.

In today's America, if a leader wants to inspire excellence, she must model it herself. She must treat her employees with respect and dignity, empower them, tell them the truth, trust them, and hold them accountable. She won't get through to everyone, but she will influence enough people to accomplish her goals. Only the people who work for you can bring about the transformational changes you seek.

6

Stakeholders: Friends and Foes

L eaders of organizations, especially large ones, hear voices. Lots of them. A cacophony. They are the voices of myriad groups and individuals who have—or want—a say in how institutions important to them are run. As I alluded to earlier, they may be legislators, boards of directors, community officials, boards of regents, retirees, alumni, the media, unions, employees, lower-level managers, students, customers, vendors, lobbyists, professional organizations, accrediting boards, investigative bodies, regulators from every level of government, activist organizations, political groups, and on and on. All the voices have different interests, authority, points of view, and agendas. Some will have formal responsibilities for an organization; many will have none. But all can be considered stakeholders and will demand attention and satisfaction. While the private sector and its bureaucracies hear many of these voices, public institutions are nearly overwhelmed by them and the time they consume. They get particularly stirred up by an agenda for change.

However demanding the stakeholders, a leader's success depends on cultivating positive relationships with them. She may not need or want their "help." She may not even like or respect them. But she likely cannot survive the open hostility of most. She must make time for them, and she must—dare I say it again—listen to them, if not always agree with them. A leader should never lose sight of the fact that some of these voices, annoying as they are at times, can actually be helpful.

Of all the stakeholders associated with public bureaucracies, elected oversight bodies—local school boards, city and county council members, state legislatures, Congress—are the most important.

Regardless of personal feelings and views, a leader must invest the time necessary to develop positive relationships with elected officials and exercise the personal discipline to avoid creating hostility and enmity. Their ability to stymie a leader's efforts is scarily broad, and she forgets that at her peril. Simply put, the leader of a public organization cannot succeed without the support of its elected overseers.

The place to start is cultivating a strong relationship with senior legislative leaders, especially those with direct oversight responsibilities. As CIA director, I initiated biweekly private meetings with the leaders of the two congressional intelligence committees, keeping them informed of everything I was doing and all matters relating to intelligence activities—an unprecedented breadth and depth of communication. It built great trust.

Reaching out to other leaders in legislative bodies also pays dividends, sometimes in unexpected ways. As DCI, I met one-on-one with senior members of Congress such as the Senate Appropriations Committee chairman Robert Byrd, the House Banking Committee chairman Henry González, and the House Judiciary Committee chairman Jack Brooks. Though they did not lead the intelligence oversight committees, they still had enormous influence over issues that mattered a great deal to the intelligence community. Brooks and González had been trying to get my predecessors to testify in front of their committees for ages, and with a handshake agreement limiting the scope of my testimony,

I agreed to appear, thus earning brownie points on the Hill that would later come in quite handy. (Brooks even gave me some of his wife's home-baked chocolate chip cookies.)

In early 1992, not long after I became DCI, *The Washington Post* published an editorial accusing Senator Byrd of forcing the CIA to build a billion-dollar logistics facility in West Virginia— just another example, according to the *Post*, of Byrd's using his position as chairman of appropriations to get more "pork" for his state. Now, in fact, Byrd was the "king of pork" when it came to getting federal dollars for his state. But in this rare instance, he was innocent; the CIA had sought his support for the facility and told him they would locate it in West Virginia, figuring that was the only way the agency would get the money. I called Byrd and volunteered to write a letter to the editor of the *Post* informing him of the facts. There was a long silence at the other end of the line, and finally he said, "You'd do that for me?" I said that I would. When my letter was published, Byrd thanked me profusely. Other senators told me he subsequently would tell Senate colleagues, "That Mr. Gates at CIA is an honorable man." This small gesture made Byrd my friend and personal ally on the Hill for the rest of my time as DCI and then as secretary of defense fifteen years later, despite his fervent opposition to the Iraq War in general and the 2007 troop surge in particular.

Few executive branch officials got along with these three powerful old lions of Capitol Hill, but I invested the time, and it paid off repeatedly.

It's also worthwhile to take time to do special (legitimate and appropriate) favors for important politicians and legislators. As DCI, I did an event for the chairman of the Senate Intelligence Committee David Boren at the Cowboy Hall of Fame in his home state of Oklahoma. Also as DCI, I agreed to appear at a special hearing of the committee in Fairbanks, Alaska, for its vice-chair Frank Murkowski. (It was summer and I just happened to be vacationing at home in the Pacific Northwest, so doing this favor for him in his home state wasn't *that* big a deal.) And I offered a ride on the CIA plane to Representative Lee Hamilton of Indiana when we were to appear together at a speaking event. (That trip was a classic case of miscommunication. Indiana University was in Hamilton's congressional district, and I had earned a master's degree there. It was only when the plane turned north out of Washington, D.C., that we learned we had both unwittingly accepted an invitation from Indiana University of Pennsylvania.) Anytime a top leader can speak in a member's district or elevate his or her profile at home, he will bank credit.

Developing special relationships with key members of the state legislature should be a no-brainer for the head of any public university or any local or state enterprise. Not much attention had been paid to state senator Steve Ogden, who represented the district in which A&M was located, an especially serious oversight because he chaired the Texas Senate Finance Committee. Before I even arrived in College Station, I called Ogden and asked him to be my mentor on legislative matters inasmuch as I was new to Texas. I had no "asks," which I think made him more receptive to my initiative. He was quite smart and influential, and we developed a strong relationship that benefited the university the entire time I was there. I also cultivated the leaders of the higher education committees in the state legislature, another no-brainer.

I won an additional strong supporter in the state senate, Royce West, an African-American who represented a large district in the Dallas area. During my first week on campus, he called me to a hearing in Austin focused on A&M's wretched record in contracting with "historically underutilized businesses," that is, minority-owned firms. I told him I would fix it and within a few months could point to considerable progress. He never forgot that I had delivered on my promise and would be an important defender when I announced my unorthodox approach to improving campus diversity.

When traveling around Texas as president of A&M, I would often invite local state legislators—and other local leaders as well—to university-sponsored community events. While at A&M, I agreed to an invitation from the legendary former Texas governor Dolph Briscoe (a Democrat and devoted University of Texas alumnus) to speak to new Eagle Scouts in his hometown of Uvalde.

I wrote very critically in my book *Duty* about Congress, expressing quite directly my disgust with how it did its business— or didn't. However, I think most senators and representatives were surprised by what I said because I had worked so hard at hiding my feelings when I was secretary of defense and, in fact, had worked quite successfully with Congress in that role. I was cordial, respectful, candid, responsive, and conciliatory. Because that kind of behavior was required to get what I wanted and needed from Congress, I had to bury my real feelings very deep. As a result, I had an unusually productive working relationship with the congressional leadership and the four committees (two in each house—Armed Services and Appropriations) with primary jurisdiction over the Department of Defense. I was aided indirectly by the fact that my predecessor as defense secretary, fairly or not, was viewed as openly contemptuous and dismissive of members of Congress of both parties, who were all too happy to see him go. So, admittedly, I had a relatively low bar to clear, at least at the beginning.

As secretary of defense, I would routinely visit members of Congress in their offices, where they would often have photographs taken of me greeting some of their local constituents. For the record, most of them serve lousy coffee.

Whether the elected oversight body is a town or city council, state legislature, or Congress, the leader of a public bureaucracy is well advised to follow the path I took in terms of respect and conciliation. Their members can make a leader's life miserable if they smell disrespect or arrogance because such bodies not only provide the money, but can summon a leader to countless hearings, cut his budget, stall his appointments, publicly berate him, and so much more. The Geneva Convention rules don't begin to cover what annoyed legislators and other elected officials can do to uncooperative, disrespectful leaders of bureaucracies.

Almost every government entity at every level has people, places, and events legislators are eager to know, tour, or experience. The opportunities are legion for a leader to reach out. It's best for the leader to get legislators on her turf when the legislature is in recess (so there is ample time and no interruptions) and she is not asking them for anything. Call it "gardening," as a former secretary of state used to say about routine diplomacy. (Forget the obvious wisecracks about fertilizer.)

Granted, all this politicking is a pain in the ass. But paying attention to key legislators, building strong relationships with them, investing time with them outside hearings, showing them respect, and building them up in front of their constituents are important investments that pay off in diverse ways. They can result in support for funding or problem avoidance. A leader, when appropriate and relevant, also should cultivate cordial relationships with key staff members of important legislators. They can be immensely influential and, like their bosses, have egos that like to be stroked. Think of such relationship building as an insurance policy; it may have little immediate value but can pay off later.

There are some absolute no-no's for a leader—regardless of whether in the public or the private sector—in dealing with elected officials. Never, ever lie to them or mislead them. Never embarrass them in front of their peers or the public. Never promise something you can't deliver. A leader must never be disrespectful or offensive in a hearing, no matter how ugly the elected inquisitors might be. Never speak critically of them publicly (unless as a leader you are leaving or have left your job and don't want another). A leader has to avoid placing them in situations that are potentially compromising ethically (free tickets and such); a legislator may be at fault for the breach, but he won't forget the leader who put him in harm's way. One other thing: A leader must never forget that legislators are elected by the same people he has been appointed to serve. They are the people's representatives and, for that reason alone, warrant a leader's respect and deference, however hard that sometimes is.

Leaders in the private sector can benefit from the foregoing recommendations as well. The no-no's certainly apply, but so do the suggestions for establishing relationships when you're not facing a problem with Congress, a state legislature, or local elected councils and when you are not asking them for anything. The private sector has to be especially cautious when it comes to plane rides, gifts, and so on, but invitations to company-sponsored local charitable events, celebrations, tours, and briefings all potentially offer opportunities to reach out and establish relationships.

Leaders in mature industries in America have long recognized the need to maintain close and cordial relationships with legislative bodies at every level of government. One of the primary purposes of each of thousands of private sector trade associations is to promote legislation advantageous to their respective industry and to prevent deleterious actions. Lobbyists and governmental-affairs employees are paid to do the same thing and to establish the kinds of relationships I have been writing about—and to prevent their CEO from being hauled into a hearing and made a public whipping boy or girl. New industries, such as tech and Internet companies, for too long thought they could ignore politics and politicians and just focus on changing the world. They, too, have gradually awakened to the difficulty legislators can cause them and have joined their more-established business counterparts in hiring substantial representation in state capitals and Washington. My advice to the leaders of all major companies is to get more personally involved in this process, spend some of your own time getting to know key legislators—especially before you need them. And make sure your subordinates and staff dealing with legislators follow the "to dos" and "no-no's" I have described here.

And a lesson for all, but especially those in business: For heaven's sake, if called before an elected body to testify, be modest, truthful, humble, and forthright. Be mindful of the political and public context of your presence at the hearing. Remember why you are there. If you are seeking a multibillion-dollar bail-out, drive a car or take a Greyhound bus to Washington, not a flock of corporate jets as auto executives did in 2009. The lions in the congressional Colosseum feasted well that day. That's an extreme example of cluelessness, but whether it's a town council, a state legislature, or Congress, business and public sector leaders must use common sense and behave appropriately in light of the circumstances they face. As the military would say, in front of an elected body, a leader needs to minimize his target profile.

Dealing with elected overseers is not for the queasy or pure of heart. The most important thing to remember is that only very rarely does anyone get all she wants from a legislature. Every inter-action a leader has will be transactional, a negotiation, and she needs to have determined her priorities before going in—what she is prepared to concede, what compromises she is willing to accept. If a leader believes so strongly in the righteousness of what she has proposed that she is unprepared to compromise, if her approach is all or nothing, she will nearly always wind up with nothing. A good leader needs to have figured out what is the irreducible min-imum she can live with, whether the issue is the budget, authority to do something new, or fighting off some legislative encroach-ment on executive authority. Ronald Reagan, often considered an ideologue, was in fact quite pragmatic when it came to Congress. If he could get 60 percent or so of what he wanted, he was content to ink the deal—and then come back for the rest later.

On the very rare occasion when an issue is of such vital inter-est to a public sector leader, whether on its merits or symbolically, that he cannot compromise, he can so indicate that by announc-ing his willingness to resign over the matter. But the issue had better be a big one where public opinion (and the media) are on his side and the politicians involved see personal consequences for them in provoking the resignation. This is high-stakes poker because the legislators probably couldn't care less whether a leader stays or goes. His potential departure has to be seen by them as politically costly. The threat to resign is usually a card that can only be played effectively once. And if things don't go the leader's way, he must quit. Failure to do so will leave a leader on the battlefield disarmed and without allies, totally ineffective.

A leader can strengthen his hand in dealing with elected overseers by allying with others—especially those seen as competitors or rivals—when there are common interests at stake. It always surprised legislators in Texas when the president of the University of Texas at Austin and I would work or testify together on a subject. And I was always helped when, both as DCI and as secretary of defense, I testified together with the secretary of state or other senior State Department officials. Legislators legitimately get frustrated with lack of interagency cooperation or when institutions engage in a dog-eat-dog fight for their own parochial interests. The politicos notice when the leader of a big institution argues publicly on behalf of another. My speech as secretary of defense in November 2007 calling for significantly more resources for the State Department and the Agency for International Development not only made a big splash at the time; it resounded through Congress for years to come. In dealing with legislatures, sometimes a leader can do his own cause a lot of good by supporting someone else's. Such "broad-mindedness" is so unusual—if not shocking—it almost always has a positive effect.

Mostly, I have been talking about techniques I have found useful in getting legislators to do what the leader of a public institution wants them to do—more often than not relating to money. But a leader will also face another kind of challenge with elected overseers: harebrained legislative ideas that have some public appeal but are potentially destructive to what the leader is trying to accomplish, contrary to sound management practices, or just plain stupid. On more than one occasion, self-anointed experts in Congress would push hard for specific kinds of impractical weapons systems or for unworkable changes in acquisition procedures. Stopping such proposals from gaining momentum and potential passage is sometimes complicated. I dealt with this sort of thing all too often—undesirable and often unworkable restrictions on operations, directives to buy certain kinds of equipment, legislative micromanagement. Blocking bad legislation is often as important as getting good things passed.

Other lawmakers are usually your strongest allies in blocking something odious from being enacted. There are countless ways in legislatures to derail bad ideas, and if you take the time to explain to the leadership and committee chairs the negative consequences of such proposals, those leaders will very often find a way to put the ideas on a procedural path to oblivion. This is especially true on under-the-radar issues, harder for high-profile ones. Members generally don't like to embarrass their colleagues, so this tactic needs to be used judiciously. But a reminder here: a leader must have previously cultivated a relationship of trust with those same leaders so they are inclined to take her concerns seriously.

Sometimes, bad ideas move forward in the legislative process. A leader will need to work with allies in the legislature to revise a bill in ways that render it harmless or manageable. Leaving implementation to the discretion of an executive at some level can neuter bad law. If circumstances allow, if the proposed legislation really shines and stinks in the moonlight, a leader can enlist the help of the media, editorial pages, and the commentariat in generating publicity (bad laws are usually pretty self-evident) and opposition.

It's tough dealing with elected officials. They are often not knowledgeable about the bureaucracies they oversee (or the businesses they seek to regulate), and their priorities—usually and above all getting reelected or moving up the electoral ladder—will frequently not coincide with any leader's. They may see a leader's institution simply as a pawn in the unending chess game of seeking political advantage—or as a competitor to other interests of greater importance to them. But to lead change effectively, one must play the legislative game.

Even if a leader can't stand the politicos, he must reach out to them anyway and paste on a smile when doing so because, in any public institution, he cannot succeed without their support.

Treat appointed oversight boards and regulators as you do legislators because they sometimes have even more direct authority to control or shape what you do.

A leader attempting to reform an institution must try to win the support—or at least acquiescence—of supervisory bodies. A leader who incurs their hostility could quickly find herself not just unable to effect change but out of a job. If a leader can't find ways to work with such overseers in good conscience, she must leave.

Leaders of bureaucracies must report to appointed boards of dizzying variety. They exist at every level of government. In the private sector, there is a broad array of regulatory bodies at every level of government, not to mention a company's board of directors. When I was DCI, in addition to Congress I reported to the President's Foreign Intelligence Advisory Board, the Intelligence Oversight Board, and various ad hoc panels set up by the president or Congress for specific purposes. At A&M, I reported to a board of regents (nine people appointed by the governor, confirmed by the Texas Senate), the Texas Higher Education Coordinating Board, a regional board of accreditation, and others I have long since repressed. I actually had the fewest oversight boards as secretary of defense—just two advisory groups and the occasional ad hoc group appointed by the president or Congress to investigate or assess specific problems.

The quality of the people appointed to these oversight boards varies dramatically. As described earlier, over four and a half years I had some regents at A&M who were smart, well-informed, principled, selfless, and constructive. I had others who were political hacks, egotists, rude and bullying, ignorant of higher education, cowardly, and ethically challenged. On one occasion, a regent called on behalf of Governor Perry to lean on me to appoint a friend of the governor's as vice president for student affairs, a case of pure and inappropriate patronage as far as I was concerned. I told him a formal search was under way that comprised faculty, students, staff, former students, and others and that I would not bypass that process. I said that if the governor felt so strongly, he should send me his friend's résumé—under the governor's signature—and I would forward the package to the search committee and encourage fair consideration for the candidate. He never did so. The committee ultimately recommended, and I appointed, a professionally qualified person to the position. At their very next meeting, the regents changed the rules so that they would approve all such future appointments (and thus be able to respond to the governor's preferences). Incidentally, the VP for student affairs I appointed was hugely successful and very popular but was abruptly fired soon after I left to become secretary of defense. The governor's pal was quickly appointed to take his place.

This wide range of attributes and flaws of the board of regents was characteristic of virtually every appointed oversight board I worked with over several decades. It applies at the local level as well.

As with legislatures, leaders of bureaucracies must work with these appointed panels. Some, like university regents, have enormous power to control what the leaders reporting to them can do. Their control is exercised routinely and often extends to day-to-day operational matters: no aspect of the organization is beyond their purview. They are significantly more intrusive than legislatures, and there are far fewer procedural tactics to keep them from taking action. Appointed regulatory boards, similarly, can have enormous capacity to create problems for the private sector. The wise leader must work with such boards. To create goodwill (and room to maneuver), develop personal relationships, keep the regulators well-informed, be transparent and honest, and put the board members in contact with your best professionals. Listen to them.

The CIA director Bill Casey taught me an important lesson when it comes to listening, one that I found applied especially to such boards (and a broad range of other interlocutors as well). Most people, he told me, will listen to a speaker and if they disagree with part of what he or she says will reject everything said. Bill advised me not to focus on what I disagreed with but to see if there were one or two kernels of information or wisdom worth seizing on—finding a little wheat amid all the chaff. Just because 95 percent of what someone says is nuts, he would say, laughing, doesn't mean you should ignore the 5 percent that might be useful. (He was always handing me pamphlets or books to read, warning, "This guy is crazy, but there's an interesting idea on page *x*.") The same principle applies to both legislators and appointed boards. Latching onto an overseer's idea will allow a leader to build rapport with that person and demonstrate he was actually paying attention, and, who knows, the idea might even be a good one.

A reform leader should view the media as important means for getting his message out to his own workforce and to the public about what he is trying to do.

A leader mustn't think in terms of "using" the media—which they will see through and resent—but rather, through access, transparency, and candor, educating them about the changes being made and why. This applies equally to local community journals and national television networks.

In both the public and the private sectors, there is an overwhelming propensity to see the media as a hostile force. I have a different view. From my earliest days as secretary of defense, I told senior military and civilian officials and even cadets and midshipmen at the service academies that "the press is not the enemy and to treat it as such is self-defeating." Good reporting repeatedly alerted me to problems in the Department of Defense and on the battlefield that I would not have learned about otherwise. In each case, I publicly credited the press.

I advised senior officers that when their office was contacted by a journalist about a problem or investigative endeavor, they should not go into a defensive crouch or offer an immediate denial. Rather, first they were to find out for themselves whether the allegation or story was true. They were to get the facts. If the story turned out to be accurate, I urged them to acknowledge this publicly and indicate what they intended to do about the problem or situation. If the allegation were false, they would have the facts to prove it (as opposed to reacting immediately in ignorance). This is good advice for the private sector as well.

All that said, a call from a reporter, much less *60 Minutes,* can usually throw an entire organization into defensive chaos. Granted, there is often ample reason for such trepidation. Even at the national level and in the highest-quality outlets, outside a dedicated press contingent—such as at the Pentagon and the State Department—it is increasingly rare for reporters to be deeply knowledgeable about their beat. As issues become more complex, both public and private institutions have reason to worry about the quality of reporting on what they do. (When I was a member of the board of independent trustees for the Fidelity mutual funds, I was stunned at how little many reporters, even those writing for business and financial publications, understood about how the mutual fund industry works.) Sometimes it is because the reporter or the outlet has a hostile bias, but even more often it is concern about the reporter's skills—whether he can get the facts right. Journalists are offended when government departments or businesses hand out "fact sheets," but the reality is that, without them, getting the statistics and facts of a specific matter correct often seems to be a challenge. (By the same token, the leader better make damn sure his fact sheet is accurate, comprehensive, and straightforward; too many are selective, misleading, or wrong.) At the local level, all too often someone who attended a school board meeting will not recognize the session from the write-up in the local paper the next day. When I am asked by a reporter if he or she can record an interview, my response has always been "Please do."

And then, of course, there *is* the problem of bias. Virtually no cable channel or blog is viewed as objective, and many viewers and readers think the same of the national news networks and newspapers. Partly, I suppose, this is due to the growing penchant to only view or read sources that one agrees with. Leaders in both the public and the private sectors are justifiably concerned about whether their actions will be reported accurately and fairly.

The result of all this is the ubiquity of public affairs and communications offices in virtually every organization larger than a mom-and-pop grocery store. While I wish I could say that their goal is simply to get fair media treatment for their organization, in reality their efforts are often focused mostly on promoting their agency, department, or company (and its boss), "spinning" whatever the outfit is doing to get the most favorable coverage possible. They are expert at evasive or partial answers, shifting blame for problems to others outside the organization, serving up vacuous and nonsubstantive talking points, and playing favorites among journalists in search of friendly reporting. All too often, these antics are attempted by people without the experience, intelligence, or dexterity to pull them off, and so the media coverage gets even worse as a result. Some organizations tell outright lies. So it's a vicious circle. Bureaucracies want favorable treatment but are often evasive and avoid taking blame—on or off the record—for anything that goes wrong. This is especially true of their leaders, who often are seeking higher positions or office and want no blemishes on their records. Reporters, naturally, resent the games bureaucracies play with them.

Too often companies—small and large, publicly and privately held—assume that because they are nongovernmental, they have no need or obligation to engage with the media or explain themselves to the public. Companies with that attitude regularly pay the price at some point in the form of legislation that doesn't go their way, an adverse local government or regulatory ruling, or, most often, skeptical if not hostile press coverage.

I have certainly had my share of media coverage over the decades, sometimes harshly critical, sometimes laudatory. I know which I liked more. (And anyone, even an old hand, who says that a negative story, especially one impugning competence or character, doesn't get under his skin is kidding either himself or everyone else.) Most of the news coverage of what I was trying to do in all three organizations I led was pretty positive. I think there are lessons to be drawn from my experience that leaders in both the public and the private sectors can use. I approached the media as a fact of life: they are always significant factors for those in leadership positions. Wishing them away is silly. Resenting them or taking on a bunker mentality will only hurt you in the end (see Nixon, Richard). You need to deal with them. In fact, the media can be the best vehicle a leader has to communicate his actions, his thinking, and his intentions for change. Most senior bureaucrats see the media as a liability and a threat; I believe they can also be an asset, especially for a change agent. The reformer needs to take advantage of all the tools at his or her disposal.

Particularly in the wake of the end of the Cold War, as mentioned earlier, I felt we at the CIA had to be more open to the media—and thus the public—about what we were doing and why collecting and analyzing intelligence continued to be important. The public had tolerated such a secret organization (and our periodic missteps) during the forty-five-year-long existential conflict with the Soviet Union but, I thought, was going to be significantly more skeptical about the need for the agency after the collapse of our primary adversary. So I undertook the measures described earlier to lift the veil of secrecy about the CIA, its historical record both analytically and operationally, and how it continued to contribute to national security. Dramatically greater accessibility to the CIA for the media was central to achieving my objectives. Through them, we had the opportunity to better inform

Americans about our role and thereby (hopefully) gain their support—or at least their toleration.

The media were also central to achieving my agenda at Defense. Media coverage of congressional hearings and press conferences provided the public with my messages about our strategy and tactics in Iraq and Afghanistan, where we were making progress—or not—and the need to end the wars in a way that did not affect our broader global interests. When I announced major program cuts in 2009, I counted on the media's reporting to help create a positive public reaction that would put pressure on Congress to be supportive. And I hoped that media reporting on our efforts to help wounded warriors as well as those still in the fight would provide reassurance to both the troops and their families.

On many of the larger issues I was addressing at the Pentagon (and everywhere else I led), I counted on media coverage of my major speeches to spread the message about changes needed or under way to audiences far broader than those sitting in front of me. I wanted the public to know what I was trying to do, and I used that transparency not just to inform but also to generate outside support for my agenda and to make internal opposition more difficult. A media strategy that focuses on a bureaucracy working to improve its performance and be more responsive to citizens—to do the right thing—is highly likely to generate positive coverage, and this will help a leader internally and with external stakeholders. In large bureaucracies, people will usually just nod their heads in meetings and mumble assent to what the boss is saying—and go on doing what they were doing before. But when a leader goes public with his or her views—or criticism, no matter how tactful—of how the organization is working, it's a sign that he or she means business, in effect airing the dirty laundry in public. That raises the stakes for everyone involved.

I did this repeatedly, including with respect to my dealings with much of the air force leadership in 2007 and 2008. When it came to my priorities—immediate battlefield needs over potential future conflicts—they just weren't "getting it." In my speech to the Air War College in April 2008, delivered with press in the auditorium, I spoke of "pulling teeth" to get air force reconnaissance assets to the battlefield, throwing down the gauntlet after weeks of useless meetings and briefings. It also sent a message to those on the front lines—and their families—that I had their backs.

Investigative efforts on the part of the media can cause problems, but they also may well inform you of a problem you didn't know you had or of opportunities to be seized. As I have written, it was a *Washington Post* series that alerted me to the scandalous treatment of outpatient wounded warriors at Walter Reed Army Medical Center. Spurred by those stories, we responded seriously and quickly and received a lot of favorable coverage at the same time the plight of our wounded troops received public attention. Similarly, I would not have known about the capabilities of the MRAP vehicles had it not been for a story in *USA Today*.

I learned that after the story about MRAPs was published, the Pentagon's public affairs office—accustomed to a more reactive, defensive posture—immediately went into "rapid-response" mode to rebut the article. The notion that *USA Today* raised an important issue with respect to troop protection seemed not to have been considered. In reality, the bureaucracy had dragged its feet getting these lifesaving vehicles to the war zone, and no amount of denial and spin would change that.

I wish dealing with the media were easy and straightforward. The challenge comes when the reporter is on a short deadline and a leader doesn't have enough time to ascertain the facts, thus leaving her with a noncommittal quote, which is never a good place to be. It makes her sound wishy-washy or, worse, evasive. Or a reporter won't believe her and will go ahead with the story anyway, maybe not even including what she had to say. Sometimes a reporter will run a story without ever talking to her. All these things happen, and the leader has no control. She just has to cope as best she can. But she will be making a mistake if she allows those situations to make her resentful or defensive in dealing with the media or lead her to clam up. She will be the loser. The media are stakeholders. They can—and will—have an impact on a leader's ability to achieve change in any institution. As the old saying goes, "Never argue with people who buy ink by the barrel" (or, today, control endless hours of airtime or millions of page views). Fighting with the media or treating them as the enemy gives them a foil and will leave a leader the worse for it. To be effective, a leader has to use her media coverage in advancing a reform agenda. As when dealing with other stakeholders, a leader must play the long game and not get diverted by one or another bad experience. The press must be given access and spoken to honestly and candidly. Transparency is the watchword. As is telling the truth. Give the press public credit when it is due.

Legislatures, oversight boards (and regulatory bodies), and the media are probably the three most important stakeholders with a claim on a leader's time and to which he needs to be responsive for success. But they are far from alone. So a word about several others he really can't ignore.

Any leader in a big organization must deal with the local community. Most people are familiar with "town and gown" issues affecting universities and the communities where they are located. But other large bureaucracies have similar challenges. For the leader of any large organization, public or private, managing the chemistry with the local community will be time-consuming and require political finesse. This is especially true if an organization is located in a small or medium-size town where it is one of the largest—if not the largest—employer. An effective leader in an organization must try to keep relations with the community on friendly terms—or at least minimize hostilities.

There is a leadership challenge on both sides of the fence—local business and community leaders and leaders of big institutions located in town. Problems will arise that beggar the imagination and would test the wisdom of Solomon because, above all, the locals are ambivalent about the presence of the big organization.

On the one hand, they need it: It is usually an economic lifeline—sometimes the only one—for a town or neighborhood. It is a major source of help and donations for every kind of good cause, and its employees are usually deeply involved in the community.

Yet residents see the presence of such institutions as a major daily hassle. The big business, state or federal institution, university, or military installation causes traffic jams; doesn't pay local property taxes (or, if a business, pays too little); causes environmental problems; behaves "arrogantly" and "secretively" and is "uncaring" about local problems; pays salaries that "distort" the local housing market. If the institution is one of some forty-two hundred two- and four-year colleges or universities in America, it typically has thousands of young people between eighteen and twenty-five living in the community. They park their cars in creative places, don't exactly tend carefully to the places they rent—inside or out—adore loud music, drive like they were in NASCAR, and usually consume copious amounts of alcohol, especially on weekends. They sometimes engage in social activities their older, more staid neighbors find inappropriate and offensive (especially if those activities take place in their shrubs or on their lawn). Moreover, these educational institutions have a penchant to throw their weight around when they want something, to develop commercial real estate or off-campus housing that competes with local businesses, and to engage in other practices the community regards as preemptory or presumptuous.

If the major installation is a military facility, its eighteen- to twenty-five-year-olds will hit town for recreational purposes. There will be warplanes and helicopters flying too low, restricted airspace, or limits on public access to favorite hunting grounds, as well as environmental and other issues. Activists who are opposed to nuclear weapons (or weapons of any sort) being near their homes and opposed to any military presence at all will be vocal. As secretary of defense, I was routinely briefed on disputes between military installations and nearby neighbors and towns.

The point of this rather superficial overview of problems associated with local communities as stakeholders is simply as a reminder that they matter and, if neglected, can cause a leader innumerable headaches. On the other hand, they can also be real assets in dealing with state legislatures or congressional delegations. A business or government leader goes a long way in winning over local communities and officials by giving them some of her time, being transparent, taking their concerns seriously, and responding constructively. She must look for opportunities to involve members of the community and their leaders in activities sponsored by her institution. Similarly, she and her senior colleagues should get involved in the community. Attendance at meetings of the chamber of commerce, the Rotary, and other civic organizations gets noticed, as will support of local charities, Little League, and so on. Gestures of respect toward the community by the leader of the biggest employer in town can pay disproportionate dividends.

I had little experience working or negotiating with unions (although some would apply that label to university faculties), but based on observation from a safe distance, it seems to me that most conflict between local or state government leaders (including university leaders) and unions—except for the public teachers unions—is about pay, benefits, and job security. Many city and state governments in past years made generous commitments to employees in those areas—particularly pensions—that have now become onerous, even unsustainable fiscal burdens.

Reform leaders should regard unions as stakeholders who must be taken into account. A leader should figure out what reform measures he can detach from hot-button issues such as pay and benefits and make those changes independently. He must demonstrate how changes that improve efficiency and performance can reduce costs and enhance public support—thereby enhancing job security. If reducing the number of employees is necessary, as suggested earlier, a leader must try to make the process as humane, transparent, and painless as possible. I realize this all sounds terribly rational and sensible in situations where both of those qualities are usually in short supply. But the more a reformer can stifle his rhetoric and try to make the union leadership a partner in making needed changes, the better his odds of success. Let the politicians debate the role of unions in government agencies. As far into the future as most reformers can see, unions will be a fact of life. They are not to be ignored. A leader must figure out a way to work with them. As with all stakeholders, persuading them that constructive change and improved performance are in their own self-interest is vitally important.

———

There are two other groups of stakeholders most leaders will likely never encounter, but for leaders at nearly all levels in higher education or the military they are critically important. So, please indulge me while I speak to those folks—although others may find this aspect of two huge types of institutions of more than passing interest. I am speaking of alumni and retirees.

No college or university head can neglect the alumni. Most leaders, especially outside universities, don't understand how important these folks can be. Many graduates from a university or college remain interested in what goes on there. Cultivating these people can be time-consuming and sometimes a nuisance, but it's worth it. The leader's reassurance to them that he intends to make a good organization even better, that in doing so he will be respectful of the traditions and culture of the place, and that he does not plan to plow over their hallowed grounds can pay big dividends.

As state funding for public higher education continues to drop, the importance of alumni and their financial gifts continues to rise. They are now more important than ever. But their contributions of time and resources come with a price tag: a greater voice in what goes on at the university—athletics, academic programs, management, policies, and even matters relating to the faculty and students. If a leader has an ambitious agenda for change, he will hear plenty from alumni, both in support and in virulent opposition. Alumni will clog his e-mail, his phone lines, and his waiting room, all in an effort to weigh in with their views on what he is up to. And lest he even think about being dismissive, they also have influence with his board of regents and with the state legislature.

As I mentioned earlier, A&M was an all-male military college until the mid-1960s, and participation in the Corps of Cadets was mandatory. Nearly all of the university's most revered traditions derive from the corps, even though it now accounts for less than 5 percent of the student body. The corps is still seen as "the keepers of the spirit," the heart and soul of what it means to be an Aggie. A&M's older, and many of its most influential, alumni were in the Corps of Cadets.

When I became president of A&M in 2002, the corps was going through a rough patch in terms of recruitment, academic performance, and publicity. In order to enlist the necessary support of older, more conservative Aggies for me (an outsider) and for many of the changes I wanted to make at the university, I decided to adopt the corps, to become its biggest booster on campus, to protect it, to improve its academic performance. Accordingly, I attended virtually every corps event. I ate lunch with cadets regularly in their dining hall. I ran with them early in the morning. More significantly, I also engaged the old Aggies by forming a presidential "board of visitors" to advise me on growing the corps and making it more appealing to incoming freshmen. I selected for the board about twenty of the former students most ardently supportive of the corps, and I asked that each donate $20,000 a year, all of which would be used to recruit more kids to the corps.

The members of that board, some of the most influential and generous alumni, would become some of my strongest supporters at the university, mainly because they saw how much I cared about the corps. That support would become essential as I tackled controversial issues such as increasing racial and ethnic diversity. My love of the corps was genuine, but it also served a broader purpose.

One important constituency unique to colleges and universities are the sports fans. Any president of a big public university who is not a visible supporter of athletics is in trouble. As the former president of the University of Texas at Austin Peter Flawn wrote in his primer for university presidents, "If you are a sports enthusiast and enjoy intercollegiate athletics, so much the better; if you are not . . . fake it." When I arrived in 2002, there was a sense on the part of many Aggies that the university's athletic program was stagnant—they were right; it was not well run—and, most important, the football program needed to be reenergized. My first fall, I replaced the athletic director and, at football season's end, fired the head coach. As I told the media, I had overthrown the governments of medium-size countries with less controversy. Nonetheless, I had shown that I took athletics seriously, thus winning over another constituency.

Retirees are generally not an important stakeholder in most private and even public institutions, but they are a powerful constituency for the military services (and Defense Department more broadly), the CIA, and some other outfits. Foremost, of course, are the veterans' service organizations (VSOs) such as the Veterans of Foreign Wars and the American Legion. These groups have enormous clout in Congress, particularly when it comes to pay and benefits for service members and veterans. As the then Speaker of the House Nancy Pelosi once told me, when it comes to military compensation and benefits, "We primarily pay attention to the VSOs"—that is, as opposed to the secretary of defense.

In addition, each service has multiple external, private organizations that closely monitor the health of the service, whether it's getting its fair share of the budget, whether the secretary of defense favors one service over another, and if Congress is being helpful or not. While these groups have a far broader base than just retirees (such as representatives of the defense industries), like alumni at a university, they have real influence—in Congress, inside the Pentagon, and certainly among veterans. They have professional publications of their own to either praise or excoriate decisions affecting their service. In a speech to the Navy League, I once referred to the need to reconsider the way we use and deploy aircraft carriers. I heard about that one for months. Likewise from army retirees when I canceled that service's Future Combat System, the centerpiece for army modernization yet vastly over-priced and failing to adequately protect soldiers from IEDs and other threats. I had, according to one retired general, "gutted the entire future of the Army." And the response of retired air force fighter pilots to my capping production of the F-22 fighter jet was equally hyperbolic about what I had done to the future of America's air superiority.

Even retired intelligence officers have their own organizations. While these organizations generally stay out of the political fray, they often invite currently serving senior intelligence officers to speak at meetings, and individual attendees make their views known on such occasions as well as in contacts with journalists and legislators.

In addition to alumni and retirees, leaders of public and private bureaucracies will have professional societies to deal with, as well as activists with a focused agenda (like environmentalists). If something happens that gets a leader or his business or institution into the national news, he will get more "help" than he needs from advocacy groups, lawyers, specialized organizations, and celebrities. When A&M was providing shelter in our basketball arena for hundreds of evacuees fleeing Houston in anticipation of Hurricane Rita, university police removed a man claiming to be transgendered from a women's shower room after an elderly woman evacuee complained. I got an earful from advocacy groups about that episode (as a result of which we subsequently provided separate facilities).

———

All stakeholders have the potential to be supportive and helpful—but also to wreck a leader's plans. Each kind of bureaucratic institution—indeed, every organization, public or private—will have its unique batch of such groups. But no matter how different they may be, the best approach is to treat them with respect, transparency, an open door, an open mind, and a willingness to take time to listen. Take them seriously, take their concerns seriously, and, wherever possible, try to address their issues and implement some of their suggestions. That is the way a good leader can make friends and allies. What turns off all stakeholders and makes them into antagonists is condescension and being ignored. When it comes to stakeholders, abide by the law of the conservation of enemies: make as few as possible. What can seem like a nuisance in the short term will pay off in the long term.

7

The Agent of Change:
"Mirror, Mirror on the Wall"

Now we come to the critical factor in leading bureaucratic reform: the leader himself, the potential single point of failure. Many senior government and business officials have written about their experiences as leaders and offer their observations on how to be successful. But American popular culture offers its own comedic insights into what works and what doesn't. Casey Stengel, the legendary manager of the New York Yankees and Mets, once ascribed his success to "keeping the guys who hate you away from the guys who are undecided." The famous football coach Vince Lombardi would warn his team, "If you aren't fired with enthusiasm, you'll be fired with enthusiasm." The film director Alfred Hitchcock wrote, "There's nothing to winning, really. That is, if you happen to be blessed with a keen eye, an agile mind, and no scruples whatsoever." Perhaps my favorite tongue-in-cheek formula for successful leadership, though, is attributable to the humorist and writer on bureaucratese James Boren, who wrote, "When in charge, ponder; when in trouble, delegate; when in doubt, mumble."

Real leadership, however, is a rare commodity. Believe me, I know. I have worked for eight U.S. presidents—including four in the White House—and observed or worked with fourteen secretaries of state, thirteen secretaries of defense, nine chairmen of the Joint Chiefs of Staff, fourteen national security advisers, ten directors of the CIA, and more generals, admirals, and ambassadors than I can count. I have known scores of university presidents and served on the board of directors of companies large and small. And I have had the opportunity to interact with many foreign heads of government and historical figures, including Margaret Thatcher, Mikhail Gorbachev, Anwar Sadat, Vladimir Putin, and Yitzhak Rabin. To say their styles of leadership varied would be something of an understatement. But my focus here is on what I believe to be the characteristics of leadership needed in America, both in our governmental institutions at all levels where reform is of the essence and in the private sector.

I've already discussed some of the qualities required for successfully leading reform—vision, strategic thinking, attention to implementation, transparency, treating people respectfully, political finesse with stakeholders. What I want to discuss now is not the tools and tactics of successful leadership but rather the personal qualities I believe necessary to effectively lead enduring change. How does a true leader conduct himself?

The best leaders have their egos under control.

They empower subordinates who are given the lion's share of credit and accolades when success comes. Such leaders are strong enough and confident enough to stay in the background while subordinates are praised. A leader's primary goal should be to get the job done, not personal glorification or self-satisfaction.

When King Louis XIV of France received word in 1704 that his army had been defeated at Blenheim by the British, he is said to have complained, "How could God do this to me, after all I've done for Him?" Unfortunately, like Louis, too many leaders are so full of themselves they think they're doing favors for God—and everyone else—just by their very existence and by doing the job they're in. Everything is about *them*. Egotism is easily detected, and it's often the little things that give it away. Fury over minor inconveniences, temper tantrums over trivial matters, indifference to the needs or feelings of others. I've been told about cabinet officers, generals, admirals, and business executives who were abusive to staff or flew off the handle because the crust wasn't removed from their sandwich bread, the mustard was misplaced on the dinner tray, rain was wrecking their hairdo, the wrong kind of bottled water was served, too much condensation had accumulated on their glass of ice water (really!), their chauffeured SUV wasn't there at exactly the moment they were ready, or the departure of their personal plane was delayed by weather.

As secretary of defense, I once made a surprise secret trip overseas and was accompanied by a four-star admiral whose headquarters was outside the Pentagon. The air force folks who fly military VIPs (and members of Congress) keep a list of the personal preferences of their regular "customers," and when the crew chief of the plane I was using learned at the last minute that this admiral was to be on board, he nearly had a meltdown. Apparently, the admiral had a pages-long list of dining, drinking, and other preferences, and the crew chief had no time to fulfill his wants and so anticipated a real ass chewing. I told him to relax. As long as my list was fulfilled, he didn't need to worry about the admiral's. And my standard list of preferences for overseas travel had only two items on it—Grey Goose vodka and a piece of lemon to go with it. The crew chief was genuinely shaken nonetheless.

Egotists are incredibly sensitive to slights. Being seated too distant from the top person in a meeting or at a dinner, or being at a table of people they consider inappropriately low-ranking compared with their own stature, will set them off. I've seen powerful men literally weep when informed they were not invited to fly on Air Force One or not on the list for a state dinner. Years ago, one very senior State Department official was so obsessive about getting into meetings with the president that the Secret Service joked that if one of them saw a lump under the carpet in the West Wing moving in the direction of the Oval Office, he was to step on it—it had to be this official, whom they nicknamed "the ferret." Similarly, if the same fellow wasn't invited to a state dinner at the White House, it was rumored the Secret Service would double-check the waiters' identities to make sure he wasn't disguising himself to gain entry.

Egotists treat subordinates badly. Joseph Persico wrote in *Roosevelt's Centurions* that General George Marshall disliked "the truculent personality—the man who confused firmness and strength with bad manners and deliberate discourtesy." Ulysses S. Grant wrote in his memoirs, "It did seem to me, in my early army days, that too many of the older officers, when they came to command posts, made it a study to think what orders they could publish to annoy their subordinates and render them uncomfortable." He also wrote that Lincoln's secretary of war Edwin Stanton "cared nothing for the feelings of others" and that General George Meade "was unfortunately of a temper that would get beyond his control, at times, and make him speak to officers of high rank in the most offensive manner."

Sadly, behavior that was offensive in the nineteenth century is commonplace in the twenty-first. The consequences go well beyond morale and working conditions. The last thing the egotist wants is candor, particularly if that includes implied criticism or even a hint that the boss is somehow shy of perfection in all things. It stifles creativity. If someone comes up with a good idea, the egotist is quick to dismiss it because it was someone else's—or take credit for it with superiors. The sharpest, best people will do whatever they can to avoid serving with such people. Subordinates will hesitate about making decisions for fear of the egotist's wrath at independent thinking or action, much less the consequences of something going wrong. In short, the environment created by an egotist is the antithesis of what is required to lead reform successfully. An egotist cannot help being an autocrat, the type of boss who unilaterally decides what changes are needed and implements them by fiat from above—the thunderbolt approach to leading change. It is nearly always guaranteed to fail.

The handmaiden of egotism is arrogance, and we see the results of arrogance every day in the news. I mean executives in both government and the private sector who come to believe that the rules governing others don't apply to them, that they are so smart they can avoid getting caught, or at least evade the consequences of wrongdoing. Whether it's presidents lying or breaking the law, governors and members of Congress getting caught with their hands in the cookie jar, or the heads of major companies going to jail or being forced to resign because of fraud, insider trading, or other lawbreaking and wrongful acts, arrogance is at the root of their crimes.

But you don't have to be a criminal to be arrogant. Like everyone else, I've worked with and for such people throughout my career. You can't tell arrogant leaders anything they don't already know. They disdain advice, especially from underlings but even from peers and superiors. They often operate just barely inside the rules. They are supremely self-confident, amazingly lacking in self-awareness, incapable of introspection, and generally unpleasant to deal with. They are usually bullies. And they can be found throughout the ranks of management, not just at the top.

Arrogant egotists also are people who crave power. Like a black hole in space, they draw to themselves all decision-making authority and constantly seek to expand their bureaucratic empires, to continue growing their power. They weaken everyone around them. The power hungry have no sense of limits.

An arrogant egotist is exactly the wrong person to lead reform in a bureaucracy.

A leader, or those who aspire to that role, regardless of whether in the public or the private sector, must have integrity.
Every leader in public service and business will at some point

need to stand apart and alone—to speak truth to power and to do the right thing. That can be a very lonely place. But it is where leaders who can effectively reform institutions are found.

In *King Richard II*, William Shakespeare wrote, "Mine honor is my life; both grow in one; / Take honor from me, and my life is done." Yet the concept of personal honor seems rather quaint nowadays. In fact, one rarely hears of it anymore. It meant everything to our Founding Fathers. "A young man should weigh well his plans," John Adams wrote to his son Thomas. "Integrity should be preserved in all events, as essential to his happiness, thro every stage of his existence. His first maxim then, should be to place his honor out of the reach of all men." The Declaration of Independence concludes with the signatories pledging to one another "our Lives, our Fortunes and our sacred Honor."

Honor is defined as "honesty and integrity in one's beliefs and actions," integrity being "adherence to moral principle and character." Words like these are not heard much in our public discourse today. But I believe these words and what they represent are the bedrock of effective leadership. If you seek to lead men and women, you must persuade them to follow you. That means they must trust you. Herbert Asquith, British prime minister from 1908 to 1916, wrote, "To speak with the tongue of men and angels, and to spend laborious days and nights in administration, is no good if a man does not inspire trust." A leader's actions must match his words. People must believe he means what he says, that his promises matter and are not just idle rhetoric. Integrity in action becomes moral authority, and it is moral authority that moves people to follow someone even at personal risk or sacrifice—or even when they disagree.

Sadly, there are far too few leaders today publicly noted for their personal integrity and who carry the mantle of moral authority. It seems that every time we pick up a newspaper, turn on the television, or go online, we read about yet another government or business leader who has been caught lying, cheating, or stealing. But even more pervasive, though less obvious yet no less damaging, is a willingness to look the other way when others are behaving dishonorably, to pretend that certain villainous acts are okay because others are doing them, or to believe that dishonor in one's personal life can be isolated from one's professional life.

My personal lesson in doing the right thing came during the Iran-contra scandal that broke in 1986, a scandal involving a secret effort to fund the anticommunist contras in Nicaragua with the profits from arms sales to Iran. It almost resulted in President Reagan's impeachment. The CIA director, William Casey, orchestrated the effort in league with the national security adviser, keeping it secret from all but a few people in the CIA and elsewhere in government. I had been Casey's deputy (for five months) and testified before the special counsel Lawrence Walsh that I had first learned the outlines of what was going on in October 1986. At that point, I informed Casey (who did not let on that he already knew about the scheme), as well as the agency's general counsel, and, following the latter's advice, informed the national security adviser (not realizing he was deeply involved in the matter). Walsh was convinced I had been told about the arms-for-profit deal a few weeks earlier, but he could never prove it. I never denied that I might have been told a few weeks earlier, but simply did not remember any such conversation. Over the years to come, others in the agency who had been in on the Iran-contra deal testified that I had been kept in the dark. While uncertainties about what I knew and when I knew it derailed my nomination to replace Casey as DCI in the spring of 1987, as more information came out, members of Congress continued to trust me. I remained as deputy DCI under Bill Webster and would be confirmed in 1991 as DCI under President George H. W. Bush.

I relate this story because, through this searing experience, I came to realize that while I had done nothing wrong, *I hadn't done enough right.* After informing the already-aware Casey, the CIA general counsel, and the national security adviser about what I had learned, during the month that followed before the scandal broke publicly, I did nothing else. I didn't go to the White House

counsel, to the chairmen of the congressional oversight committees, or to the attorney general. I told myself for years that I only
knew part of the story, I was no lawyer and didn't even know if
laws had been broken (the agency's general counsel did not tell me
he thought the activity illegal), and I had no reason then to mistrust Casey's professed ignorance of the arrangement. But when
it was all over, I knew, in my heart of hearts, by my own standard
of conduct, I had somehow fallen short. I swore it would never
happen again.

For most at or near the top of the bureaucratic heap, it is not
the great crime that undermines integrity but the little things that
erode it. When I became DCI, my personal secretary from time to
time would come into my office and share the latest gossip about
which senior CIA officials were having affairs. I told her to stop.
I said that such information made it very difficult for me to work
with those men because if their wives couldn't trust them, why
should I—or the country? I couldn't fire them, but I couldn't fully
rely on them either.

As secretary of defense, I became frustrated with the number of senior military officers being investigated by the inspector general for having abused their privileges and perquisites on
travel, questionable expenses, and the trappings of grandiosity. It
was not grand theft, but those people were operating at the line
of propriety—and maybe just over it. Some went clearly over
that line and were disciplined. They were spending thousands
of taxpayer dollars on slick publications celebrating their service in a senior role, elaborate farewell dinners and ceremonies,
motorcades of four or five vehicles (the chairman and I had two
each). The problem of senior officers' ethical lapses became serious enough that I discussed it several times with the Joint Chiefs
of Staff and addressed it in talks with new general officers. Even
so, the problem worsened, so much so that after I left office, the
secretary of defense and the chairman of the Joint Chiefs of Staff
appointed a senior officer to work just on this problem.

And then there is Congress. Out-and-out bribery, tens of

thousands of dollars secreted away in home freezers, sexual predators, misuse of campaign funds—the list of misdeeds (about the only bipartisan thing in Congress these days) goes on and on. But that doesn't include the legal but reprehensible hypocrisy of some of the loudest proponents of moral rectitude getting caught with their pants down (literally as well as figuratively) all too often. The only good news is that this is nothing new. More than a century ago, Mark Twain wrote, "There is no distinctly native American criminal class except Congress."

The point is that everywhere we look, leaders seem to have feet of clay. So who can young people—and others—look up to and admire as an effective leader with honor and integrity? There actually are many examples. They just don't get any publicity. I was privileged to work closely over my government career with a number of men and women of impeccable character—the national security advisers Brent Scowcroft and Zbigniew Brzezinski; the deputy DCIs John McMahon, Dick Kerr, and Bob Inman; the DCI William Webster; Admiral Mike Mullen; and my own chief of staff at Defense, Robert Rangel, to mention just a few. I had the highest admiration for many senior officers I worked with in the CIA and the Pentagon as men and women of utmost integrity. The same was true of my experience at Texas A&M. The trouble is that their character, their integrity, garner no national media attention. Thus, as role models for young people across the country, they are nearly invisible, especially compared with the ubiquity of the miscreants.

Character is sometimes described as how people behave when no one is watching. The trouble is that in an age of YouTube, iPhones, and social media, someone is watching all the time. And you'd think that people smart enough to be leaders would be smart enough to realize the chances of getting caught in flagrante delicto today are dramatically higher than ever before. Which brings us back to ego and arrogance.

Too many leaders have discredited themselves away from the workplace: honor and character are 24/7 propositions, not just for one's professional activities. If you lead a public institution, and often as well a private one, people are watching you at all times. Thomas Jefferson wrote, "When a man assumes a public trust, he should consider himself as public property." The leader of a big institution in a small or medium-size town has little privacy. The residence of the president of Texas A&M is one of the few such homes still located in the middle of campus. For nearly four and a half years, the drapes were always closed because students were continuously on the grounds. But not just students. I was sitting outside on our little, semiprivate patio one Sunday afternoon reading, only to look up and see a woman walking her dog and looking at me from about ten feet away.

Washington, D.C., and other big cities may provide most inhabitants some measure of anonymity, but whether you are a senior government official or business executive, don't kid yourself that you go unnoticed. Whether you are a powerful congressional committee chairman who, drunk, drives his car into the Tidal Basin with a stripper as his passenger, a White House aide or senator arrested in a men's room, a corporate executive fired for an affair, or myriad other embarrassments we have read about over the years, dishonor can destroy you and everything you are trying to achieve.

Self-discipline is central to the leadership of institutions and to reforming them.

A favorite saying of mine is "Never miss a good chance to shut up." I won't tell you how many times in a congressional hearing I just wanted to scream. How often in the White House Situation Room I wanted to say, "That's the dumbest idea I ever heard." How often in a briefing at the CIA or the Pentagon I wanted to tell someone where to stick his PowerPoint slides. Senior leaders want to blow off steam—shout at people—all the time. But to be an effective leader, you have to suppress those urges.

Two common threads through this book have been the needs

to listen and to empower subordinates. The corollary to both is to know when to keep quiet and when to keep your hands off the steering wheel. The temptation to weigh in with your own opinions or to take over a problem is constant. Being an effective leader, especially a reform leader, requires a lot of self-control. Silence and restraint are essential, if undervalued, tools of leadership.

Everywhere I have served, I have seen too many people in authority dominate a meeting by talking nearly the entire time and then, with five minutes left, ask for comments. By then, everyone just wants out of the room, and so no one speaks up. In other settings, some people are so eager to share their wisdom with everyone present that they ignore what others are saying and interject their thoughts without any reference to what another speaker has just said. I once belonged to a strategic study group where the practice was to turn your name placard on end to signal the chairperson you wanted to respond to the speaker. More often than not, before the speaker had even said hello, a dozen placards had been turned on end. Those who did so had no intention of responding to the speaker. They just wanted to bloviate with their own thoughts for the enlightenment of the attendees. Listening was not part of their agenda, nor was self-restraint.

It is a simple truth that when you are talking, you are not learning. I was criticized by one of Bob Woodward's sources in his book on Obama and the Afghan war for not speaking up until late in NSC meetings (except when the president called on me early). And it is true I would bide my time before offering my opinion. This had two benefits. First, it was advantageous in terms of my strategy to have the meeting conclude along the lines I preferred. By waiting to speak, I knew where the other principals were on the chessboard before I weighed in and thus could better calculate what I wanted to say and how to express it. Second, on some issues, I had not made up my mind and actually wanted to hear what others had to say. I proceeded on the radical assumption that by listening, I might learn something I hadn't thought of.

Fortunately, few readers will testify before Congress, but I think there are lessons in self-discipline from the experience that are broadly applicable for leaders—especially the importance of identifying situations when it is best to remain silent. The rule of thumb provided by White House legislative minders for nominees going before the Senate for confirmation hearings is 90/10: if the senators are speaking 90 percent of the time, things are likely to turn out just fine. They love to hear themselves talk, especially in front of a camera, and the witness who insists on interrupting them to say his or her piece is woefully misguided. I will acknowledge, though, keeping silent in the face of outrageous speeches, misstatements of fact, and unfounded allegations takes a lot of self-discipline.

I confess to a certain perverse pleasure in some of my responses during testimony. During my DCI confirmation hearing in 1991, it was late in the day and Senator Howard Metzenbaum read a long screed—on live television—about a complicated issue, a text obviously prepared by his staff. When he finally finished reading, I told him I had lost the thread of his argument and could he just tell me what his question was. I knew full well he couldn't. First one, then another of his staff came up and knelt beside him to help him formulate the question. It didn't work, and finally he just read the screed all over again. But my simple request demonstrated to all he didn't have a clue what he was talking about. Along the same lines, now and then I would get an extended speech/question from a member of Congress and I loved responding monosyllabically yes or no. They might ask me to elaborate, to which I would reply, "No." The virtue of restraint.

Self-discipline is required in other situations as well. Whether dealing with staff, the media, or others, a leader will always be tempted to let his temper fly, to yell and pound the table, to curse, to bully, to be cutting. In contrast, it didn't take too long anyplace I worked for people to learn that the angrier I was, the quieter I became. After I fired the secretary of the army over the Walter

Reed Army Medical Center scandal, he commented to the press how stone cold I had been.

Temper tantrums by a leader are an embarrassment and a waste of time and energy. But such behavior is unfortunately fairly commonplace—and with long historical precedent. Dwight Eisenhower had a terrible temper and worked all his life to control it, a monumental effort at self-discipline. The daughter of another key figure in World War II, the chief of naval operations, Admiral Ernest King, according to the writer Joseph Persico, described him "as the most even-tempered man she knew: 'He's always in a rage.' "

One of my favorite scenes from the movie *Patton* is when, after a tirade by the general, his military aide observes that sometimes his audience didn't know when he was acting. To which Patton replies, "It's not important that they know when I'm acting, only that I do." The trouble is that most leaders who fly off the handle aren't acting; they just lack self-discipline.

Restraint is a must in dealing with the media. I have witnessed and read about too many people in charge who have no use for the media and behave accordingly. In press conferences, they are condescending, insulting, evasive, and disrespectful. An ineptly framed or ill-informed question is met with derision, a critical one with scorn. The consequence in my view is nearly always short-term gain and long-term pain. No one suffers public humiliation well. And the media will always have the last word. I tried to treat the Pentagon press corps respectfully, and when occasionally a reporter might ask a clumsy question or had trouble articulating what he or she was trying to say, I did my best to figure out the question and respond seriously.

One of the reasons I believe the leader of an institution—any reformer—must exercise great self-discipline has to do with subordinates. If the boss can't control himself, that sends a signal to those at lower levels that such behavior is acceptable, and that hardly creates an environment in which inclusive, participatory reform can take place. It sounds old-fashioned, but the leader of an institution needs to be a role model.

A leader must be friendly, approachable, and accessible but ought not to allow too much familiarity. After all, he's still the boss. It may sound stuffy, but a leader has to maintain his dignity, another old-fashioned notion. He must be cautious about the activities he agrees to join. One can be totally dedicated to the well-being of subordinates without affecting to be their "pal" or "one of the boys." They don't think you are anyway. A leader has to find the thin line between being a good sport and becoming an object of ridicule for trying too hard to demonstrate he is a regular guy. Even with top-level executives, a leader must never forget they report to him and that someday he will likely make decisions they don't like, including about them. Getting too close will only make those decisions harder.

It's important for a leader to recognize there are some things he *can* do that he *shouldn't*. Just because some things are not forbidden does not mean they are permissible. A good leader doesn't encroach on other people's space—their offices, where they gather for recreation, where they live—just because he has the authority to do so. When I first arrived at Texas A&M, the vice president for student affairs asked me to join him in an unannounced late-night visit to one of the Corps of Cadets dormitories. I'd been there about thirty seconds when I realized I didn't belong. I never again made that kind of mistake.

A leader shouldn't ask subordinates to do personal favors, like running errands or some chore at her residence. She shouldn't place her staff in embarrassing situations by asking them to do something even mildly humiliating. One cabinet secretary I know of, who led a less than prominent domestic department, was notorious for a large personal staff that was used for every manner of personal errand. Some years ago, the head of a major federal agency lost his job because his wife routinely used employees to carry out personal tasks for her. When I was growing up, the key question was always, what would your mother think? Nowadays, the more apt question regarding behavior is, how would it look on the front page of the newspaper or on YouTube?

Intellectual and professional intimidation, characteristic of those who believe they are the smartest people in the room, is a poor way to solicit good ideas and avoid big mistakes.

Over the years, I have worked for and with a number of people who thought they were the smartest in the room. A couple were presidents of the United States. I can think of at least two White House chiefs of staff, a handful of cabinet secretaries, a few corporate executives, and assorted others in less august positions. A leader who feels that way has a tough time taking seriously what anyone else thinks, especially if he disagrees. Such a leader might solicit opinions from others on a particular subject, but it quickly becomes apparent to all others that his interest is phony: he believes he has already thought about everything everyone has said—and made up his mind before walking in the door. The folks who believe themselves to be the smartest in the room tend to condescend and subtly or not so subtly bully their interlocutors. Sometimes they can be downright insulting. They are not much fun to work for—or with. There is a remarkable overlap between arrogant egotists and those who believe they are the smartest people in the room. A telltale sign of both is, in the middle of a meeting, a long-suffering sigh intended to convey impatience at having to put up with inferior minds.

The Supreme Court justice Oliver Wendell Holmes Jr. once observed of Franklin D. Roosevelt that he had a second-rate intellect but a first-rate temperament. I believe most of our greatest presidents fit that description: George Washington, Abraham Lincoln, FDR, Truman, Eisenhower, Reagan. No one around any of them ever forgot who was in charge, but each surrounded himself with extremely capable people, listened to them, integrated their opinions with his own judgment and instincts, and made historic decisions. The historian Gordon Wood wrote of Washington, "Lacking the genius and intellectual confidence of the advisors, he consulted them often and moved slowly and cautiously to judgment; but when ready to act, he acted decisively, and in the case of controversial decisions he did not second-guess himself." Some senior advisers and cabinet officers of several of these presidents—Lincoln, Eisenhower, and Reagan among them—fairly openly derided their intelligence and judgment. But guess who history remembers and honors?

Leaders of institutions who approach their jobs with some humility are far more likely to get from subordinates the kinds of ideas and advice critical to success and to build a solid team than those who presume to know all the answers. No matter what room I was in, I always knew I was not the smartest person there. This was not false modesty. A D in freshman calculus and being in the presence of anyone who had mastered biochemistry, mathematics, or engineering—which I could never have done—were constant reminders to me of my limitations. What I brought into the room was a willingness to listen (I got better at that with every passing year), an ability to analyze and synthesize large and diverse amounts of information, opinions, and recommendations and come up with practical solutions to problems and proposals for reform. That, and a willingness to be bold.

Courage is essential for reform.

"Courage" is not a word that automatically pops into mind when thinking about bureaucracies. But anytime a mid-level leader tells his boss and his colleagues that the old way of doing things is no longer adequate and that change is necessary, it is a courageous act. Even when the man in charge takes a stand that most people, at least initially, oppose, it requires courage.

Acts of courage by institutional leaders for the sake of principle or the national interest are more common than you might think. But not so much when it comes to institutional reform. The truth is that dramatic reform efforts in public institutions, certainly at the federal level, are so rare that examples are hard to come by. There are more examples of significant change among governors and local leaders, whose hands are often forced and strengthened by budgetary crises.

Transformational reform takes courage because so many people have a stake—political, financial, or emotional—in the status quo. The defense of what "is" begins within the institution but then quickly involves potentially affected businesses, lobbyists, stakeholders, politics and political donors, and, perhaps most daunting of all, the legislature. A leader has to fight everyone to implement reform. The foregoing chapters have talked about the how of doing so. But the process begins with the act of courage required just to start.

Of course, if the would-be reformer isn't at least somewhat daunted by the challenge of bringing change to his institution, he doesn't understand the strength of the forces that will be arrayed in opposition. As on the battlefield, a realistic appreciation of one's adversaries is the first step toward success.

When a leader is fighting bureaucratic battles for reform, she needs a few senior associates who are trustworthy, share a commitment to her agenda for reform, and are capable of effectively implementing her decisions.

A leader's battle for bureaucratic reform will be a lonely one because she will not have many allies inside the institution—at least at senior levels. Upper-level officials will be concerned about their own careers and turf and eager to protect whatever "empires" they have assembled. Some may offer their support only selectively.

Upon taking her job, a leader may have the opportunity to fill vacant senior positions. She should look for capable, independent-minded people who share her goals but are willing to give candid recommendations for how to achieve them. As should be clear by now, I believe a leader must avoid yes-men.

Once a decision has been taken, though, those new colleagues should be committed to implementing it.

A new leader will also have to decide if she needs to replace some executives. She should not be in a rush to do so. Everyone should be given a chance to prove herself. No one should be fired just so the new woman in charge can portray herself as being tough.

At A&M, I felt there was an urgent need to send the message that a change in outlook and culture was required, and I concluded that most current senior administrators needed to go. I let a couple go pretty quickly; I told others to announce their retirement a year ahead of time so I could signal change was coming in his or her area and we could get searches under way for replacements. As I've said, I intended to reorient the entire university away from an administrator-dominant culture to one where the academic leaders dominated the decision-making process. To do that, I needed a new team of administrators.

I replaced no senior officials at the CIA when I became director and had no authority to replace the leaders of the other agencies that I nominally led. At Defense, I replaced no one when I arrived. As I said earlier, I wanted to send a message of my confidence in the incumbents. But there was a practical reason as well: with two wars ongoing and going badly, and the unpredictability of the Senate confirmation process, I wanted to take no chances on important chairs being empty. I knew I had to make a number of tough decisions on programs and issues, and I wanted a generous sampling of opinion. Meanwhile, I could determine whom I could count on in the long term. (I was immensely relieved to discover that was nearly everybody.)

In some ways, as important as who occupies the senior operating positions for a leader's success is the immediate staff with which he surrounds himself. Who they are and how they conduct themselves reflect directly on him.

I had been on the staff of one national security adviser, executive assistant to another, executive assistant to one DCI, and chief of staff for another. So I knew better than most what kind of person I wanted right outside my door. I wanted someone who was a facilitator, not a guard dog; someone who could ascertain whether a senior officer's need to see me was truly urgent and, if so, find a way to get him through my door in a timely way; someone who could identify and expedite high-priority decision papers; someone willing to ask me to clarify directions I had given—or report a dissent objectively; someone who kept the lines of communication open between my office and my senior associates. I wanted someone seen by the bureaucracy as an asset to them as well as to me. I wanted a mix of experience and new eyes and people who would be absolutely honest with me, who would tell me what I needed to hear, not just what I wanted to hear. I did not want any of my staff to be self-important or, worst of all, "wearing my epaulets"—a phrase describing staff who behave as though they have their boss's rank, treating others arrogantly and with disdain.

I wanted people competent and self-confident enough to make sure my wishes and directions were being carried out. From time to time when I was secretary, we would send one of the middle-ranking noncommissioned officers from the office into the field to help prepare for my trips. On one occasion, in Afghanistan, one of these men (all of whom I admired a great deal), Staff Sergeant Jason Easom, was doing the advance work and had a face-off with a full colonel who was working on my visit to the front lines. Jason had politely told the colonel what I wanted, but the colonel had a different plan, which he insisted upon. (He wanted me to spend most of my time in briefings; Jason knew I just wanted to visit troops.) Finally, Sergeant Easom walked over to the colonel's phone, picked up the receiver, held it out, and told the colonel, "One of the two of us can call the secretary of defense and be put through immediately." The colonel got the point and acceded to the guidance I had given Easom.

I ran a very lean front office in all three institutions I led, especially given their size. I suggest all leaders do the same. Too big an immediate staff becomes an obstacle to good communications and getting things done. After all, someone who is part of a large front office staff needs to keep busy and usually does so by bothering the rest of the institution—asking unnecessary questions, interposing himself unnecessarily in decision making, and generally creating problems for everyone, including the boss, who probably doesn't know the staffer is out there meddling in everybody's business trying to justify his position. A big staff also makes a boss look self-important and oblivious to cost, not good things when he is trying to lead reforms. With small staffs, there is much less jockeying for position or face time or petty gamesmanship. There was a lot of trust among my staffs at all three places I led and an environment that not only encouraged but was conducive to real candor. Even with a small staff, a leader can still get a mix of perspectives so that in the front office itself every problem is seen from different vantage points and experiences, a huge benefit for a decision maker.

This approach served me well. At the CIA, my personal secretary was a woman I had worked with for nearly a decade and whom I could count on to tell me exactly what she thought. (One time I wanted to go to a corporate-sponsored social event and asked the agency's general counsel if it was okay. She brought in his memo, sort of flipped it onto my desk, and rather snidely said that the general counsel had offered a wishy-washy opinion concluding that there was no problem, but she went on to say that in her opinion it didn't pass the *Washington Post* smell test. I didn't go to the event.) My executive assistant was a very bright career CIA economic analyst, Janice Williams. And, finally, I had a special assistant, Neal Wolin, a young lawyer my predecessor, Bill Webster, had brought in for a year to serve in that role—a practice he had followed with young lawyers as FBI director and then continued at the CIA. I was very impressed with Wolin and quickly moved him into a much more substantive role reviewing all paperwork coming to me with his lawyer's eye and acting as my surrogate monitoring all the task forces. (Years later he would be appointed deputy secretary of the Treasury.) Overseeing the

CIA and an intelligence community of some fifteen other agencies, a budget of several tens of billions of dollars, and more than a hundred thousand people, I had an immediate staff of three. It worked just fine.

At A&M, my staff was about the same size—a personal secretary, a director of special events, an office manager, a receptionist, and two support staff (all women). I created, for the first time at A&M, the position of chief of staff to the president, which I filled with a young lawyer from the provost's office, Rodney McClendon. I told him I knew nothing about Texas law pertaining to higher education and needed him to keep me out of trouble. He was amazingly well-informed about what was taking place on campus and was very effective in facilitating communication both from and to my office. This small group, together with the vice president for governmental affairs who shared our office suite, was brutally candid with me to the point of near insubordination on a daily basis. That small team kept me grounded, extremely well-informed, well-advised, and accessible and was an asset to the entire university community.

Finally, at Defense, the inner circle was somewhat larger but, compared with those of predecessors and successors, still quite small. The de facto chief of staff was Robert Rangel. I never heard Robert raise his voice—although one eyebrow often seemed to be especially upwardly mobile—but I think he was one of the most intimidating figures in the Pentagon because his standards for materials coming to me were so high, his discipline in keeping the trains on the track and on time was so rigorous, and his knowledge of the department and, indeed, all of Washington was so extraordinary. My confidential secretary kept the schedule and guarded the door to my office. I also had a senior military assistant, two junior military assistants, and two civilian assistants who played an instrumental role in almost every initiative I undertook.

I have described these staffs in some detail simply to underscore the point made earlier: leaders in all organizations—including the biggest ones—are well served by a small front office staff. It is more effective, and for a leader focused on transformational reform, it sends a powerful message.

In the real world of bureaucratic institutions, you almost never get all you want when you want it. A good leader must compromise, adjust his plans, prioritize, and show flexibility and pragmatism.

There is an old military saying that no plan survives first contact with the enemy. That is true in reforming institutions as well. Sometimes, a plan turns out to be unworkable for any number of reasons, from impracticality to a lack of resources or the technology necessary for implementation. Sometimes, the opposition is just too strong. When it comes to implementation of a leader's reform agenda, she needs to stay focused on her agenda or vision but flexible about how she achieves it—and sometimes either admit defeat or be satisfied with half a loaf (and come back for more later). I had to do this all the time.

One of the reforms I wanted to put in place as DCI was to move away from providing intelligence to policy makers once a day (first thing in the morning) on paper. I would tell my staff we were delivering intelligence to President George H. W. Bush the same way it had been delivered to George Washington: we wrote it down on a piece of paper, put a person in a vehicle (we *had* gotten past using horses), and carried the document by hand to the recipient. I wanted to do all this electronically, sending the information in real time to a computer on the policy maker's desk and updating it constantly throughout the day—and enabling the user to ask questions of us electronically. This effort in 1992 failed partly because of technological challenges in those days and partly because a number of our "customers" were uncomfortable receiving information in this newfangled way. This was one reform that died on the vine—then.

Another reform I pursued was to change how the intelligence community managed our photographic intelligence assets.

During the first Gulf War, there were many problems in getting reconnaissance photographs to field commanders and units in the fight. Over a period of decades, we had solved this problem in signals intelligence by giving the National Security Agency the authority to standardize transmission systems and coordinate all levels of collection, from a tactical military unit in the field to space satellites. We had no comparable organization on the photographic side, and I intended to fix that. My idea was to create a single agency—comparable to the NSA—that could coordinate all our imaging assets (a soldier with a camera, a Beechcraft airplane, satellites) and have the authority to make sure those images could be shared with the smallest units in combat. The initiative was bitterly resisted by the CIA, which wanted to maintain its independent institutional capability for photointerpretation. I wanted to integrate it into this larger, multiagency organization. I could override the CIA's objections to the new agency but not those of Secretary of Defense Dick Cheney and the Joint Chiefs of Staff chairman, Colin Powell. Both were deeply skeptical of creating a big new agency that put together nearly all civilian and military imaging assets, including the Defense Mapping Agency (highly dependent on satellite photography). I settled for half a loaf, creating the Central Imaging Office, which coordinated our photographic assets and needs of users but lacked the authority for standardization and coordination the NSA had on the signals side. My concept eventually won out, however, and the agency I tried to create in 1992 was ultimately established four years later. It is now known by the inelegant title "National Geospatial-Intelligence Agency," and its mission covers virtually everything I intended in 1992 and more.

At all three institutions I led, I told folks that between where we stood and achieving our goals was a swamp. Sometimes, you slog your way across the swamp, dealing with alligators and snakes and such. And sometimes, it's best just to walk around the swamp; it might take longer, but you eventually reach your destination without the teeth marks on your ass. The key is to keep moving forward. The smart reformer knows when to plunge into the swamp and when to take the roundabout route.

One key aspect of successfully reforming institutions, public or private, is taking the work seriously but not yourself. A leader needs to set the example of that principle.

Never underestimate the extraordinary power of humor. Of the eight presidents I worked for, two had no discernible sense of humor: Richard Nixon and Jimmy Carter. You can draw your own conclusions from that. I suspect many Americans would be surprised how much laughter there is in the White House Situation Room, even during the most tense moments. I have always believed that humor is the way sane people cope with intense pressures, with decisions involving life and death. Often, it will be just a wisecrack, a pun, or a muttered aside that provokes laughter. It may seem inappropriate, but it is in fact a useful tool.

At the end of the raid that killed Osama bin Laden, we heard that Admiral William McRaven had a six-foot-tall SEAL lie down next to bin Laden's body at our base in Jalalabad, Afghanistan, to see if it was indeed six feet tall, another effort to confirm the terrorist's identity. President Obama quipped, "McRaven can crash a $60 million helicopter but can't afford a tape measure?"

George H. W. Bush had a great sense of humor. He liked jokes, including practical ones. On his birthday, we would go out and get him risqué cards and sign the names of foreign leaders to them, and we would all roar with laughter. He created the Scowcroft Award, named for his national security adviser, Brent Scowcroft, an award that he gleefully presented to the U.S. official who most ostentatiously fell asleep in a meeting with the president of the United States. He carefully weighed the length of the nap, depth (snoring always won extra points), and quality of recovery—did you quietly regain consciousness and ease back into the conversation or come awake with a jolt that knocked over coffee? During long meetings with foreign leaders, he would carry the conversation for the first hour but then looked to the rest of us to relieve him of that chore for the duration. He would actually score us on our contribution—the amount of time we each used up. I once received high marks on time consumed but earned the comment "although you were boring as hell."

I highly prized irreverence among my colleagues, partly because I am irreverent myself. A leader should never underestimate the benefits of self-deprecating humor; making jokes or humorous observations about himself can be a powerful tonic to his team. Henry Kissinger was probably the most talented person I worked for in this regard. In all three of the institutions I led, little was off-limits, from comments about my white hair to my ridiculously unhealthy eating habits and boring suits and ties.

Almost everything about Congress was good for a laugh, and the same was true about the antics of the Texas legislature when I was at A&M. Along with the serious stuff at the CIA, we were always getting intelligence reports about the nonpublic activities of foreign leaders, some of which were hilarious.

The best corporate leaders have a good sense of humor and encourage it in others. Years ago, I was on the board of directors of a holding company that owned a kitchen appliance business. Executives would regularly demonstrate new products for this older, all-male board, including at one meeting a new model of "salad shooter" for making tossed salad. I quipped that asking that board—none too familiar with what went on in a kitchen—to evaluate such a device was like asking a teetotaler to judge the quality of a whiskey. I joined the board of a company that owned Massey Ferguson tractors and was told of a board visit to a factory before my time where the CEO mischievously organized a plowing contest to see which urbane board member could plow the straightest furrow. The results weren't pretty, but there had been a lot of laughs. These business executives and others I observed knew how to use humor to build a team.

Doris Kearns Goodwin writes about the value and importance

of humor in her wonderful book about Abraham Lincoln, *Team of Rivals:*

> Modern psychiatry regards humor as probably the most mature and healthy means of adapting to melancholy. "Humor, like hope, permits one to focus upon and to bear what is too terrible to be borne," writes George Vaillant. "Humor can be marvelously therapeutic," adds another observer. "It can deflate without destroying; it can instruct while it entertains; it saves us from our pretensions; and it provides an outlet for feeling that expressed another way would be corrosive."

My experience in public life affirms every word of that passage.

Don't overstay your welcome.

When you have accomplished your mission of reform, or taken it as far as you likely can, go home. Don't let power and position—or being spoiled by the corporate airplane—go to your head. As the old saying goes, "The cemeteries are full of indispensable men."

One of the toughest decisions in life is knowing when to dance off the stage. We have all seen political and business leaders who stayed too long. Some get so enamored of the power, perks, and privileges they just can't bear to give them up. Or they don't want to give their critics inside and outside the organization the satisfaction. And so they remain in place, a growing liability to the very institution they might have ably led for a long time. I have always thought the sweet spot was to leave at a point when people would say "I wish he weren't leaving so soon" as opposed to "How the hell do we get rid of this guy?"

The toughest decision on whether to leave is when circumstances begin to sour, trending in a direction that makes you uncomfortable, or when you disagree with important decisions by those in charge. It is the dilemma many senior public servants have faced: Do I leave as a matter of principle and because I am increasingly at odds with the initiatives, or do I continue to soldier on, hoping I can mitigate the consequences for my organization (and perhaps my country or state) by staying? It is a question every individual must answer for himself or herself. An important part of the decision for a leader at any level is to look inward and be honest with herself whether she is staying for noble or ignoble purposes.

Unlike in a parliamentary system like Great Britain's, there is not a tradition in American politics, particularly at the national level, of senior officials resigning because of a disagreement over policy or to take responsibility for a failure. Indeed, the only time in my career I can remember a cabinet official resigning over a matter of principle was when Secretary of State Cyrus Vance did so in April 1980 because he so deeply disagreed with President Carter's decision to attempt the rescue of our embassy hostages in Iran. There have presumably been others at lower levels, but even they are exceptionally rare. Probably too rare at all levels.

Only slightly less tough for any leader than leaving over policy differences is being honest with herself whether she has done all she can do to reform or change an institution—to tell herself, as she probably has told subordinates she was firing, that she doesn't have the energy or ideas or whatever else is required to take the organization to the next level of excellence, that she's made her contribution, and it's time to go.

It is sad to see someone cling to power and position interminably. Secretary of State Dean Acheson once said that "to leave a position of great responsibility and authority is to die a little." Just before President Obama announced that I would retire as secretary of defense in 2011, he was quite explicit in telling me he would have welcomed my remaining in the job. A number of friends and acquaintances asked how I could walk away from such a powerful position. But I knew it was time. At four and a half years, I had served longer in the job than all but four of my predecessors—two of whom had to resign in disgrace and one of whom was indicted.

It was not a historical record I wished to emulate. I was exhausted, and I felt pretty sure the period ahead was not going to be either pleasant or easy. Unlike Acheson, I decided to leave so I could "live a little."

What I have written here on the personal qualities I think are necessary to successfully lead reform of institutions—of bureaucracies public and private—is obviously highly subjective; some attributes are self-evident, others controversial. But, as a package, they constitute a set of values and characteristics that, I believe, stand the test of time.

In his short book *Churchill*, Paul Johnson describes what he considers the personal qualities that made Winston Churchill such a great leader:

> The first lesson is: always aim high. . . . He did not always meet his elevated targets, but by aiming high he always achieved something worthwhile.
>
> Lesson number two is: there is no substitute for hard work. . . . The balance he maintained between flat-out work and creative and restorative leisure is worth studying by anyone holding a top position. But he never evaded hard work itself: taking important and dangerous decisions, the hardest form of work there is. . . .
>
> Third, and in its way most important, Churchill never allowed mistakes, disaster—personal or national—accidents, illnesses, unpopularity, and criticism to get him down. . . . He had courage, the most important of all virtues, and its companion, fortitude. . . . In a sense his whole career was an exercise in how courage can be displayed, reinforced, guarded and doled out carefully, heightened and concentrated, conveyed to others. Those uncertain of their courage can look to Churchill for reassurance and inspiration.
>
> Fourth, Churchill wasted an extraordinarily small amount

of his time and emotional energy on the meannesses of life: recrimination, shifting the blame onto others, malice, revenge seeking, dirty tricks, spreading rumors, harboring grudges, waging vendettas. . . . There is nothing more draining and exhausting than hatred. And malice is bad for the judgment.

Finally, the absence of hatred left plenty of room for joy in Churchill's life. . . . He showed the people a love of jokes, and was to them a source of many. No great leader was ever laughed at, or with, more than Churchill.

Churchill has always been my greatest personal hero. His qualities, captured above, are those every leader in every institution should aspire to emulate. And every politician, too.

8

Money, Money, Money:
Reforming in Scarce Times

The fight for money is a distinguishing feature of bureaucracies, both in business and at every level of government.

In a big business, different components or divisions seek more resources from the corporate leadership for product development, marketing, modernizing manufacturing facilities, research, cyber security, and myriad other purposes. The elbows inside the organization can be very sharp. The CEO must decide how to allocate the company's available resources based on her judgment of what will best advance her strategy and benefit the company and its shareholders. As a corporate director, I have observed multiple business chiefs do just that, and I have seen the behind-the-scenes competition among the heads of company components to get a bigger share of the pie. The CEO's advantage over the public sector leader is that her decisions are final—unless the board chooses to fire her.

The resources available to the leader of a public bureaucracy, in contrast, depend on the whims of elected councils, legislatures, mayors, governors, and presidents. They are subject to a broad array of pressure groups and stakeholders described earlier.

Spending decisions by public sector leaders can be reversed by politicians, and those leaders also face great uncertainty about future funding, all of which makes long-term planning and reform that much more difficult.

A bureaucracy has infinite capacity to spend money—no matter how much it is given. The appetite is insatiable. Undisciplined spending habits proliferate during flush times, making the transition to hard times all the more challenging. I once observed that notwithstanding a defense budget of over $700 billion (including war funding), the "needs" identified by our military leaders could not be fully satisfied with $1 trillion. A bureaucracy—public or private—will always have a wish list of unmet needs, ranging from the "urgent" to the "nice to have."

Flush times in public bureaucracies are rare and usually associated with some sort of crisis or domestic emergency. Whether the occasion is the terrorist attacks of September 11, 2001, Hurricane Katrina or Sandy, the Veterans Affairs scandal, or a multitude of other disasters, the public demand for a quick and massive response brings a flood of dollars to departments and agencies ill-equipped to spend them efficiently. And the demand that a bureaucracy react speedily is a sure guarantee of massive waste. As we used to say in the CIA when a policy maker wanted quick results, "You want it bad, you get it bad."

The money spigot for the U.S. military and intelligence agencies subsequent to 9/11 remained wide open for nearly a decade. An entire generation of managers and leaders accustomed to an open checkbook assumed senior positions, only to be told by the president and Congress in 2010 that the bank was out of money. The national security bureaucracy suddenly had to begin to adjust itself to the kind of bare-bones diet that federal domestic departments and most state and local bureaucracies had long experienced.

The struggle for resources is a central part of every bureaucratic leader's job. I was at the CIA in the early to mid-1970s when the flow of money associated with the war in Vietnam was shut off. I became DCI at the end of the Cold War, when the flow of dollars to both Defense and the CIA began to be severely reduced—another "peace" dividend. Public universities across the country have been seeing the level of state support diminish for a couple of decades now, and Texas A&M was no different. And midway through my four and a half years as secretary of defense, the effects of the U.S. financial crisis, the Great Recession, and huge budget deficits collectively began to bring the hammer down on military spending.

Periods of budget stringency are unparalleled opportunities for reform leaders to implement changes in the bureaucracy, to make structural and cultural reforms, to increase efficiency, and to reallocate resources to new priorities.

The cold-shower reality of fewer dollars to spend is the perfect time to strike boldly against the bureaucratic status quo. It is a fact of life that because bureaucracies are so tough to change, they don't. And over time they get fat, sloppy, lazy, and set in their ways. Tight or reduced budgets afford the reformer an important weapon for forcing change. If no additional resources are available or if budgets are cut, then higher priorities, new initiatives, and new requirements must be funded by changing the way business is done or by eliminating less important programs.

I first experienced budget cutting as a new second lieutenant in the air force in 1967, when the costs of the Vietnam War were forcing severe spending cutbacks in all parts of the military not directly engaged in the war. There were significant cutbacks in travel, nonessential activities, and all manner of amenities at the Strategic Air Command base where I was stationed in Missouri. The small Plans and Intelligence office where I worked even had to give up our subscription to *The New York Times* (which meant the captain I worked for had to find some other way to occupy his mornings). At the CIA in the early 1970s, I saw the perversity of bureaucratic budgeting. We would have to cope with a scarcity of money for eleven months, and then the green eyeshade guys would decide at the last minute that the agency was going to have money left over at the end of the fiscal year—a cardinal sin—and so managers would literally walk around trying to find projects at which to throw the excess dollars.

But at no point in my career did I see bureaucratic leaders use periods of stringency as an opportunity to make important structural or operational changes. Significant cuts in national security spending in the mid- and late 1970s and the early 1990s resulted in canceled programs and constraints on noncritical spending (such as travel and conferences) but had no discernible effect on the way bureaucracies were organized or went about their business.

The bureaucratic status quo was my target in all three big institutions I led. When I was DCI, more than half of the two dozen task forces I established in one way or another addressed how the fifteen intelligence agencies I oversaw could better integrate and restructure their efforts to accommodate budget reductions at the end of the Cold War. In particular, the creation of the Community Management Staff was intended to give me a stronger, more effective way to manage the agencies' budgets than had previously existed. A presidential directive to all the relevant cabinet and agency heads to reexamine the priorities for intelligence collection was also an effort to cope with reduced resources.

At A&M, as mentioned earlier, two of my top priorities for change were adding some 450 new faculty and greatly expanding our recruitment of minority students. Both required money—a lot of it. The new faculty salaries alone would add some $10 million each of four successive years to our overall budget of just under $500 million—not to mention the cost of space to accommodate those faculty. I planned to set aside another $20 million for diversity initiatives.

Between 2003 and 2006, we eliminated more than four hundred staff positions with annual recurring savings of $12 million. In 2006 alone, we implemented actions resulting in another $9 million of annual cost savings, including reducing our utility costs by 25 percent. We outsourced a variety of services and aggressively reorganized and restructured administrative functions. Much of this work was initiated and implemented by a new senior vice president for finance, Sue Redman, whom I had hired away from a pharmaceutical company. I believed her private sector business acumen and perspective would identify significant areas in which we could reform the way the university did business, and I was not disappointed. The executive vice president/provost and vice-provost also played central roles. (I must give credit as well to the Texas legislature, which gave us a special appropriation of $20 million to help fund the faculty expansion.)

These cost-cutting measures did not reduce the university budget, but through administrative reforms and efficiencies we were able to free significant dollars to fund major improvements in the university. I directed the effort, but it was a team project that, because it included broad representation from the university community, was carried out with minimal anxiety and disruption. The endeavor also demonstrated how critical to reform are like-minded, tough-minded lieutenants.

At Defense, in 2009, I cut or capped nearly three dozen major acquisition programs that, had they been built to completion, would have cost taxpayers about $330 billion. My motive in doing this was, above all, to make decisions that should have been made in most cases long before to eliminate overcost, overdue, or no longer needed programs. A secondary motive was to demonstrate to Congress and to the public that the department could clean up its own house—always a good idea for any institution—and thereby perhaps be somewhat shielded from the obviously approaching budgetary train wreck (an embarrassingly naive idea). I admit that changing the way the bureaucracy did business was not an integral part of my decisions in 2009.

However, in 2010, I undertook another major budget initiative, this time with the sole purpose of forcing the bureaucracy to reform and change. I directed the military services to cut $100 billion in overhead costs over a five-year period. The only way to

achieve that goal was to cut administrative and staff costs, con-
solidate or eliminate functions, shutter headquarters, and change
the current way of doing business. As incentive, I promised that
for every dollar of successful cuts in overhead, I would consider
equivalent dollar requests for purchasing new or additional military capability—a direct swap of "tail" for "tooth." The services
found the $100 billion. I also directed the other parts of the Pen-
tagon to find another nearly $80 billion in overhead savings, most
of which we would return to the Treasury. In both years, the effort
produced results in large measure because of the involvement of
leaders from all over the department—and intensive pressure
from me and my office.

Regardless of the nature of the institution, the public or private sector boss must have a mechanism to ensure that elements
of the bureaucracy are, in fact, implementing the budgetary cuts
and changes they originally agreed to. It's one thing to sign up
when the trumpet sounds "charge"; it's another to stay the course
until the battle is finished. This is where accountability must be
an essential part of the leader's playbook. He must ensure the
actions he directed are being taken in full.

Cutting jobs and firing people are almost always unfortunate con-
sequences of reduced budgets. How they are done matters.

One significant area of difference between business and the
public sector is that the former routinely reduces the workforce
when revenues are down or a company is changing strategies or
merges with another. Employees in many industries—automobile
manufacturing, banking and finance, and retailing, to mention
only a few—are familiar with this reality, and leaders usually have
considerable experience in managing such reductions. Seniority
often plays an important role, and the magnitude of personnel
reductions will often vary from one part of a company to another.
The leader will make these decisions based almost entirely on

business considerations. Layoffs and reductions in force are obviously painful for the individuals involved, but the relative lack of job security is a fact of life in the private sector.

In contrast, one of the principal attractions of employment in a public sector bureaucracy is job security. Because personnel reductions are so infrequent, when they do occur the impact is significant and traumatic for an organization. While under ordinary circumstances public employees have some job protections, many discover to their dismay that those protections are pretty limited if there is a budget crunch. In these circumstances, the challenges facing the leader, his manner of decision making, and the implementation of employee reductions are quite different from in the business arena. How the leader handles such reductions will affect future morale as well as perceptions of him by those who remain in the institution.

When Admiral Stansfield Turner was head of the CIA in the latter half of the 1970s, he fired hundreds of clandestine service officers. As I understood the situation at the time, he wanted the letters of separation to include expressions of appreciation for service rendered to the country and their contributions to U.S. security. The agency lawyers apparently persuaded him that such niceties—courtesies—might give a fired officer some grounds for a lawsuit to get his job back, and so those let go received a terse, even callous, dismissal letter. The result was deep animosity toward Turner not just by those fired but by most of those who remained at the agency. As long as a leader is operating within the laws and regulations pertaining to such matters, he shouldn't let advisers deter him from—make him afraid of—treating people being let go courteously and with compassion.

When lists of people to be dismissed are assembled, a good leader will look closely at eligibility for retirement. If he has any flexibility at all, he should let those near retirement finish out their service. If they have put in a lifetime of service, they deserve consideration. Again, the rest of the employees will be watching whether a leader deals with such cases sympathetically and humanely.

A leader in either business or government needs to be cautious about offering broad-based programs for early retirement as a means of encouraging people to leave voluntarily. He will find, as often as not, that the people he most wants to stay take advantage of the chance to leave and those he most wants to go decide how much they love the place and want to stay. When that happens, the boss is left standing there looking like Wile E. Coyote who just set off a bomb under himself.

Several mechanisms are available to a leader for managing "head count" and reducing the number of employees in an organization. If the objective is simply to prevent further growth, freezing the number of positions in a component—imposing a personnel ceiling or force cap—will allow the manager flexibility to move people around, hire, and fire as long as he stays under the overall limit. A force cap also allows the leader to manage the normal ebb and flow of personnel.

If the objective is to reduce the number of employees, the best approach is to focus on weeding out the poorest performers. This has the dual benefit of likely improving overall performance and improving the morale of those who remain. Two other available, but less attractive, mechanisms for reducing numbers are attrition (not filling positions as they become vacant) and a hiring freeze. There are downsides to using either. Above all, attrition takes personnel decisions—who should stay, who should go—out of the leader's hands and leaves him at the mercy of the decisions of others. Using attrition also means the fewer remaining employees will be asked to work harder and do more unless the way the work is done is changed. A freeze on hiring, especially in a big organization, disrupts the recruitment and training process that continually feeds new blood into the institution. A leader ought not to keep it going too long—say, more than a year.

I have used all these techniques to reduce personnel. Predictably, weeding out poor performers was the most effective but also the most difficult on both employees and supervisors. Telling someone smart enough to be hired by the CIA and perhaps work there for years that he isn't good enough to stay is painful for both the employee and his supervisor. Although we reduced staff by nearly four hundred at Texas A&M, we managed all but about three dozen through attrition and a yearlong hiring freeze. I imposed a force cap at the Pentagon in 2010 as part of the broader effort to reduce overhead costs, and there weren't too many yelps.

Whether in the private or the public sector, a leader should use any reduction in workforce to reform the way the organization does its work. Don't maintain the status quo structurally and operationally, simply asking fewer people to do more work in the same old ways. That is not fair or efficient. It also represents a missed opportunity. Look for a better way.

As with the reform agenda itself, transparency in budget cutting is the only way to build trust in a bureaucracy.

How much transparency is possible depends on the nature of the organization. Disclosure of details in the CIA budget, for example, could reveal major new allocations for a covert operation or new investments in satellites. Too much transparency by a company could expose investments in new products or changes in strategy that would provide advantages to competitors.

Still, broadly speaking, when it comes to budget cutting in public or private bureaucracies, it is important to remember that uncertainty creates anxiety and saps morale. Whether the question is which programs will be eliminated or which employees let go, everybody is stressed until the final decisions are made and announced. As long as the uncertainty continues, efficiency will plummet as rumors fly and people are distracted by speculation on what will happen—and whether they will soon be out of a job.

On budgetary matters, I told the senior leadership at Texas

A&M, we need have no secrets, no "black boxes." We briefed deans, faculty, and students on the budget options we were considering, how we would pay for new initiatives, how much tuition and fees might rise, and the impact of state appropriations on our choices. All basic budget options, recommendations, and decisions were examined by the Finance Council mentioned earlier, and its ideas and recommendations were taken into account.

At the CIA and Defense, there were obvious security and other practical constraints on how much budgets could be discussed in detail with the entire workforce. That said, within the intelligence community, at my direction the Community Management Staff shared information and options widely with the agencies, and I sought the views of those agencies' leaders frequently as we formulated decisions. Even with so many highly sensitive programs, I tried to run, at a senior level, as open a process as possible.

Both Congress and various military service and Defense staffs were highly critical of what they termed my excessively secretive approach to major budget decisions, especially the major initiatives in 2009 and 2010. Guilty as charged. As described earlier, I did exclude many staff people in Defense from the process and even required the senior-most officers to sign nondisclosure agreements (as did I). Otherwise, as always before, options under consideration would have quickly leaked and given the opposition on the Hill and elsewhere the opportunity to thwart decisions affecting their parochial interests. That said, I involved virtually all of the senior military and civilian leaders of the department in developing every option and in formulating recommendations for my decisions. There was ample and open debate in 2010 in the course of some sixty meetings on every subject under review. And every senior civilian and military leader had multiple opportunities to weigh in. The openness of the process (at least at senior levels), I believe, played a big role in the absence of leaks and the support of the military services for my decisions in congressional deliberations. (I acknowledge that all involved also knew that after their intensive involvement and chance to be heard in the process, I would not have tolerated them undercutting my subsequent decisions.)

Few institutions require the secrecy of the CIA or the Defense Department on budget matters. Involving as many senior personnel as possible and making the process open to them are important to their support of a leader's subsequent decisions—and to their ability to inform and reassure their employees. The more information a leader shares, the more he can inform his people about the choices the institution faces and the options he is considering, the more he can allay some of the uncertainty that inevitably accompanies tough budget decisions. The more he can say about the size of personnel reductions, and how those decisions will be made, the more he can reduce anxiety. The worst of all possible worlds is a black box approach, where a leader and a small group of his staff make budget decisions without broad involvement of others in the organization and then spring decisions on people without warning. Even on budgets, trust is the coin of the realm. More information equals more trust in any organization.

Salami-slicing budgets—each component gets a thin cut—is a formula for broad institutional mediocrity and is the antithesis of reform and striving for excellence.

Too many leaders faced with budget cuts give directions as though they were talking to their barber: "Just a little off the top." Across-the-board cuts to accommodate a budget reduction are, for a leader, by far the easiest because each department is cut roughly equally, leaving everyone a little unhappy and everyone experiencing some pain. Congress—all elected officials, in fact—loves this salami-slicing approach because it fulfills the law of the conservation of enemies: no one gets too pissed off. Too many leaders of institutions like it for the same reason.

There is just one problem: It is the worst possible approach from the standpoint of accomplishing an organization's mission and for carrying out reform. It is, I reminded people, managerial cowardice.

The journalist Thomas L. Friedman has written, "What is leadership if not the framing of concrete choices for the public and then urging one over another." I opposed across-the-board cuts in every institution I led. This was demonstrated most vividly in the spring of 2011 when President Obama "asked" me to cut an additional $400 billion from Defense over the following ten years. I told him the only way to do that responsibly was to commission a strategic review by the department of the choices that would need to be made. We had to be able to tell the president and Congress what military missions we could no longer carry out with reductions of that magnitude and assess the risks associated with those choices. In short, he and we needed to make hard choices about strategic priorities and military capabilities; we could not rely on across-the-board cuts that would weaken critical capabilities. (That, by the way, is just what has happened under "sequestration," which is congressionally mandated salami slicing: everything is cut the same, from the smartest and most important things the military does to the dumbest and least important.)

When it comes to budgets, and especially cutting them, the leader must establish priorities; some activities are core to the mission of the organization, and others are not. But establishing priorities, saying one program or one part of the enterprise must be protected from budget cuts, is tough because you will antagonize everyone not included in the highest-priority category. Establishing priorities sends the message that some functions aren't as important as others, and that too creates ill will. Even so, a leader needs the intestinal fortitude to make the cuts where they should properly be made, come what may.

Waste, fraud, and abuse are favorite targets of politicians and the media and are usually lumped together as a single category of bureaucratic malfeasance. All three exist in every bureaucracy, but each is quite different from the other, and so is the remedy.

Of the three, waste is by far the most universal and costly. When it comes to eliminating waste, given the forces arrayed in opposition to change, a leader must be fearless. I don't think anyone intentionally sets out to waste money. It is just inherent in the nature of bureaucracies, both public and private. People get committed to programs, and when those programs are no longer needed or go off track, they probably rightfully believe that their jobs depend on keeping their program alive—even if on life support. People also get comfortable doing business in particular ways, and when, over time, those ways become increasingly inefficient or fail to provide quality service, they have no interest in changing the status quo. Or senior officials see others of similar rank with certain perks and privileges and want the same and then push the envelope to get a little more. Others just think that a posh office or house is their due. Or folks recognize that a particular program is wasteful, but because it is a pet project of a powerful member of Congress or a state legislator, or of a higher-level boss in the private sector, it continues to be funded. In other words, one man's "waste" is another man's job or useful project.

A reformer looking for waste in bureaucracies has a target-rich environment. Examples abound. I suspect more university presidents have lost their jobs because of overspending on building or decorating their official residence and/or their office than all other causes combined. (Of course, the luckiest university president is the one whose predecessor has been fired for such excesses: the successor gets all the benefit with none of the grief. Still, the money is gone, wasted.) Less blatant is the money wasted because managers are preoccupied with protecting their turf and sole control of their own support functions. Too often, each college or administrative unit in a university insists on having its own computer model, its own external support contract for office equipment like copiers, and the like. It's as much about control as anything—that, and a lack of confidence that centralized support will be as responsive as needed. Consolidation and outsourcing of support services would save most schools—and many other organizations—a great deal of money, and a large number have taken this road. (But somebody had better pay attention to quality and speed of service from that low-bidding outsourcer.)

When it comes to waste, the all-time champion is the Department of Defense. The biggest waste of all, of course, is in the form of major acquisitions that are unneeded or have been poorly managed and the cost has exploded. Programs I canceled for those reasons included a new presidential helicopter, six years behind schedule and the cost of which had doubled to $13 billion; the missile defense "kinetic energy interceptor," a five-year "development" program in its fourteenth year whose cost had nearly doubled to $8.9 billion; an airborne laser, deployed on ten to twenty Boeing 747s at a cost of $1.5 billion each, with a range of just fifty miles; and nearly thirty more such programs. These and dozens of other acquisitions gone wrong cost the taxpayers many billions of dollars. Each had its defenders inside the Department of Defense, as well as in industry and in Congress.

Then there is congressionally mandated waste. A good example is the first-generation C-5A Galaxy cargo aircraft, which the air force cannot afford to keep flying—and it doesn't—but which Congress won't allow to be decommissioned. The only time these giant planes move is when they are towed around the tarmac. Even as Congress cut the defense budget by hundreds of billions of dollars and manpower by the tens of thousands, its unwillingness to allow the department and the military services to close unneeded bases and facilities all across the country is mind-boggling. The military estimates that nearly a quarter of its facilities are unneeded and should be closed. The list of legislatively required waste is a very long one.

Needless to say, there is enormous waste internal to the Defense Department as well. When we could identify $180 billion in overhead cuts in five months of work, the potential for dramatically greater savings is evident. As I said at the time, we had to go from a culture of spending to a culture of saving. Figuratively speaking, as the deputy defense secretary Gordon England was fond of saying, there is a river of money that runs through the Pentagon—hundreds of billions of dollars in routine spending that rarely gets close scrutiny. Some is in large chunks, but much of it is in relatively smaller accounts that are nearly invisible given the size of the overall budget. To get at those funds, and decide what is necessary and what is not, is very hard work. But it can be done.

To make the cuts we did in a number of areas, the department and the military services had to rethink how we did our business and make significant structural and procedural changes. The only way Defense could manage the additional $400 billion in cuts directed by the president—and even more through congressional sequestration—without seriously weakening America's national security was through radical reform and getting at that river of routine spending, both efforts that could only be led from the top.

Abuse and fraud demonstrate a lack of honor and integrity and, as such, can cast the responsible individuals, an entire organization, and its leadership in an unfavorable light. Both are, at minimum, violations of a trust and cannot be tolerated.

Allegations of fraud and abuse make for stirring political rhetoric, but I think their significance in contributing to misspent money and poor performance is greatly overdrawn. Fraud is taken very seriously and regularly punished. In every institution I have led, I have seen employees—including some fairly senior officials—fired and some prosecuted for falsely reporting time and attendance, for false claims relating to travel and other expenses, for misuse of official aircraft and vehicles. More broadly, there are many documented cases of government officials who have taken bribes or been guilty of conflicts of interest, been caught, and sent to jail. Interestingly, government seems more willing to prosecute small-scale thieves (and even more significant ones) than business, where there is a penchant simply to fire a miscreant rather than invest the time, trouble, and money to take him or her to court.

In the overall scheme of things, I suspect the dollar cost of abuse is not significant (especially when compared with waste). I think the term, in the context of "waste, fraud, and abuse," applies mainly to rule breaking and violations of fiduciary responsibility that do not rise to the level of fraud or criminality. This term applies, in my view, especially to a number of the cases in recent years of senior military officers exceeding propriety when it comes to use of staff for personal errands, improper use of government resources, lavish entertainment, and questionable use of government aircraft for personal purposes. But many others in every bureaucracy—public and private—indulge in these and similar abuses. No one goes to jail for these offenses, as in the case of true fraud, but people do get formal reprimands, lose their jobs, and sometimes must pay restitution.

———

Leaders in the public sector face multiple budgetary challenges their counterparts in business are spared. Foremost is that the budgets of virtually all public sector organizations are subject to approval by elected bodies. That means great uncertainty from year to year as to how much money a leader and his organization will get. Such uncertainty makes even medium-term planning and strategy formulation tough. Also, elected overseers usually provide little flexibility to change ways of doing business, to deal with new priorities, or to restructure organizations—a particular challenge for the reformer. Perversely, efficiency and careful stewardship of taxpayer dollars more often than not are penalized, not rewarded. If a leader manages carefully and ends the fiscal year without having spent every dollar he was budgeted, the powers that be will likely conclude he was given too much money and will therefore cut his allocation for the next year. On the other hand, the lousy manager who spends his entire allocation and perhaps then some will likely get a sympathetic hearing for an increase in budget next time around.

These challenges are not insurmountable. With patience and the investment of a lot of time, a leader can overcome these obstacles.

———

Not many leaders see budget cuts as an opportunity, but, to paraphrase the English writer Samuel Johnson, "Nothing focuses the mind like a hanging." Budget stringencies offer a leader of reform the best chance to refocus the organization, redefine priorities, and—especially when cuts are involved—change outdated, inefficient, and wasteful ways of doing business. All these actions can be done while an organization's budget is stable or during those rare periods when it's growing. But it's a lot harder to make big changes in fat years than in lean years. Because most public bureaucracies are going to have a lot of lean years ahead, reformers will have ample opportunities to put the above-mentioned suggestions to work.

9

Reform: The Never-Ending Story

The reality of reforming bureaucracies is that when a leader thinks he is done, *he* probably is done. If a leader has implemented everything on his list of reforms and has nothing else to propose, it is time for him to leave. Transformation is an unending process, not a once-in-a-lifetime experience, and that is how a leader must think of it.

The external environment is always changing, creating new challenges and new opportunities at every turn. Additionally, there must be another law of physics that over time even reformed bureaucracies are magnetically drawn back toward their natural state: torpor, complacency, protecting the status quo, inertia, and inefficiency. The most successful businesses continuously reinvent themselves, never resting on their successes. Just look at companies like IBM led by Ginni Rometty, Apple under Steve Jobs and Tim Cook, Amazon and Jeff Bezos, or General Electric under Jeffrey Immelt. But after a period of reform and change, too many organizations in the private sector and nearly all in the public sector fall prey to that putative law of physics: they tend to get comfortable with the new status quo and defend it as passionately as they did the old way of doing things. That means a leader must always have an unfinished agenda in a continuing quest for excellence and success. Like the legendary captain of the ghost ship the *Flying Dutchman*, the reformer never makes port.

The leader of an organization is the engine of change and reform, and his work is never done. If his yellow tablet keeps filling up with ideas, he should keep on truckin'. But if a leader cannot sustain his enthusiasm, energy, and creativity to keep making his institution better, he needs to step aside for someone who can.

Whether leading a bureaucracy for a short time or a long time, the reformer must never lose his zeal for continuing improvement. As he implements his initial agenda for change, he must also be cognizant of changes going on externally—and backsliding internally—and always adding to his to-do list. He must constantly stir the pot in the search for ways his organization can do its job better. He must be disruptive.

A good leader must keep coming up with new perspectives, new ideas, new improvements. I have served on the board of directors of companies where the person in charge has been doing the job for decades and is still the most restless, energetic, and innovative person in the company. A leader has to keep listening, remain open-minded toward new ideas from others, always be on the hunt for better ways to get the job done. She has to keep reinventing herself as well as the organization. She has to look hard in the mirror to be sure she is still hungry enough to lead. Only a committed leader can keep an organization—a bureaucracy—on its toes, continuously adapting, innovating, improving. She has to be continually evaluating subordinates, sending away those she hired who have flagged and who can lift their organization no further, and hiring new potential leaders to restoke the fires of enthusiasm and performance.

At the CIA, I began with fourteen task forces but within weeks saw the need for even more far-reaching change and added ten more areas in need of reform. I returned to Texas A&M from every vacation with a yellow tablet filled with notes on additional changes I thought were needed and on ways to improve on what we were already doing. When given a significant extension as secretary of defense by President Obama, I worked with my team long and hard on "Gates 2.0"—what I was going to do with the additional time I had been given in terms of internal changes and reforms. When I left as DCI and president of Texas A&M, I was just getting warmed up in terms of additional reforms and changes. I worked on such an agenda at Defense for two and a half years before deciding the time had come to pass the baton to a fresh runner.

The best business leaders are always searching for new concepts, new products, new ways of doing business. Brinker International, which owns the Chili's restaurant chain and others (and where I served on the board), proudly displays in the foyer of its headquarters the logos of a number of restaurant brands it has bought and subsequently sold—evidence of the continuing search for innovative concepts and new approaches to expanding the business and a willingness to walk away from unsuccessful initiatives. For nine years, I was an independent trustee (board member) of Fidelity mutual funds, a huge enterprise whose parent organization, led by Ned Johnson, was always testing new investment ideas as well as better ways to serve customers. Johnson's vision, for example, led Fidelity to invest massively many years ago in building the support structure to manage 401(k) investment plans for other companies, and to this day it continues to hold the biggest market share in that business. Who would have thought that Starbucks, a coffee company, would pioneer the use of mobile phone order and pay in a retail environment? Successful business leaders are never satisfied with the status quo. Time and again, at the end of a company's best year ever, I have seen perpetually discontented CEOs warn their boards and employees against complacency and demand new ideas for change and growth.

An acid test for a leader when deciding whether to go or stay is whether he can critically assess the changes *he* has implemented—his ideas—and see ways to improve upon them. If he can cycle back after considerable time in the job and be as tough and objective judging his own handiwork as he has judged that of others, then he probably still has the moxie to continue. If a leader finds himself defending the status quo he created, if he can't look at the people he appointed to senior positions and critically assess whether they are growing and getting stronger and leading effectively or topped out, if he looks at what he has done and those he has appointed and pronounces all is fine and dandy, it's almost certainly time to move on.

———

The first and continuing responsibility of the leader is to understand the implications of a changing environment for his organization, to anticipate new needs, and to keep developing fresh strategies. The leader's second important responsibility is to look for ways to continuously make the organization more user-friendly, more efficient, and more cost-effective.

Once a leader has carried out his initial set of reforms, often to correct obvious problems, how should he decide what needs to be done next? What should his second act look like? Part of the answer to that is easy: there will always be new problems, and external circumstances will always be changing. His challenge is to figure out how to constantly adapt the organization in response.

A leader in both the public and the private sectors today faces an unprecedented pace of change in technology, workplace culture, customer expectations, and the political and business environment. Particularly as government—local, state, and federal—intrudes further into people's daily lives, their impatience with cumbersome, unresponsive, rigid, and frustrating bureaucracies will only grow. Adapting to this new world is a huge problem for public sector bureaucracies, as we saw so vividly in the scandals surrounding the Department of Veterans Affairs in 2014, the online rollout of ObamaCare, and the response to Hurricanes Katrina and Sandy. That list of unsatisfactory governmental performance is, to vastly understate, incomplete.

In a fast-changing world, the CIA's priority targets for intelligence collection must be adjusted constantly, and the techniques for doing so altered to reflect new technologies and new circumstances. The CIA was slow in detecting the emergence of Islamic fundamentalism in the late 1970s and failed to predict the Iranian Revolution—or the consequent sudden loss of technical collection sites in the northern part of Iran vital to tracking Soviet missile developments, capabilities we quickly recovered through an unprecedented partnership with China. As we moved beyond the Cold War, information about the new threats America faced was often not to be found on the diplomatic circuit, so the CIA had to significantly increase the use of men and women operating independently of U.S. government organizations. The wars in Iraq and Afghanistan led to radically new ways to fuse real-time intelligence and military operations in a virtuous cycle. At the end of 2013, the situation in eastern Ukraine was probably not high on the CIA's list; just a few months later, it was likely near the top. Same thing with the emergence of the Islamic State terrorist group in Syria and Iraq. In the world of intelligence, adaptability is critical.

It's similar for the military. The record of both civilian and military leaders over the past forty years in predicting where we would use force next—or even within the ensuing six months—has been perfect: we have never once gotten it right. Not in Grenada, Haiti, the Balkans, Somalia, Panama, Iraq (three times—1991, 2003, and 2014), Libya, or Afghanistan. As tensions heat up with Russia over Ukraine and with China over the South and East China Seas, we will need to rely on the most modern combat capabilities, hopefully only for deterrence. And as the threat of violent Islam spreads to Nigeria, Kenya, Mali, and elsewhere in Africa, the training and equipment required will be very different from that needed to deal with the militaries of large nation-states. Thus the need for adaptable military capabilities.

Even in a university, new academic programs, new technologies, new financial challenges, the changing needs and interests of students, and the question of whether most four-year degrees are worth the cost require an organizational and conceptual agility now and in the future unheard of in earlier decades.

———

To better carry out the second task of making the organization more user-friendly, more efficient, and more cost-effective, over the years I saw experiments with one fad after another. Management by objective. Zero-based budgeting. Benchmarking. My approach is simpler and draws on techniques I described earlier. The leader should keep his eye focused on the mission of the organization and remember that it is the people working for him who deliver that mission. He should ask those on the front lines, those who interact with the public or other customers, to identify obstacles to getting their jobs done better and more efficiently.

The Japanese some time ago developed a business practice called *kaizen*, which basically means continuing change for the better in all aspects of an organization—engineering, information technology, financial, commercial, customer service, and manufacturing. Many companies around the world have adopted the practice, which includes a very open process encouraging suggestions for improvements large and small from employees at every level, including especially on the shop floor—the folks on the front lines. Developed for business, the concept of *kaizen* seems to me to have equal value for public sector bureaucracies as well.

The central idea behind *kaizen* is very important: understanding that everything in an organization can always be improved and that people at every level can make a contribution. It is in keeping with my view that the reformer's work is never done. How do you instill in a bureaucracy this notion of ongoing and dynamic change, which is so alien to bureaucratic culture?

As with the Japanese use of *kaizen*, a leader should provide incentives for his employees to come up with ideas on how to improve performance. She shouldn't just put up a suggestion box. She needs to get people at all levels thinking and working as a team—not just in the old rhetorical, locker-room way, but in the way they work together every day. Leaders need to break down silos and stovepipes and get people thinking beyond their own narrow piece of the action, get them thinking about how the organization as a whole can do better. People need to be incentivized to think "outside their lane."

Managers at all levels should regularly sit down with their folks and talk about ways to do the work more efficiently and better serve the public—the customer. Those managers must be held accountable for continuously seeking out ideas for improvement and implementing those ideas. A leader must publicly recognize and reward employees and managers whose suggestions are implemented. As I said earlier, it is not systems that deliver the mission but people. Using techniques I have described, a leader has to get them on board in his effort to constantly challenge the status quo.

———

When it comes to management techniques for improving performance, one familiar slogan is to "measure what you value and value what you measure." Used properly, metrics can be invaluable in tracking and evaluating performance in myriad categories. However, in my experience, the danger is that people get so focused on successful statistical outcomes they fail to see how excessive reliance on numbers can distort reality and lead to unintended consequences.

Because U.S. military headquarters in Vietnam decided the number of enemy killed was an important indicator of success during the war, getting that number as high as possible led to exaggerated body counts and often counting civilian casualties as enemy deaths. These, in turn, misled senior officials into thinking we were doing better than we actually were. In too many universities, the worthwhile objective of increasing minority enrollment often led to a numbers game, where the premium was on the number of such kids admitted with little attention to the likelihood of their being able to graduate. Universities and colleges also manipulate statistics and definitions in order to improve their standing in the rankings. Even the Boy Scouts suffered when, more than twenty years ago, so much emphasis was placed on increasing membership that some Scout councils engaged in fraudulent practices with regard to enrollments just to get the numbers up and be suitably rewarded. Everyone is familiar with complaints about standardized testing in schools as a means to evaluate student progress and teachers, thus leading the latter to "teach to the test" rather than more broadly educating students. In the air force, the demand for near-perfect test scores by airmen in the ICBM force led to widely publicized cheating scandals. In the VA system, numbers were fudged to show that veterans were getting appointments within the fourteen-day goal set by the leadership when, in fact, they were not. And, as I wrote in *Duty,* the military health-care system cited numerous statistical analyses to demonstrate that changing the medevac time in Afghanistan from two hours to one hour wouldn't really matter in terms of survival rates—while ignoring the impact on morale of the soldiers and marines on the front lines. By the same token, in many areas of business, whether in manufacturing or services, increasing gross numbers—in sales or other categories—can mask a decline in quality that endangers the brand (as happened with U.S. car manufacturers in the 1970s–80s).

In these and countless other cases, meeting a metric became an end in itself, and organizations went terribly wrong. But even in situations where there is no fraud or cheating, a priority on meeting statistical benchmarks can be distorting if not destructive—as in the medevac case. Metrics are a tool. Their use, or misuse, reminds me of a line by the Scottish literary figure Andrew Lang, who said of someone, "He uses statistics as a drunken man uses lampposts—for support rather than for illumination."

Never look at numbers in isolation from other considerations in evaluating performance, including intangibles such as quality of product or services, morale, friendliness, and that special effort by an employee to help someone; while it takes extra time (and thus may blow the hell out of the response time metric), it transforms a cold bureaucracy into a willing and warm operation with a human face. Use metrics for illumination, not support. That will benefit both business and the public sector.

The leader needs to keep a cold, hard eye on his initiatives and be honest enough with himself—or open to the views of colleagues—to admit something isn't working and then pull the plug fast.

In companies as well as government, I have seen leaders stick with a bum idea too long, all too often because it was their brainchild. A leader should recognize that not every idea and initiative will pan out, and move on.

Senator Roscoe Conkling of New York once said, "When Dr. Johnson defined patriotism as the last refuge of a scoundrel, he was unconscious of the then undeveloped capabilities and uses of the word 'Reform.' " I have been around long enough to fully appreciate the law of unintended consequences, even of reform. And I can bear personal witness to the fact that change is not necessarily always for the better. So how do you avoid changing things for the worse? As the historian E. H. Carr observed, "Change is certain. Progress is not."

I have sought in these pages to link "change" with "reform," to make clear that the change I advocate is intended to improve the performance of an organization and, in the case of public institutions, also to make them more responsive to the people they were created to serve. But that is not always the way change works out. Everywhere I have worked, I have seen leaders make changes that were misguided and retrogressive. From ill-conceived reorganizations at the CIA to ill-informed and wrongheaded decisions by administrators and the board of regents at Texas A&M, virtually unworkable congressionally mandated restructurings in the executive branch, and specific decisions within Defense, I have seen the results of bad decisions regarding change.

The list of misguided decisions in business also is a long one. Think about the Ford Edsel in the mid-1950s or New Coke in the 1980s. More broadly, consider some of the big retail chains facing challenges wherein a new CEO took them down the wrong path of change that worsened the problem or, in some cases, even destroyed the company. As a board member of the TRW corporation, I witnessed a wrongheaded strategic decision on an acquisition that ultimately led to the demise of the hundred-year-old company. There have been big mergers that never really worked out, and of course the financial meltdown in 2008 was due in large measure to really bad business decisions.

In no case, public or private, did the decision makers intentionally head the organization in the wrong direction; to a person, I suspect they thought they were making things better or a wise business move. So how does a leader avoid constantly roiling the waters for no purpose other than the appearance of change, and how does he avoid making changes that turn out badly?

Acknowledging that there are no guarantees in life, especially when it comes to avoiding mistakes, I believe there are ways to minimize change going wrong. Every decision involves risk, but a leader can mitigate that risk by continuing throughout her tenure to use the techniques described earlier to test every idea for change she or others have. Specifically, she should be open and transparent about what she is considering, consulting widely within the organization and with her stakeholders. She must listen to her employees and encourage constructive criticism and candor. Abraham Lincoln captured this approach thus: "I am never easy when I am handling a thought, till I have bounded it north, and bounded it south, and bounded it east, and bounded it west." The opinions a leader gets on each proposed change may not affect her decisions at all, or they may lead her to revise her plan or cause her to abandon it altogether. But if she proceeds, she will have had the benefit of thorough scrutiny, and she will have a pretty good idea of potential risks, vulnerabilities, weaknesses, and criticism.

Face it. Being a disruptive reformer is a high-wire act, no matter how long one does it. Even if a leader has been in the job for some time and has already successfully implemented numerous reforms, each new change she seeks might well be the wrong move. And if she doesn't have some failures along the way, she's probably not being bold enough.

If you are the leader of an organization, public or private sector, with a strong culture and traditions (that would include, by the way, most universities and colleges), you need to identify those elements of the culture that you must embrace, support, and try to strengthen and those that must be changed to enable future success. If you are seen as a champion for the core elements of the culture, you will encounter less resistance to changing less central aspects.

Throughout these pages, I have focused on reform—how to start it and how to keep it going, on the need never to become satisfied or complacent. But amid all the change, you need to identify the traditions and those aspects of institutional culture that are core to your organization's past—and future—success. Not every public bureaucracy or private company has a strong culture, but many do.

All three of the institutions I led have exceptionally strong cultures and hallowed traditions. The most important cultural feature of each, though, is common to all three: a powerful sense of family. That same feature figured prominently in *In Search of Excellence* in the authors' discussion of what qualities were characteristic of the most successful companies.

In each organization I led, there is a commitment to taking care of one another at all times but especially in adversity or times of need. At the CIA and in the military, because of the inherent risk in the profession and the reality of human loss, the ranks close around the wounded and the families of the fallen. The pag-

eantry of military funerals is well-known, less so are the CIA's
Memorial Wall and Book of Honor remembering those killed
while working for the agency. Behind the scenes, both organizations have far-reaching programs to support the families of those
who are deployed overseas. Even more important, military and
agency families are simply there for each other in good times
and bad.

Similarly, at Texas A&M, the university's most significant traditions revolve around the Aggie family. When a current student
dies, no matter the cause, an evening ceremony called Silver Taps
is held at the center of the campus the first Tuesday of the following month in his or her honor. The student's family usually is
there, and on average more than ten thousand students attend the
memorial, its silence broken only by the playing of taps. And once
a year, Aggies gather to remember all of their number who have
died during the past year. This Muster ceremony draws twelve
thousand students and others on the main campus, and similar
ceremonies are held the same day in some four hundred locations
worldwide. On a more upbeat note, the so-called Aggie Network
is the envy of many schools because of the willingness of those
long graduated to help new graduates find jobs. The Aggie ring is
a passport to jobs, friends, and help, a visible symbol of the enduring strength of the Aggie family.

All three institutions have traditional ceremonies and rites
celebrating their history, their uniqueness, and their service to the
United States (seven members of Texas A&M's Corps of Cadets
received the Medal of Honor in World War II). Those in each
organization believe fervently that those on the outside cannot
possibly understand what makes it different and singular. On the
downside, pride begets insularity, and long-standing but inappropriate practices and behaviors are tolerated because they are
"a tradition."

All three institutions I led have faced important cultural challenges. For example, changing the culture at the CIA to be more
open in its dealings with Congress has been a work in progress since

the mid-1970s. Getting the clandestine service to welcome women as case officers overseas was a protracted struggle. For a long time, analysts regarded the operations folks as "knuckle-draggers" and were, in turn, regarded as naive, ivory-towered academics. Getting the four military services to work more closely together has been the work of more than six decades and continues still. Acceptance of gays and women in the military, the latter's role in combat, and the prevention of sexual assault have been long-standing struggles in the Department of Defense. Texas A&M has had its own cultural issues but was placed on the right track by the tough-minded, reform-oriented president of the university in the 1960s, Earl Rudder, who inherited an all-male military school, and proceeded to admit women, make participation in the Corps of Cadets voluntary, integrate the school, and begin to hire a world-class faculty. Students at the time thought he was destroying the place and everything it stood for, but his historic reforms probably saved the institution and still managed to preserve the core of its culture. Detested then, he is revered today.

More than a few companies have successfully created a strong company culture, complete with pep rallies and intense focus on customer service and satisfaction. The strongest business culture I have encountered is at Starbucks where, as mentioned earlier, I serve on the board of directors. The twin pillars of the Starbucks culture, in my view, are taking exceptional care of employees in terms of benefits, respect, and opportunities and a strong commitment to corporate social responsibility and leadership. There is a true sense of family. I am confident that other companies have a similarly strong culture, probably in greater numbers than the public expects.

My approach in each place I led was to do everything possible to strengthen those aspects of the culture focused on the institutional family—and associated traditions—and pride in public service and sacrifice while working to eliminate activities and behaviors detrimental to future success. I tried to break down insularity, build bridges to other institutions whose cooperation was important, and be more transparent to the public and the legislature.

The reforming leader faces a delicate task in bringing significant change to an organization without undermining or calling into question the institutional tenets that have been central to past success and the loyalty of its people.

The agent of change in bureaucracies should regard reform—institutional transformation—as a marathon, not a sprint.

I wondered from time to time in my leadership roles whether the pace and extent of change I was pushing was overloading the organizational circuits—whether I was piling too much on the plates of my lieutenants and those who worked for them.

Previous changes at the CIA and in the intelligence community more broadly had been largely slow and evolutionary. There would be flurries of activity under directors such as Admiral Stansfield Turner, William Colby, and James Schlesinger (in his very brief tenure) and various reorganizations. But all in all, in terms of the way business was conducted day to day, change was quite incremental—that is, until I launched all those task forces that touched on almost every aspect of the intelligence business and involved a significant number of subordinate managers and staff. The short deadlines clearly pushed everyone as well. The initial round of task forces had all completed their work by the summer of 1992, but that fall I was readying an entirely new round of reforms, some of which were as far-reaching as the original agenda. When George H. W. Bush lost his presidential reelection bid, I decided to retire and leave office with him. I always imagined there was a sigh of relief that the yellow tablet full of new changes departed with me.

A rapid program of reform and change is a rare phenomenon at a big university. Because there are so many constituencies involved with widely varying interests, agreement on almost any change is difficult to achieve, much less implement. At A&M,

the initiatives to expand the faculty by 450, begin construction on hundreds of millions of dollars' worth of new academic buildings, change the role of faculty and students in decision making, create a new kind of degree program for undergraduates, increase diversity, and much more put a huge new burden on faculty, staff, and administrators. As just one example, hiring a new professor involves a faculty search committee, the department head (or chair), and the dean and can be quite time-consuming for those participating in the process. The faculty in the College of Engineering alone was faced with hiring over 100 new faculty members in a four-year period. When I left the presidency of A&M to become secretary of defense, my tablet was still full of ideas for further change.

People at Defense were, I think, also weary when I departed in 2011. The department was in the eighth year of the Iraq War and the tenth year of the war in Afghanistan. Both the senior military and the senior civilian leadership had been deeply engaged in the time-consuming and stressful 2009 exercise that resulted in cutting or capping three dozen major acquisition programs and the 2010 effort to cut $180 billion out of the bureaucratic overhead. In the spring of 2011, the president asked that another $400 billion be cut from the budget over the ensuing ten years. When I left, we were nearing completion of the yearlong effort to replace "Don't Ask, Don't Tell" with open acceptance of gays in the military. But unlike at the CIA and A&M, there would be no prospect of a breather when I left Defense as the leadership had to continue the war in Afghanistan and complete a strategic review of how to accommodate the additional budget cuts—including what capabilities and missions to give up—and then there was the madness of sequestration that fall (with another $500 billion budget cut).

Public bureaucracies are unaccustomed to rapid or intensive change, but I think that is because they experience it so rarely. They are like out-of-shape runners called upon to compete in a 10K race. At one point, I thought that the period of rapid change at both the CIA and Texas A&M might require a subsequent period of consolidation for people to integrate and assimilate all the changes. Now I believe a rest period—a moratorium on change—is an invitation to relax and fall back into old, bad habits.

In contrast, those working for successful businesses are under constant pressure from competitors, the marketplace, and investors to continuously change and innovate; if they slow down or relax, they will no longer be successful. They cannot get tired or rest.

In the public sector, a single burst of energetic reform should be the starting point for developing a culture of dissatisfaction with the status quo and a long-term, day-in, day-out commitment to searching for better ways to serve the public—the customer. The reform leader should be ruthlessly self-critical in addressing whether he has the energy and the ideas to sustain continuing improvements and, if out of gas, he should get off the road. His change agenda should be aligned with the core values and culture of the organization and use the synergy of the two working in tandem.

10

A Flaming Heart

My first leadership position was as a patrol leader in Boy Scout Troop 522 in Wichita, Kansas. Nothing develops or tests leadership skills like trying to get people to do what you ask when they don't have to—especially if they are twelve or thirteen years old and you are just a year older. My first leadership training course was in July 1959, the national junior leader training program at Philmont Scout Ranch in New Mexico. I was fifteen. That was the last formal leadership or management training I had.

The Internet and shelves in bookstores are full of books telling people how to be leaders and managers. Nearly all colleges and universities have degree programs on the subject, and many companies and government agencies offer—or require—those climbing the ladder to take such training. Yet I think too often leadership and management are treated synonymously when they are, in fact, very different.

My dictionary defines a manager as a "person charged with control or direction of an institution or business . . . one who handles, directs, governs or controls in action or use." God knows, good managers are vitally important. Every enterprise—whether

business, university, government agency, or other institutions—
needs people with management skills: finance, marketing, logistics,
human resources, information technology, planning, communications, procurement, recruitment, manufacturing, operations, and
all the rest. All are endeavors requiring real skill and real competence, and all are essential to the success of any undertaking.

I believe, however, that leadership is much more than the sum
of these skills, much more than managing well. The best definition of a "leader," as described early in these pages, is "one who
guides, one who shows the way." We surely need good managers
here in America, but we are desperate for leaders.

While my formal training in leadership began and ended in
the summer of 1959, in reality my education in leadership has continued for the last fifty-five years. From effective bosses and bad
ones, from working for so many presidents and observing countless other leaders at home and abroad, from watching multiple
corporate and university executives, I have learned what makes
good and even great leaders. And I have tried to distill those lessons here.

Dwight D. Eisenhower wrote to his son in 1943, "The one
quality that can be developed by studious reflection and practice
is the leadership of men. . . . The idea is to get people working
together . . . because they instinctively want to do it for you. . . .
Essentially, you must be devoted to duty, sincere, fair and cheer-
ful." Devotion to duty. Sincerity. Fairness. Good cheer. These
are not qualities taught in school. Formal education can make
someone a good manager, but it cannot make a leader, because
leadership is more about the heart than the head. How does any
organization teach courage, integrity, a love of people, a sense of
humor, the ability to dream of a better future? How can any training program inculcate personal character and honor?

Core to leadership is the ability to relate to people—to empa-
thize, understand, inspire, and motivate. Years ago, I read a
story that during the American Revolution, General Washington was making his rounds through a camp of soldiers when one

private, John Brantley, who had gotten a little drunk on stolen wine, asked Washington if he would have a drink with him. The general declined, saying, "My boy, you have no time for drinking wine." As he began to ride away, Brantley yelled, "Damn your proud soul—you're above drinking with soldiers." Washington turned back, saying, "Come, I will drink with you," and a jug was passed around. As Washington rode away, Brantley called out to him, saying, "Now I'll be damned if I won't give the last drop of my heart's blood for you." A personal touch earned loyalty unto death. That's not learned in a classroom.

If you fundamentally don't like or respect most people, or if you think you are superior to others, chances are you won't be much of a leader—at least in a democracy like ours. Just because you are high on the organizational ladder and can tell people what to do doesn't make you a leader. Just a boss.

Unfortunately, we are living through a period when improving people's lives through institutional reform is exceedingly difficult. Most Americans these days don't see many organizations trying to make their lives easier. Indeed, they are pretty disgusted with all of the bureaucracies they see complicating their lives and with those who lead them—elected and appointed officials as well as those in charge of big organizations in the private sector. At the federal level, Congress, taken as a whole, is about as popular as head lice. Yet more than a hundred years ago, Mark Twain wrote, "Suppose you were an idiot. And suppose you were a member of Congress. But I repeat myself." Members of Congress focusing on parochial interests and getting reelected rather than the national interest goes back to the beginning of the Republic.

While observers like to point out (correctly, in my view) that both Presidents George W. Bush and Barack Obama have been deeply polarizing, they tend to overlook the reality that of thirteen U.S. presidents over the last eighty years only Eisenhower, Ford, and Bush 41 did not evoke deep animosity—even loathing—from partisans in the other party. At his nadir, neither Bush 43 nor Obama reached the low level of public support and disdain President Truman encountered. As I wrote in *Duty*, my own father, a small-business Republican, referred to FDR as "that damned dictator," and I was ten before I realized Truman's first name wasn't "goddamn."

Still, during 1947–48, at a time when politics was every bit as polarized and ugly as today, and with the Republicans controlling both houses of Congress, Truman sent historic proposals to the Hill to create the Marshall Plan, establish NATO, restructure our entire national security apparatus (the National Security Act of 1947), and provide aid to Greece and Turkey (the foundation of our containment policy toward the Soviet Union). All were enacted into law—thanks especially to the support of the Republican senator Arthur Vandenberg of Michigan and the Republican congressman Richard Nixon.

During my career, our national political life was shocked by the Vietnam War and then Watergate (and Nixon's resignation), both episodes characterized by pervasive lying by public officials and resulting in a dramatic increase in public mistrust of government. In subsequent years, oil embargoes, interest rates and inflation (both above 15 percent), the Iran-contra scandal, Clinton's impeachment, going to war in Iraq based on wrong information, the Great Recession, and one scandal or failure after another have hammered home to the American people again and again the message that government is corrupt, its leaders lie, and most are incompetent.

And yet, despite all that, as in 1947–48, there were enough members of Congress during the turbulent 1990s and early years of the twenty-first century willing to reach across the aisle and work together so that essential business—such as approving budgets—was accomplished and important legislation passed, including the Clean Air Act Amendments under Bush 41, welfare reform under Clinton, legislation in 2001–2 to protect the nation against terrorism, and much more, all with significant support from both parties. That was because of a few dozen senators and representatives—I call them bridge builders—who placed the national interest above party interest in order to do the nation's business. Such people are, today, an endangered species.

Although nasty politics, self-interested members of Congress, and presidents provoking deep hostility are nothing new in American political life, the near-total refusal in recent years to reach across the aisle to achieve agreement on legislation needed to move the country forward or protect its interests *is* new—and dangerous. Moderation has become synonymous with having no principles and compromise with selling out. Failure to pass even routine budgets for government departments year after year, much less tackle tough issues like immigration, the deteriorating national infrastructure, underperforming schools, and long-term fiscal problems, represents the worst sort of dereliction of duty by our political class.

Over the last few years, between the scorched-earth tactics being used by both parties to win control of Congress and the uncompromising stance of both the hard Left and the hard Right, nothing is getting done—unless, like "reform" of the Veterans Administration, opposition would be suicidal or, in the case of the Affordable Care Act, legislation affecting every American and 15 percent of the economy is passed without a single vote from the other party. If you add to the mix two presidents who have not been much interested in investing the time and energy to forge compromises on the Hill or, facing resistance, simply gave up, we see why the government truly is in a ditch.

Volumes have been written about our national political malaise, and, admittedly, the causes and history are much more complex than I have described. But the resulting paralysis is apparent to all, and forecasts of the chances of the situation improving anytime soon vary primarily only in degrees of pessimism.

The natural assumption, under these circumstances, would be that anyone with aspirations to reform a bureaucracy—at least in the federal government—would, like Don Quixote, simply be picking up a lance and tilting at a windmill. And to be sure, pessimists abound. Francis Fukuyama wrote in the September/October 2014 issue of *Foreign Affairs* that demands for more legal checks on the executive branch have reduced "the quality and effectiveness of government" and yet greater demand for government services has imposed "new mandates on the executive, which often prove difficult, if not impossible, to fulfill." Both processes, he contends, "lead to a reduction in bureaucratic autonomy, which in turn leads to rigid, rule-bound, uncreative, and incoherent government." Fukuyama quotes the scholar Paul Light that, "Federal employees appear to be more motivated by compensation than mission, ensnared in careers that cannot compete with business and nonprofits, troubled by the lack of resources to do their jobs, dissatisfied with the rewards for a job well done and the lack of consequences for a job done poorly, and unwilling to trust their own organizations." Fukuyama would probably apply much of that dreary assessment to local and state employees as well.

However, after spending a lifetime in public service and working with many state and federal workers in diverse departments and agencies of government, I believe Fukuyama is wrong in the assertion they are more motivated by compensation than mission. While I agree with his description of the challenges they face, I am convinced most of those employees continue to do their jobs because they believe in the mission of their organization. And therein is the opportunity for the bureaucratic reformer.

Moreover, the picture is brighter at the state and local levels. Many states have constitutional requirements for a balanced budget, thus forcing legislatures to make tough and timely decisions, regardless of which party has control. And at both the state and the local levels, there are many experiments under way in reform and governance that hold the potential for problem solving at those levels. Also, because governors and municipal executives must deliver services directly to citizens (and voters), those holding such offices tend to be fairly pragmatic in their actions if not their ideology. If street crime skyrockets, the garbage doesn't get picked up, or snow doesn't get plowed quickly, a mayor is in trouble no matter what his or her political coloration.

I have written this book because I believe that the challenges of public service such as Fukuyama describes can be overcome by talented leaders and, most important, that solving our larger political problems is not a prerequisite for bureaucratic reform—for doing what government does better, cheaper, faster, and in a more "user-friendly" way and holding people accountable for performance both good and bad. Such optimism is uncharacteristic for me. Many years ago, *The Washington Post* called me the "Eeyore" of national security. Like A. A. Milne's character in *Winnie-the-Pooh*, I was able, the paper said, to find the darkest cloud behind every silver lining. But when it comes to changing bureaucracies for the better, I am optimistic.

A politically dysfunctional environment is not, in itself, an insurmountable impediment to bureaucratic reform. After all, there wasn't exactly a lot of reform going on before government paralysis. At all levels of government and however rancid the country's politics, the suggestions in these pages will stand the reformer in good stead wherever she sits.

However great the public's dissatisfaction with the public sector, the private sector doesn't fare much better. It's not just huge frauds like Enron (2001), WorldCom (2002), and Bernard Madoff's multibillion-dollar Ponzi scheme that have hurt the reputation of the business community. There have been gross management failures in big industries such as automobile manufacturing and in financial institutions, the latter—along with misguided (and often self-serving) government and political decision making—leading to the Great Recession, which reduced the household net worth of most Americans, threw millions out of work, and wrecked retirement plans for millions more.

While the media have focused on mismanagement and lawbreaking, far more widespread in business in my view has been a failure of leadership and, too often, a failure of character: arrogance, egotism, obliviousness to the fate of employees, failure to hold people accountable for behavioral or financial misdeeds, belief that high position warrants entitlement, and so much more. Regardless of one's opinion on the cause or extent of recent growth in pay disparities between executives and those who work for them, the highly negative public perception is all too real. Just as government is paralyzed by self-serving, power-hungry politicians, private sector executives are seen as equally self-serving, greedy, and believing themselves entitled to be held to a different standard of behavior from ordinary folks.

On the other hand, the business executives I know personally are men and women of strong character and high integrity, personally enormously generous to worthy causes, conscientious about the well-being and future prospects of their employees, concerned about what ails our society—and deeply involved in trying to find remedies. But again, that is not the broad public perception of the top rung in the private sector. And just like negative perceptions of politicians, that is a problem for our society, a leadership problem I believe the suggestions in this book can help address.

———

I conclude with a few words specifically addressed to public service. The columnist Walter Lippmann wrote long ago, "Those in high places are more than the administrators of government bureaus. They are more than the writers of laws. They are the custodians of a nation's ideals, of the beliefs it cherishes, of its permanent hopes, of the faith which makes a nation out of a mere aggregation of individuals." If you scratch deeply enough, you will find that most of those in public service—"the custodians"—no matter how outwardly tough or jaded or egotistical, are in their heart of hearts romantics, idealists, and optimists. They actually believe it is possible to make the lives of their fellow citizens better and the world a safer place. But an important part of what makes America unique is that our nation's ideals, hopes, and faith are manifested not only in individuals but in our institutions.

Accordingly, we can only bring our ideals alive, fulfill our hopes, and strengthen our faith as a country by improving the institutions that are the instruments through which we can achieve those goals. I have loved each of the organizations I have led—the CIA, Texas A&M, the Defense Department, and now the Boy Scouts of America. But my love of and dedication to them have not blinded me to their shortcomings and need for change and reform. Most of the big changes I have led to improve those institutions have worked and often have endured because I applied the approaches and techniques described in these pages.

Bureaucratic reform can be accomplished even in rough political waters. Indeed, politics is just one of multiple obstacles facing a leader when it comes to challenging the status quo. Accordingly, there are no excuses for not starting today.

The question is whether new leaders, agents of change, are up to the challenge. Harry Truman once said, "Every great achievement is the story of a flaming heart." The task of reforming institutions is a difficult one. A leader's heart must be on fire with belief in what she seeks to do. Changing institutions is a battle, and she must undertake it with courage, strength, and conviction. She must believe in it before she can persuade others to believe in it. She must be prepared to put her job on the line for it if she is to ask others to risk their careers and reputations to help her.

Woodrow Wilson wrote, "When you come into the presence of a leader of men, you know you have come into the presence of fire—that it is best not incautiously to touch that man—that there is something that makes it dangerous to cross him." The reformer must be very tough and, from time to time, ruthless. She will sometimes stand absolutely alone in pressing for change. She must hold people accountable and be prepared to remove those who are opposed or who cannot do the job. She will encounter criticism—sometimes vicious and personal—along the way. The path of the reformer of institutions is never easy and rarely downhill.

I entered public service nearly fifty years ago because, when I was a college student, President Kennedy urged us to ask not what our country could do for us but what we could do for our country. I remained in public service because President George H. W. Bush reminded us that "public service is a noble calling." And so, especially to young people, I would paraphrase John Adams's admonition to his son, quoted earlier: If the wise and honest among you refuse to serve, others will not. And we will all be the poorer for it.

The Nobel laureate Anatole France once wrote, "To accomplish great things, we must not only act, but also dream; not only plan, but also believe." To those who believe our institutions can be better than they are, I say, Dream. Believe. Plan. Act.

Acknowledgments

In writing this book, I have drawn on memories and experiences stretching back to childhood. The lessons taught and example shown by my mother and father with respect to character and integrity, how to treat other people, and the joy of living have shaped my entire life.

How do I thank the countless men and women who, over the course of my professional life, have taught and influenced me, from my first CIA cubicle mate and lifelong friend, the late Barry Stevenson, to those in uniform who so inspired me as secretary of defense? I have been fortunate to have mentors, coaches, partners, and friends everywhere I have worked in government, universities, and on corporate boards. Their influence, collectively and individually, is reflected on every page of this book.

I asked several people to review this manuscript, and I want to thank them for making the time and effort to help me: Pete Chiarelli, Benton Cocanougher, Ryan McCarthy, Rodney McClendon, Geoff Morrell, Michael O'Quinn, Robert Rangel, Harry Rhoads, Thayer Scott, and Neal Wolin. Obviously, responsibility for any errors or mistakes is mine alone. Thanks also to my assistant, Keith Hensley, for his help in preparing this book and for managing my life and my time so I could actually get it done.

Both the CIA and the Department of Defense reviewed the manuscript to prevent the disclosure of classified information, and I thank both for their expeditious responses. Needless to say, all statements of fact, opinion, and analysis are mine and do not reflect official positions or views of the CIA or the Defense Department. Similarly, nothing in the contents should be construed as asserting or implying U.S. government authentication of information or as endorsement of my views.

Special thanks to Wayne Kabak of WSK Management, who has represented me for more than twenty years and through three books. He is a very special friend. I also want to thank Jonathan Segal of Alfred A. Knopf, an always constructive and superbly gifted editor who has guided me through two books. Jon, I raise my martini glass to you. I also want to thank Sonny Mehta at Knopf for his confidence in me for both this book and *Duty*, as well as others at Knopf for their contribution.

Finally, I want to thank Becky, my wife of nearly fifty years, who has been my love, my companion, and my best friend through many trials and adventures. She has always kept me grounded and made home and a loving family a sanctuary for me from the pressures of some very stressful jobs. Her generosity and kindness toward others have set an example I have tried—not always successfully—to emulate. When I asked her to marry me so long ago, I promised our life together would never be boring. I believe I have kept that promise.

Index

accountability, 96–97, 124–29
Acheson, Dean, 183–84
across-the-board spending cuts, 196–97
"Action This Day" tabs, 97
Adams, John, 22, 162, 228
ad hoc groups. *See* task forces
Affordable Care Act (ACA), 4, 96, 206, 223
Afghanistan, 20, 30–31, 216
    extended tours of duty, 84–85
    intelligence operations, 207
    ISR support, 73, 147–48
    medevac times, 74–75, 210
    MRAP vehicles, 51, 73, 148
    wasted development funds, 4–5
agenda. *See* goal setting
Air Force, 147–48, 210
airport security regulations, 4
alumni and retirees, 14–15, 152–55
Amazon, 25, 202
analysis processes, 87–90
anticipating change, 206–8
Apple, 25, 202
Arab Spring movement, 24–25
arrogance, 161
Asquith, Herbert, 162
Austin, Lloyd, 111
auto industry bailouts, 138

Barzun, Jacques, 18, 25
Begin, Menachem, 24
Berra, Yogi, 38
Bezos, Jeff, 25, 202
bin Laden, Osama, 180
blaming the bureaucrats, 102–4
blogs, 16

Bonaparte, Napoleon, 5
Boren, David, 133
Boren, James, 157
Bowen, Ray, 33–34
Boy Scouts of America, 8, 210
Brantley, John, 221
bribery, 200–201
Brinker International, 205
Brooks, Jack, 132–33
Brzezinski, Zbigniew, 107, 165
budgets. *See* spending decisions
bureaucratic failure, 3–22
    analysis paralysis, 87–89
    blaming the bureaucrats, 102–4
    costs of, 6
    egotism and arrogance, 158–61
    failures of leadership, 157–85
    investigative bodies, 89
    obstacles to reform, 6–7, 9–19
    partisanship, 221–25
    private sector, 5–6, 225–26
    report writing, 101
    scandals, 4–5, 56–57, 72, 125, 148, 206–7,
      225
    spending decisions, 187
Bush, George H. W., 46, 163, 178, 216,
    221–22
    Gulf War of 1991, 32, 179
    NSC of, 66, 86–87
    on public service, 228
    sense of humor, 180–81
Bush, George W., 61, 85
    defense budgets, 187
    people skills, 102, 107
    as Texas governor, 36

Bush, George W. *(continued)*
  unsuccessful wars, 20, 30–31, 216
  See also Afghanistan; Iraq
Byrd, Robert, 132–33

C-5A Galaxy cargo aircraft, 199
cabinet secretaries, 13
candor, 118–22
Capone, Al, 107
Carr, E. H., 211
Carter, Jimmy, 180, 183
Casey, George, 121
Casey, William, 19, 40, 101, 114
  Iran-contra scandal, 163–64
  on oversight boards, 143
Centers for Disease Control (CDC), 4
Chamberlain, Neville, 118–19
character, 165–66
Cheney, Dick, 179
China, 207
Churchill (Johnson), 184–85
Churchill, Winston, 97, 184–85
CIA, 7–9, 19, 216
  anticipating change, 207
  appointing senior officials, 174
  budgets, 187–88
  candor, 121–22
  Congressional oversight, 132–34
  front office staff, 176–77
  goal-setting, 28, 30–31
  implementation task forces, 66–68
  institutional culture, 213–15
  openness initiative, 57–58, 82–84,
    146–47
  oversight boards, 141
  performance evaluations, 115–16
  retirees, 154–56
  secrecy policies, 57–58, 80–81, 146,
    195–96
  spending decisions, 189, 195–96
  strategic process, 40–41, 45–46, 48, 51,
    57–58, 60
civil service. *See* public service careers
Civil Service Reform Act of 1978, 18–19
Clapper, Jim, 112
Clinton, Bill, 222
Cocanougher, Benton, 77
Cocks, Barnett, 65
Colby, William, 216
Cold War, 24, 30, 80–81, 146, 188–89, 207,
  222
communication skills
  listening, 26–28, 117, 166–67, 172

winning support and cooperation,
    28–29, 40–49, 99
  See also people skills
Community Management Staff, 189, 195
Congress
  budget sequestration, 197, 217
  ethical lapses, 164–65
  mandated waste, 199, 201
  oversight role, 132–41
  partisanship, 221–25
  Pentagon budget, 9–11, 135, 195–96, 199
  private-sector relationships, 137–38
  testifying before, 168
  unworkable proposals, 139–40
Congressional Budget Office, 89
Conkling, Roscoe, 211
consensus, 86–87
Cook, Tim, 202
courage, 172–73
crisis management, 56
cultures of insularity, 17–18

deadlines, 66–67, 89–90, 216–18
decisiveness, 94–96
Declaration of Independence, 162
Defense Mapping Agency, 179
de Klerk, F. W., 24
Dempsey, Martin, 111
Deng Xiaoping, 24
Department of Defense, 7–9, 20, 217
  anticipating change, 207
  appointing senior officials, 174
  budget cuts of 2010, 7, 32, 51, 61, 190–91,
    200, 216
  budgets, 187, 188
  candor, 120–21
  "Don't Ask, Don't Tell" policies, 77–79,
    217
  front office staff, 175, 177
  goal-setting, 29, 30–33
  implementation task forces, 71–75
  institutional culture, 213–15
  leaks, 84–86, 195
  media coverage, 143–45, 147–48
  Office of Cost Assessment and
    Program Evaluation, 71–72
  organizational structure, 50–51
  performance evaluations, 115
  planning for future wars, 20, 31–32,
    55–56, 147–48
  program cuts, 61, 85–86, 88, 155, 217
  secrecy policies, 80, 195–96
  spending decisions, 190–91, 195–96

strategic process, 44–45, 51, 55–57, 61
   veterans and retirees, 154–56
   Walter Reed hospital scandal, 4, 56–57, 72, 148, 168–69
   wasted dollars, 199–200
   wounded warrior initiative, 55–57
Department of Veterans Affairs. *See* Veterans Administration
disruptive leadership. *See* restless leadership
"Don't Ask, Don't Tell" (DADT) policies, 77–79, 217
Dover Air Force Base, 74
Duty: Memoirs of a Secretary at War (Gates), 135, 222

Easom, Jason, 175
Eban, Abba, 86
Ebola crisis, 4
economic incentives, 18–19
egotism, 158–61
Eisenhower, Dwight, 169, 171–72, 220, 221
elected bodies, 132–41
   See also Congress
electronic communications, 178
Ellington, Duke, 90
Emmanuel, Rahm, 56
employee morale, 99–101
empowerment, 109–11, 124
England, Gordon, 200
Enron, 225
evaluations, 114–17

F-22 fighter jets, 155
Facebook, 25
Fannie Mae scandal, 124
Federal Emergency Management Agency (FEMA), 4
Fidelity, 205
firing employees, 108, 116, 127–29, 191–94
Flawn, Peter, 139, 154
flexibility, 24–25, 178–80
Flournoy, Michèle, 113
follow-through, 96–97
force caps, 193
Ford, Gerald, 221–22
Ford Motor Company, 25
Fox, Christine, 72
France, Anatole, 228
fraud and abuse, 200–201
Freddie Mac scandal, 124
Friedman, Thomas L., 197
From Dawn to Decadence (Barzun), 18, 25

Fukuyama, Francis, 224–25
Future Combat Systems, 155

Gates, Bill, 25
Gates 2.0, 31–32, 205
gays in the military, 215
General Accounting Office, 89
General Electric, 202
General Motors recall of 2014, 124
goal setting, 23–38
   acting alone, 37–38
   assessment phase, 29–35
   communicating goals, 28–29
   giving credit, 28
   listening phase, 27–28
   prioritizing problems, 37
   recognizing external circumstances, 37
   revisions/changing course, 211–13
Goldwyn, Samuel, 119
González, Henry, 132–33
Gorbachev, Mikhail, 24, 158
Gramm, Phil, 36
Grant, Ulysses S., 160
Great Recession, 4, 222, 225
Gulf War of 1991, 32, 179
guts, 94–96

Ham, Carter, 78
Hamilton, Lee, 134
Hasan, Nidal, 115
Helms, Richard, 119
Hewson, Marillyn, 25
hiring freezes, 193
Hitchcock, Alfred, 157
Holmes, Oliver Wendell, Jr., 86, 171
honor, 162, 165–66
Hoover, J. Edgar, 100
hostile-takeover approach, 26
humor, 180–82
Hurricane Katrina, 4, 187, 206–7
Hurricane Rita, 155–56
Hurricane Sandy, 187, 206–7

IBM, 202
Immelt, Jeffrey, 202
implementation techniques, 63–97
   analysis *vs.* paralysis, 87–90
   consensus problems, 86–87
   deadlines, 66–67, 89–90, 216–18
   decisiveness, 94–96
   follow-through, 96–97
   inclusiveness, 63–64, 85–86

implementation techniques *(continued)*
  micro-knowledge *vs.*
    micromanagement, 90–94
  outside panels, 72
  progress reports, 96
  task forces, 63–80
  transparency, 80–86
inclusiveness, 63–64, 85–86
  kaizen (everyone can make a
    contribution), 208–9
  listening, 26–28, 117, 166–67, 172
  task forces, 65–80
inertia, 96
Inman, Bob, 19, 40, 114, 165
*In Search of Excellence: Lessons from
    America's Best-Run Companies*
    (Peters and Waterman), 100, 213
inspectors general, 89, 164
institutional culture, 17–18, 53–62, 213–16
integrity, 161–66
intellectual modesty, 171–72
Intelligence Oversight Board, 141
Internal Revenue Service (IRS), 4
investigative bodies, 16–17, 89, 164
investigative journalism, 148
Iran-contra scandal, 163–64, 222
Iranian revolution, 207
Iraq, 20, 30–31, 216, 222
  extended tours of duty, 84–85
  Gulf War of 1991, 32, 179
  intelligence operations, 207
  ISR support, 73, 147–48
  MRAP vehicles, 51, 73, 148
  post-invasion planning, 4
  wasted development funds, 4–5
Islamic fundamentalism, 207

job cuts, 191–94
Jobs, Steve, 25, 202
job security, 12–13, 14, 192
Johnson, Jeh, 78
Johnson, Lyndon B., 4
Johnson, Ned, 205
Johnson, Paul, 184–85
Johnson, Samuel, 202

kaizen, 208–9
Kearns Goodwin, Doris, 181–82
Kennedy, John F., 102, 227–28
Kerr, Dick, 165
King, Ernest, 169
Kissinger, Henry, 87, 101, 181
Kohl, Helmut, 24

labor unions, 13–14, 151–52
Lang, Andrew, 210
Larrabee, Eric, 118–19
layoffs, 189–94
leadership definitions, 23, 220
leadership skills and principles, 8–9,
    20–22, 157–85, 226–28
  acting alone, 37–38
  anticipating change, 206–8
  appointing immediate staff, 50–51,
    173–78
  belief in mission, 224–28
  courage, 172–73
  crisis management, 56
  decisiveness, 94–96
  ego control, 158–61
  empathy, 220–21
  flexibility and pragmatism, 178–80
  humor, 180–82
  integrity, 161–66
  intellectual modesty, 171–72
  knowing when to leave, 182–84, 203–6
  listening skills, 26–28, 117, 166–67, 172
  managerial experience, 12
  metrics, 209–11
  micro-knowledge *vs.*
    micromanagement, 90–94
  ongoing reform, 203–18
  people skills, 98–130
  political relationships, 35–36, 54, 131–49
  pragmatism, 24–25
  prioritizing problems, 37, 51–52
  readiness to resign, 138–39
  recognizing external circumstances, 37
  restlessness, 204–6
  self-discipline, 166–71
  spending decisions, 186–202
  vision, 23–24, 29–35
  See also reforms of bureaucracies
leaks, 16, 84–86
leavetaking, 182–84, 203–6
legislative bodies, 132–41
  See also Congress
Light, Paul, 224
Lincoln, Abraham, 171–72, 182, 212
Lippmann, Walter, 226
listening skills, 26–28, 172
  performance evaluations, 117
  self-discipline, 166–67
little Stalins, 104–6
local communities, 149–51
local government, 224–25
Lockheed Martin, 25

Lombardi, Vince, 157
Louis XIV, King of France, 158

Madoff, Bernard, 225
Mandela, Nelson, 24
Marsh, Jack, 72
Marshall, George C., 118–19, 160
Marshall Plan, 222
McClendon, Rodney, 47, 177
McMahon, John, 165
McNamara, Robert, 85
McRaven, William, 180
Meade, George, 160
media, 16–17
    bias, 145
    investigative journalism, 148
    leaks, 16, 84–86
    relationships with, 143–49, 169
Metzenbaum, Howard, 168
micro-knowledge, 90–94
micromanagement, 90–94
Microsoft, 25
money. *See* spending decisions
morale, 99–101
Mulally, Alan, 25
Mulcahy, Anne, 25
Mullen, Mike, 78, 120, 165
Murkowski, Frank, 133
Murphy, Mary Claire, 112–13

National Geospatial Intelligence Agency,
    179
National Security Act of 1947, 222
National Security Agency (NSA), 179
National Security Council (NSC), 19, 40,
    80, 86–87
NATO, 222
Nixon, Richard, 101, 119, 146, 180, 222

Obama, Barack, 29, 61, 85, 112, 167, 183,
    205, 221–22
    "Don't Ask, Don't Tell" policies, 78–79
    Middle East policies, 39
    Pentagon reforms under, 31–33, 197, 217
ObamaCare (Affordable Care Act), 4, 96,
    206, 223
obstacles to reform, 6–7
Odierno, Ray, 111
Ogden, Steve, 134
ongoing reform, 203–18
    anticipating change, 206–8
    kaizen practices, 208–9
    metrics, 209–11

rapid deadlines, 216–18
    restless leadership, 204–6
Option B, 87
organizational rearrangements, 58–59
oversight functions, 9–11, 132–43
    See also Congress; stakeholders

paralysis by analysis, 87–89
Parker, Dorothy, 89–90
partisanship, 221–25
Patton, 169
Pelosi, Nancy, 154
Pentagon. *See* Department of Defense
people skills, 98–130
    building employee morale, 99–101
    criticizing privately, 102–4, 107–8
    empathy, 220–21
    empowering subordinates, 109–11,
        124
    encouraging advancement, 112–14
    encouraging candor, 118–22
    encouraging time off, 123–24
    expecting accountability, 124–29
    firings, 108, 116, 127–29, 191–94
    giving credit, 102–4, 107–8, 111–12
    performance evaluations, 114–17
    respectfulness, 104–9
    winning support and cooperation,
        40–49, 99
performance evaluations, 114–17
Perry, Rick, 35–36, 141–42
Persico, Joseph, 160, 169
personal qualities of leaders, 157–85
    appointing immediate staff, 173–78
    courage, 172–73
    ego control, 158–61
    flexibility and pragmatism, 178–80
    humor, 180–82
    integrity, 161–66
    intellectual modesty, 171–72
    knowing when to leave, 182–84, 203–6
    listening skills, 26–28, 117, 166–67, 172
    self-discipline, 166–71
Peters, Thomas J., 100
Petraeus, David, 111
political appointment process, 12–13
political pressure, 35–36, 54, 76–77
    legislatures, 131–41
    media relationships, 143–49, 169
    oversight boards and regulators,
        141–143
    See also Congress
Powell, Colin, 179

pragmatism, 24–25, 178–80
President's Foreign Intelligence Advisory
  Board, 141
Prior, David, 34
private sector, 5–6, 225–26
  ad hoc task forces, 64, 75–76
  boards of directors, 10–11
  candor, 122
  fraud and mismanagement, 225
  humor, 181
  innovation and change, 6
  institutional culture, 215
  job security, 13
  media relationships, 145–46
  ongoing reform, 202–3, 218
  people skills, 102–4
  political relationships, 137–38
  spending decisions, 186
  transparency challenges, 81–82
process of change. *See* implementation
  techniques
professional organizations, 155–56
progress reports, 96
public service careers, 5, 9, 21–22
  belief in mission, 224–28
  job security, 12–13, 14, 192
  performance bonuses, 18–19
Putin, Vladimir, 158

Rabin, Yitzhak, 158
Rangel, Robert, 165, 177
Reagan, Ronald, 24, 40, 171–72
  Congressional negotiations, 138
  Iran-contra scandal, 163–64, 222
recession of 2008–9, 4, 222, 225
Redman, Sue, 190
reforms of bureaucracies, 9–22
  goal setting, 23–38
  implementation techniques,
    63–97
  obstacles, 6–7, 9–19
  as ongoing process, 203–18
  strategy formulation, 39–62
  See also leadership skills and
    principles
reorganization, 58–59
resignation threats, 138–39
respectfulness, 104–9
restless leadership, 204–16
  anticipating change, 206–8
  changing course, 211–13
  commitment to institutional culture,
    213–16

kaizen (everyone can make a
    contribution), 208–9
  metrics, 209–11
  restraint, 166–71
retirees and alumni, 14–15, 152–55
Richard II (Shakespeare), 162
risk avoidance, 16–17
risk-taking, 95
Rodriguez, David, 111
Rogers, Will, 5
Rometty, Ginni, 202
Roosevelt, Franklin D., 118–19, 171, 222
Roosevelt's Centurians (Persico), 160
Rudder, Earl, 215
Rumsfeld, Donald, 44–45, 135

Sadat, Anwar, 24, 107, 158
Sandberg, Sheryl, 25
Schlesinger, James, 216
Schultz, Howard, 25, 82
Scowcroft, Brent, 66, 107, 165
Scowcroft Award, 180–81
secrecy policies, 57–58, 80–86, 146
Secret Service, 4, 159–60
self-discipline, 166–71
sense of humor, 180–82
September 11, 2001 attacks, 4, 187
sequestration, 197, 217
sexual assault prevention, 215
Shakespeare, William, 162
shared governance, 42, 68–69
Shinseki, Eric, 119
silo busters. *See* task forces
Socratic method, 66
Soviet Union
  CIA files on, 82
  Cold War, 146, 207, 222
  collapse, 30, 67–68, 80–81
spending decisions, 186–202
  across-the-board approaches, 196–97
  fraud and abuse, 200–201
  personnel reductions, 191–94
  priority-setting, 197
  reform opportunities, 188–91
  transparency, 194–96
  waste, 198–200
staff appointments, 50–51, 173–78
staff management. *See* people skills
staff reductions, 189–94
stakeholders, 131–56
  alumni and retirees, 152–55
  elected oversight bodies, 132–41
  local communities, 149–51

media relationships, 143–49, 169
oversight boards and regulators, 141–143
professional organizations, 155–56
unions, 151–52
Stanton, Edwin, 160
Starbucks, 25, 215
State Department, 139
state government, 224–25
statistical outcomes, 209–10
status reports, 96
Stengal, Casey, 157
strategy formulation, 39–62
  announcing the plans, 59–62
  considering institutional culture,
    53–62, 213–16
  front office staff, 173–78
  prioritizing and sequencing, 51–52
  reorganization approaches, 58–59
  senior staff, 50–51
  staff support and cooperation,
    40–49, 99
  thinking time, 49–50
Syria, 207

task forces, 63–80
  consensus, 86–87
  deadlines, 66–67, 89–90
  defensive role, 76–79
  duration, 73–74
  leaders, 66, 73
  members, 65–66
  outside panels, 72
Team of Rivals (Kearns Goodwin), 181–82
temper tantrums, 104–5, 168–70
terrorist groups, 32
Texas A&M University, 7–9, 19–20, 216–17
  alumni, 14–15, 152–55
  anticipating change, 208
  appointing senior administrators, 174
  bonfire tragedy, 34
  candor, 121–22
  Corps of Cadets, 153–54, 214, 215
  diversity initiative, 53–55, 96–97
  front office staff, 177
  goal-setting, 29, 33–36
  implementation task forces, 68–71,
    76–77
  institutional culture, 214–15
  living wage debates, 76–77
  oversight boards, 141–42
  political relationships, 35–36, 76–77,
    134–35, 141–42
  shared governance, 42, 68–69

spending decisions, 189–90
staff reductions, 189–90, 193
strategic process, 42–44, 46–48, 51–55,
  60–61
transparency initiatives, 83–84, 194–95
Vision 2050 report, 33–35
Texas state, 15
Thatcher, Margaret, 24, 158
toxic bosses, 104–6
transparency initiatives, 15–16
  reform implementation strategies, 80–86
  spending decisions, 194–96
Truman, Harry, 109, 171, 222, 227
Turner, Stansfield, 192, 216
Twain, Mark, 42, 165

Ukraine, 207
unions, 13–14, 151–52
U.S. Agency for International
  Development (USAID), 139

vacations, 123–24
Vance, Cyrus, 183
Vandenberg, Arthur, 222
Veterans Administration, 4, 210
  reforms, 223
  scandal of 2014, 124, 187, 206
veterans' service organizations (VSOs),
  154–55
Vietnam War, 187, 188, 209, 222
vision. *See* goal setting

Walsh, Lawrence, 163
Walter Reed Army Medical Center
  scandal, 4, 56–57, 72, 148, 168–69
Washington, George, 118, 171–72, 178,
  220–21
wasted dollars, 198–200
Watergate scandal, 119, 222
Waterman, Robert H., Jr., 100
Webster, William, 107, 163, 165, 176
West, Royce, 54, 134
West, Togo, 72
Williams, Janice, 176
Wilson, Woodrow, 227
Wolin, Neal, 176
women in the military, 215
Wood, Gordon, 171–72
Woodward, Bob, 167
WorldCom, 225
Wounded Warrior Task Force, 55–57

Xerox, 25

ROBERT M. GATES was appointed the twenty-second secretary of defense (2006–11) by President George W. Bush and is the only secretary of defense in U.S. history to be asked to remain in that office by a newly elected president. President Barack Obama was the eighth president Gates served. President Obama awarded him the Presidential Medal of Freedom, America's highest civilian honor, on Gates's last day in office. Before becoming secretary of defense, Gates was president of Texas A&M University. Prior to that, he served as interim dean of the Bush School of Government and Public Service at the university from 1999 to 2001. Gates joined the Central Intelligence Agency in 1966. In 1967, he was commissioned a second lieutenant in the U.S. Air Force. He spent nearly nine years at the National Security Council, serving four presidents of both political parties. He served as deputy director of central intelligence from 1986 until 1989 and as assistant to the president and deputy national security adviser for President George H. W. Bush from 1989 to 1991. Gates served as director of central intelligence from 1991 to 1993. A native of Kansas, Gates received his bachelor's degree from the College of William & Mary, his master's degree from Indiana University, and his doctorate in Russian and Soviet history from Georgetown University. He was installed as chancellor of the College of William & Mary in February 2012 and became national president of the Boy Scouts of America in May 2014. He is the author of *From the Shadows: The Ultimate Insider's Story of Five Presidents and How They Won the Cold War* and *Duty: Memoirs of a Secretary at War.*

A NOTE ON THE TYPE

This book was set in Minion, a typeface produced by the Adobe Corporation specifically for the Macintosh personal computer, and released in 1990. Designed by Robert Slimbach, Minion combines the classic characteristics of old style faces with the full complement of weights required for modern typesetting.

Composed by North Market Street Graphics,
Lancaster, Pennsylvania

Printed and bound by Berryville Graphics,
Berryville, Virginia

Designed by Cassandra J. Pappas